Cybersecurity and the Art of Cyberwar

The art of war is of vital importance to the state. It is a matter of life or death. Hence, it is a subject which can on no account be neglected.

—**Sun Tzu**

Why are we calling this war? It's because the conflict in cyberspace is a matter of national concern, and we are, most assuredly, losing the current struggle. So, what do we do? The person who best understands war is a 2,300-year-old Chinese general who saw conflict as more about process and strategy than fighting. Which, in essence, is the holistic concept.

Hence, this book is founded on two principles. First, cybersecurity is a state, not a technical solution. Accordingly, people and organizations must take active steps to both design and sustain a consistently secure operational process. Second, it's given that you have not attained the desired state if you have failed to deploy all of the controls necessary to achieve it.

The catch-all term for such an approach is "holistic." A holistic control architecture is the only way to achieve adequate protection. Therefore, holistic cyber defenses embody a single, unified system of electronic, behavioral, and physical controls that enforce continuous security across all common attack surfaces.

Why does the solution need to be holistic? It is because the cybersecurity function is responsible for securing three distinct and disparate types of attacks – electronic, human, and physical. And just as in war, the adversary doesn't care which attack surface they breach. They only want your stuff, and they will do whatever it takes to get it. In that respect, then, the only practical approach to cybersecurity is to create an integrated, appropriately tailored defense against any viable threat ... electronic, human, or physical.

This book describes the lifecycle process for conceptualizing, implementing, and maintaining a holistic control solution. It centers on a well-defined process for planning, building, and ensuring comprehensive, in-depth cyber defense. In that respect, then, we will demonstrate why holistic security is the only way for an organization to identify and address all valid threats to its digital resources.

Security, Audit and Leadership Series

Series Editor: Dan Swanson, Dan Swanson and Associates, Ltd., Winnipeg, Manitoba, Canada.

The scope and mandate for internal audit continue to evolve each year, as does the complexity of the business environment and speed of the changing risk landscape in which it must operate. The fundamental goal of this exciting series is to produce leading-edge books on critical subjects facing security and audit executives and practitioners. Key topics addressed include Leadership, Cybersecurity, Security Leadership, Privacy, Strategic Risk Management, Auditing IT, Audit Management and Leadership, and Operational Auditing.

Fire Brigades to Firewalls: *A Public Safety Guide to Cybersecurity*
By John Kuforiji

Bridging the Gap: *Strengthening the Bond between Audit Committee and Internal Audit*
By Denise Cicchella

CISO: *Evolution of a Vocation*
Confessions of a Recovering CISO
By Ron Baklarz

Dark Faces in Cyber Places*: Shattering Stereotypes and Leading with Legacy in Cybersecurity*
By Devon Bryan

Logic Before Language: *Rethinking AI in the Age of Illusion, Bertrand Russell and the Future of Real AI*
By Martin Milani

Relevant Impact: *A Field Guide to Integrated Assurance*
By Patrick M. Hayes

Cybersecurity and the Art of Cyberwar
By Dan Shoemaker, Tamara Shoemaker, and Amir Jabri

Cybersecurity and the Art of Cyberwar

Dan Shoemaker, Tamara Shoemaker, and
Amir Jabri

CRC Press
Taylor & Francis Group
Boca Raton London New York

CRC Press is an imprint of the
Taylor & Francis Group, an **informa** business

Designed cover image: Jacob M. Green

First edition published 2026
by CRC Press
2385 NW Executive Center Drive, Suite 320, Boca Raton FL 33431

and by CRC Press
4 Park Square, Milton Park, Abingdon, Oxon, OX14 4RN

CRC Press is an imprint of Taylor & Francis Group, LLC

ISBN: 9781032993096 (hbk)
ISBN: 9781032993089 (pbk)
ISBN: 9781003603412 (ebk)

DOI: 10.1201/9781003603412

Typeset in Sabon
by Newgen Publishing UK

Dedicated to the next generation of cybersecurity professionals: may your curiosity stay sharp, your ethics remain strong, and your work help safeguard the systems that keep our world running.

Contents

Foreword

Computing went from laboratory curiosity to civilization infrastructure in a single human lifetime. What began 70 years ago with a few room-sized machines has exploded into billions of devices integrated into every aspect of modern life – commerce, communication, governance, finance, education, and entertainment. No technology in history has achieved such ubiquity so quickly – or created such profound vulnerabilities in the process.

As computing has evolved from a tool to a basic infrastructure, the value it manages and creates has grown exponentially. So has its attractiveness as a target for everything from vandals to nation-state agencies. Rapid technological evolution, personnel shortages, and poor security risk management have produced an unending stream of breaches and compromises. Law enforcement and digital forensics haven't kept pace, enabling most threat actors to act without accountability.

Given this context, nation-state actors have been developing capabilities to leverage cyberattacks for espionage and active conflict, spawning corresponding interest in wide-scale defenses. This attack/defense dynamic has been studied under the rubric of "cyberwar" by many martial scholars, and militarists globally have established units trained as "cyber warriors."

Yet, what many people accustomed to traditional warfare miss is that the battle has already been joined! This isn't a single campaign by a single adversary under a single flag. It's a multitude of actors conducting everything from reconnaissance to establishing footholds to wars of attrition to large-scale assaults – targeting home systems and national agencies alike. It's constant, escalating, and often invisible because of stealth, inadequate defenses, and sheer background noise. If these were kinetic attacks, we would be traumatized by their frequency and scope.

This book frames what's happening to all of us collectively as "cyberwar" against a multitude of opponents. It offers a thoughtful yet readable discussion of defensive thinking, operational security, and threat response. The authors recognize that effective defense doesn't necessarily require national-level resources – but it does demand understanding threats and structuring appropriate responses. They present defense as a continuous process, not a final goal, and this work will help you craft a workable approach to that process.

Our computing landscape resembles medieval villages more than fortified kingdoms. We need sturdy walls and local militia, not distant standing armies. When besieged – whether by brigands, hordes, or organized armies – outside knights won't save you. You must guard your own gates.

In 70 years, computing transformed from curiosity to battlefield. The next few decades will determine whether we master the defensive arts sufficiently to preserve what we've built, or whether our dependence on vulnerable infrastructure becomes a civilizational liability. Whether you're protecting a home network or managing a multinational IT infrastructure, you'll find actionable advice in these chapters.

The cyberwar isn't coming; it's here. You're already a combatant, whether you've recognized it or not. Treat this book not as a manual for some future threat, but as a field guide for the conflict already underway, written by experienced strategists. Our adversaries are real, numerous, and relentless. Our defenses must be too.

Eugene H. Spafford
December 2025

About the authors

Dan Shoemaker, PhD, is a Full Professor and Director of the Graduate Program in Cybersecurity at the University of Detroit Mercy (UDM), where he has served for more than 40 years. He was a Distinguished Visitor with the Institute of Electrical and Electronic Engineers (IEEE) Computer Society for two terms. He served as Principal Investigator and Senior Research Scientist for the National Security Agency's Center of Academic Excellence in Cyber Defense at UDM's Center for Cyber Security & Intelligence Studies for over 14 years. He also served for 26 years as Department Chair of the Computer and Information Systems Program in UDM's College of Business Administration.

At the national level, he served as the Co-Chair for Workforce Training and Education for the U.S. Department of Homeland Security Software Assurance Initiative, where he was a contributing author of the DHS Software Assurance Common Body of Knowledge (CBK). He also helped author the DHS Information Assurance Essential Body of Knowledge and has served as a subject-matter expert (SME) for the NIST NICE Workforce Framework for Cybersecurity and the ACM/IEEE/AIS Joint Task Force on Cybersecurity Education (CSEC2017). In addition to his academic and policy work, he is a prolific author of leading cybersecurity textbooks published by Cengage, McGraw-Hill, and Taylor & Francis/CRC Press.

Tamara Shoemaker is a nationally recognized cybersecurity educator and program builder dedicated to closing the cyber workforce gap. She previously directed the Center for Cyber Security & Intelligence Studies at the University of Detroit Mercy. She served as Program Manager for the Auto-ISAC Automotive Cybersecurity Training Program in partnership with NHTSA. She is the founder of the Michigan CyberPatriot Program, which engages more than 1,000 middle and high school students each year through hands-on cybersecurity education, summer camps, and competitive learning experiences. She also serves as the President of the Michigan Midwest Regional Chapter of CISSE (MCISSE), is a founding board member, and a national "Emerging Leader" with the Air & Space Force Association.

A co-author of *Teaching Cybersecurity*, she is a passionate advocate for empowering the next generation of cyber defenders.

Amir Jabri is a seasoned information security and technology leader with over two decades of experience designing cybersecurity and technology strategies for highly regulated industries, including aerospace, healthcare, semiconductors, and government.

He holds a master's in information assurance and a bachelor's in information technology with a security focus, complemented by elite certifications such as CISSP, CISM, and CRISC.

He excels in risk management, cloud technology, and security across AWS, Azure, incident response, governance, and compliance frameworks like NIST and ISO 27001, mentoring teams to enable secure digital transformation. LinkedIn www.linkedin.com/in/amirjabris

ABOUT THE DESIGNER

Jacob M. Green is an illustrator and recent high school graduate currently studying digital art at the College for Creative Studies-Detroit, one of the nation's leading colleges of art and design. He has been drawing since he could hold a pencil and has a strong interest in animation, game design, and art education. A natural teacher, Jacob eagerly absorbs knowledge – collecting facts the way other students collect Pokémon cards. This is his second book illustration; his first was *Teaching Cybersecurity*, also written by the Shoemakers, which focuses on equipping educators with tools to teach cybersecurity in K–12 classrooms globally.

AI statement

We used ChatGPT 5.2 to provide the alt-text for the figures in our book on the Open platform ChatGPT with a private account.

Chapter 1

Introduction

Cyber defense is a topic of importance

Figure 1.1 A black-and-white pencil drawing of a crossroads with a wooden signpost at the center. One arrow-shaped sign points left and reads "SAFETY," while the other points right and reads "RUIN," symbolizing a choice between two divergent paths.

THE INVISIBLE WAR WE ARE LOSING

> *The art of war is of vital importance to the state. It is a matter of life, or death, a road either to safety or to ruin. Hence, it is a subject of inquiry which can on no account be neglected.*
>
> —Sun Tzu

Conflict in cyberspace is costly. If you doubt that, consider the fact that last year we lost approximately $6 trillion worth of value to the actions of our adversaries. In effect, the equivalent of the entire GDP of England and France simply evaporated into virtual space. Yet, nobody seems to have noticed.

DOI: 10.1201/9781003603412-1

I mean, seriously!! ... Given that degree of loss, one would expect promises to "get to the bottom of things" or perhaps a declaration of war. Instead, there has been nothing, nada, zilch ... just hazy press releases declaring that we have a problem and herds of companies selling snake oil as an easy solution ... and the situation continues to get worse.

So, why is this disaster not a vital public concern? It's because cyberattacks have no visible consequences ... or at least the kind that an ordinary person would see as a loss. In fact, it's possible to lose everything that you own without knowing that you've actually been attacked. Since all of the valued objects are still there, it's just that they've either been compromised or copied. That kind of cost is hard for folks to understand. Burned-out buildings and wrecked tanks ... THOSE are easy to see and value, whereas the loss of $6 trillion worth of abstract value – now THAT's hard to get your mind around.

This book is founded on two pragmatic principles ... both of which must be true for you to consider yourself sufficiently protected in cyberspace. First, cybersecurity is a state, not a function. Thus, people and organizations must take active steps to both achieve and then maintain a secure state. And second, by implication, a proper state of protection has not been attained if you have failed to take every action that is required to achieve it.

Those two conditions might seem self-evident and perhaps even a bit silly. Nonetheless, it must be kept in mind that virtual objects are susceptible to three distinct types of attack: electronic, such as classic hacking; behavioral, such as social engineering; and physical, such as natural disasters or theft. Therefore, logically, the cybersecurity solution must embody a tangible set of suitably designed and fully interoperable controls that protect against adversaries in each of those domains.

So, in effect ... if you want to be secure, then you must deploy an effective control to secure every point of vulnerability in your protection scheme. This means that every reasonable gap in an organization's cyber defense has to be identified and mitigated by effective controls. And if you haven't done all that is necessary ... then your organization is, by definition, vulnerable. Consequently, you must, at a minimum, deploy measures to detect and mitigate all feasible forms of electronic, human, and/or physical mischief that might reasonably be expected to impact your virtual assets.

That statement also probably seems self-evident. But there is one real-world constraint that prevents us from implementing what appears to be an obvious solution. That is the fact that the field of cybersecurity is stovepiped. Meaning that responsibility for building a complete and integrated architecture of controls is assigned to different, often competing, parts of the organization. For instance, information technology (IT) handles electronic security, while physical security handles physical attacks.

Why do we fail to grasp the obvious? It's due to our inability to fully understand the nature of the threat. The popular view of cybersecurity is that it ensures just the electronic aspects of the organization. That sounds reasonable. The assets we are discussing are all stored, processed, and transmitted electronically. So, the only security we need is electronic, right?

Unfortunately, this overlooks the fact that the people who install and operate these electronic countermeasures, as well as the physical locations where they reside, are also susceptible to subversion or attack. Therefore, those points of direct access also require the installation and maintenance of reliable controls.

The problem is that the cybersecurity protection operations, meaning the IT units, are only focused on the electronic attack surface. So, they, quite rightly, don't view themselves as being responsible for implementing controls to mitigate behavioral or physical threats, which, of course, presents an engraved invitation to the hacker community to run a social engineering exploit on that unprotected aspect of the organization.

So, why is that dangerous thinking allowed to persist? Let's use an old Indian proverb to illustrate the reason. In that old tale, six blind men are asked to describe an elephant based on what they are touching. Thus, the one holding the trunk thinks it's a snake, the one holding the ear thinks it's a leaf, the one touching the side thinks it's a wall, and so on. The point is that "Although they were all perfectly correct, they were also entirely wrong."

That's the current mindset in the field of cybersecurity. In effect, there is a lack of awareness of the need for close cooperation among a diverse set of players, all of whom have something essential to contribute to the overall solution. Instead, the requirement to secure vulnerabilities in the organization's non-electronic attack surfaces is vaguely presumed to be the responsibility of line managers, or human resources people, or sometimes the physical security function. The problem is that in most organizations, these functions are located in different parts of the building, or if the organization is large enough, on other continents. And even worse, the critical players rarely think about, or even want, to cooperate.

Hence, computing and communications security is an IT function. Accountability to ensure the trustworthiness of the people operating that equipment is a human resources obligation. And of course, the security of the actual building and its equipment resides with physical security.

So, the network security function does a fine job of ensuring the network. But it won't background the network manager or control the perimeter of the actual building. Similarly, human resources doesn't see protecting electronic access to the network or physical protection of the physical location as their responsibility. Likewise, no sane physical security director would want anything to do with the knotty problems of bent insiders or the intricacies of system configuration.

I hear you asking, "Who's responsible for knocking down the stovepipes?" Well ... we know for sure that the people running our organizations don't see it as their problem. For instance, only 38% of the top executives surveyed by ISACA (Information Systems Audit and Control Association) felt that they were accountable for taking substantive action regarding cybersecurity. Therefore, even with the clear evidence that very bad things are happening in cyberspace, you could reasonably characterize the current C-suite's response as "detached."

The reason for this detachment is that executive managers aren't even close to understanding the issues associated with implementing a defense against threats across three disparate attack surfaces. It's sort of like asking them to play three-dimensional chess. Therefore, instead, executive management has adopted the narrative that the company is conducting due diligence if it deploys an electronic defense.

That carefully crafted definition of responsible practice likely allows those individuals to sleep better at night, and it undoubtedly gives them plausible deniability if the lawyers show up. But realistically ... a purely electronic solution will counter perhaps one-third of all potential attack vectors, and that doesn't come close to adequately ensuring security.

So, what's the current strategy for defense in cyberspace? Well ... let's use a grizzly bear to illustrate that thinking. Grizzly bears are as fast as racehorses, at least over a short distance. So, if you are out hiking and you happen to run into a grizzly bear, you won't be able to outrun it. But practically, all you have to do is outrun another member of your hiking group if you want to escape the bear. So, companies spend just enough money to ensure that another organization is easier to breach. It's sort of the cybersecurity equivalent of "hiking with the fat kid."

Saltzer and Schroeder, who wrote the first principles for cybersecurity back in 1974, codified that thinking with a principle called "work factor." In essence, the modern adversary won't waste their time pounding their head on a robust firewall. Instead, they will hunt around for a point of access that is either open or inadequately secured. So, you can assume that you are safe if you have secured more electronic access points than another organization.

A cyber defense entirely based on electronic countermeasures might have made sense before the advent of advanced behavioral and physical exploits. However, losses due to non-electronic attacks, such as insider theft, supply chain hacks, and simple internet scams, are not strictly speaking electronic, which is why the most successful real-world exploits now target the behavioral and physical attack surfaces.

THE ADVERSARY DOESN'T CARE

Your adversary's goal is to gain unauthorized access to your system by any means possible. So, the adversary will employ "anything that works." Hence, any hole in the protection scheme, whether electronic, behavioral, or physical, is a potential point of vulnerability for the entire system. Or in simple terms, any electronic, human, or physical vulnerability that permits unauthorized access essentially negates all of the measures set up to secure the other two attack surfaces. That is the reason why a well-defined and comprehensively interacting array of countermeasures is absolutely essential.

In simple terms, since the adversary will exploit any available point of entry, the organization's defensive perimeter must incorporate every control necessary to ensure the integrity of the protection scheme. This is the reason why a fully integrated set of interoperating control behaviors is essential for a comprehensive solution.

Then those controls need to work together to safeguard all three potential forms of compromise. Thus, the absolute requirement for comprehensive control of the defensive perimeter ought to make it clear that we need to redefine our present cyber defense doctrine to ensure that all feasible attack vectors from every valid source are identified and mitigated as part of the overall cybersecurity solution.

In essence, the only effective cyber defense is a comprehensive one. Thus, the profession of cybersecurity must adjust its understanding to address and counter the complete set of vulnerabilities that exist in the organizational protection perimeter, not just the electronic ones. Or, to continue our analogy, organizations need to see and deal with the entire elephant.

UNIFYING APPROACHES

The meta-process that creates a fully comprehensive and unified solution is generically referred to as "convergence." Convergence describes the unified point of control that is always necessary to deploy and oversee a complex, rational, strategic, and cybersecurity protection scheme – one without exploitable gaps. It involves systematic steps to merge all relevant electronic, personnel, and physical security functions into a unified organizational system.

In reality, the steps necessary to achieve convergence are just as complex as the system design process. Mechanisms must exist to monitor the practical day-to-day cybersecurity operation at every potential point of access, across the entire organization. These mechanisms must provide an integrated set of mutually supporting control countermeasures, while also ensuring that all stakeholders are held accountable for secure performance.

Logically, a single control point is necessary for the coordination because the organization's monitoring and enforcement requirements are always cross-functional. That is, normal business activities involve the participation of more than one unit – for example, both human resources and IT must cooperate to ensure proper identity management.

So, by its very nature, comprehensive cybersecurity control deployment and sustainment must cross unit boundaries. This involves establishing a formally authorized strategic process with the mandate to build a wholly integrated protection scheme that fully embodies each of the organization's three attack surfaces into a single, collaborative protection scheme and then enforces that scheme across every aspect of the organization's operation.

To ensure the proper execution of all control activities, the organization must also identify and address every inherent interdependency between controls. Nonetheless, control interdependencies are challenging, as control interoperation typically involves multiple attack surfaces, such as using a social engineering exploit to install a rootkit. That complex relationship makes the cybersecurity function responsible for ensuring a three-dimensional problem. In this respect, a converged approach is the only mechanism available to ensure optimal situational understanding and response.

The catch-all professional term for a converged approach is "holistic." Holistic cyber defense involves a single unified system of electronic, behavioral, and physical controls that enforce continuous security across all common attack surfaces. Hence, holistic defenses comprise discrete, well-defined, and rational actions, which are explicitly targeted to address every meaningful threat. Holistic security is consistently implemented as a system. In that respect, then, the end product of the holistic security approach is an integrated, appropriately tailored defense against any viable threat ... electronic, human, or physical.

This book describes the approach that is required to conceptualize, implement, and maintain a properly holistic control solution. It centers on a well-defined process for planning, building, and ensuring comprehensive, in-depth cyber defense. In essence, we will demonstrate why holistic security is the only approach that enables an organization to identify and address all valid threats to its digital resources.

IT'S WAR FOLKS

> *If I know how you choose to defend yourself, then I know how to attack you.*
>
> **—Sun Tzu**

Let's be clear here ... the actions that threat actors take against your virtual assets are by definition adversarial. And just as in war, your adversary's only goal is to defeat you by any means possible. So, just as in conventional warfare, the adversary will conduct a thorough reconnaissance of your system before initiating any attack. The aim of that initial exploration is to identify the most effective way to attack you. A purely electronic solution will inevitably create exploitable gaps. That is why investing solely in electronic controls, without considering and securing the other two attack surfaces, is a recipe for failure.

Please note ... this does not imply that electronic attacks aren't a serious problem and that electronic control systems aren't necessary. The

Mitre Corporation's ATT&CK matrix framework lists 14 attack categories, which encompass 196 unique attack vectors. These attacks are further subdivided into 411 behavioral techniques, every one of which could potentially require a countermeasure. In fact, the sheer volume of harmful behaviors associated with electronic exploits should indicate the magnitude of the overall problem.

However, the infinite catalogue of harmful human behaviors, as well as physical threats, could fill volumes, and none of these factors have been effectively categorized or countered by standard best practices. And yet, every one of those yet undescribed threats is a risk, and all of them should, at the very least, be considered when putting together an effective cyber defense. This is not an issue that will be resolved in one book. However, awareness of the scope and complexity of the problem is necessary to create a successful process.

Finally, why are we discussing war here, instead of crime? According to the Federal Trade Commission, an identity is stolen every 22 seconds. That will affect the person it happens to, and the outcome can be catastrophic for that individual, which makes it a crime. However, targeted cyberattacks against U.S. infrastructure and large corporations can permanently alter your way of life or significantly impact the entire economic structure of the Country.

Take supervisory control and data acquisition (SCADA), for instance. Those little systems regulate everything that you assume will always be there ... heat, light, water. But because they are simple industrial controls rather than general-purpose computers, very few of those vital digital components are protected in any meaningful way. This makes them vulnerable to a Pearl Harbor-style attack. That would be an act of war by most definitions, and those exploits occur daily. We are already engaged in a cyberwar.

In general, adversarial actions of that type are prompted by two very human motives: geopolitical advantage or financial gain. Just as in the James Bond movies or the old-time bank robbers, the most harmful types of attacks are carried out by competent and organized groups. Worse, due to the global reach of the internet, many of these groups operate from locations, such as China, Korea, Russia, Eastern Europe, Iran, and even Africa. So, in essence, the adversary's cultures may vary as much in motive, intent, and outcome as they would in the real world. However, they share a common aim: social chaos and/or profit.

The primary concern is that cyberattacks are not part of the physical world. So, the measures that your adversary will employ to attack you are not as easy to distinguish as they might be in the real world. For instance, launching a missile in your direction – now, that's clearly an attack. However, it's difficult to categorize exploits like financial attacks. However, it's worth noting that these are the ones that currently cost us $6 trillion a year. In fact, the opportunities for financial gain are so great that highly organized criminal enterprises have established themselves worldwide. The result has been that the skill level, personality traits, and modus operandi of the adversary now comprise a vast spectrum of potential attack types. So, in order to design and deploy an effective solution you must first understand the challenging variety of threat actors.

DOCUMENTING THE THREATSCAPE

It's given, then, that your system can be compromised in many "interesting" ways, from remote hacks to simple smash-and-grab theft. Accordingly, your protection scheme must incorporate all feasible business, environmental, and human countermeasures necessary to mitigate any significant attempt to steal or compromise virtual assets.

Still, if you think that the answer is to deploy controls to defend all of the legitimate attack surfaces, you need to keep in mind that there are far too many potential points of attack to defend. Consequently, to develop an informed and intelligent response, it is necessary to understand the adversarial context. That complete collection of potential threats is termed "the threatscape."

The problem is that businesses don't have the slightest idea what data they possess, nor do they know what specifically threatens their virtual assets. That is because most organizations don't adequately:

- **Scope:** e.g., specifically identify and label their assets
- **Value:** they have a shifting concept of what useful information they possess
- **Assess the risks:** they have a limited view of the ways that their assets are threatened
- **Assign accountability:** make the right people responsible for ensuring against loss.

Hence, to adequately address the problem, the business must:

- **Organize:** have a clearly defined and economically feasible security infrastructure
- **Prioritize:** protect all assets of value in whatever form within that infrastructure
- **Safeguard:** have controls in place to address all likely threats and incidents
- **Assure:** demonstrate that the process is continuously reliable and trustworthy over time

That requires a coherent strategy to:

- **Design:** develop a comprehensive solution composed of the right set of security controls
- **Evaluate:** objectively demonstrate the reliability of that array
- **Adjust:** continuously evolve security controls to meet the realities of the threat picture

Moreover, to be judged correct, the strategy must ...

- **Address all known security exposures** – not just the interesting or convenient ones
- **Be systematically sustainable** – as a long-term solution
- **Directly support and be traceable to** – the requirements of the business case

That is the reason why the process of cybersecurity development must originate at the top. Logically, no other location in the organization has the strategic vision or the proper authority to establish a comprehensive organization-wide solution. The people at the top are the only ones who can see and understand the entire scale of the problem, and they are the only ones with sufficient authority to ensure that the correct measures are implemented and subsequently maintained throughout the organization. They are also the only ones with the power to enforce long-term, disciplined operation.

The unfortunate part is that most top executives do not consider cybersecurity a priority. Instead, they shift that responsibility entirely to the IT function. Which, given the necessity of taking across-the-board security actions, is a de facto guarantee of failure. IT practitioners don't know any more about securing personnel and physical attack surfaces than the folks at your local Burger King.

First and most importantly, the IT function doesn't have the authority to install and maintain a complete and integrated set of assurance measures for players who do, such as human resources or physical security. And finally, and most relevantly, IT is not in the club, which means the IT function is not seen as directly relevant to the business's goals, like generating revenue. But that perception will have to change if leadership wants to keep the money it has.

IT rightly does electronic security. Therefore, making IT accountable for securing attack surfaces that they are not responsible for and don't fully understand is a blindly irresponsible allocation of roles and duties by top management. The result is inevitably going to be that the solution will be piecemeal, and the adversary will find plenty of gaps to exploit.

For instance, effective access control implies that all appropriate and reasonable practices have been deployed to meet a minimum standard of due care for virtual asset protection. Therefore, no matter how adequate the electronic role-based access controls may be, they are useless without the cooperation of the human resources function to manage role assignments.

The due care obligation ensures that all necessary control processes required to address all likely threats and attacks on all three attack surfaces have been incorporated through a coherent system design and fully integrated into day-to-day operations. The ability to demonstrate due care is vitally important to most organizations now, due to the increasing legal liability that proof of negligence brings. And since ignorance of the requirement is no defense against liability. It is essential to maintain a coherent set of control elements to ensure a legally trustworthy, long-term security system.

THE HOLISTIC SECURITY LIFECYCLE

To secure ourselves against defeat lies in our own hands.

—Sun Tzu

It is a significant challenge for every business to establish an effective system of controls from scratch. The assurance of due care in virtual asset protection practice is especially difficult because the process itself involves a blend of technology, people, and practices. Therefore, a well-defined and widely understood model for creating and documenting effective practices is essential. A complete and rational protection scheme provides documented proof that due care has been adequately considered and sustainably addressed. Needless to say, though, that isn't an easy task.

Logically, every control element within the protection scheme should have a targeted purpose, and each should contribute measurable value to the outcome. Therefore, the development of sustainable protection requires a carefully coordinated effort between classic architectural and design elements. That is the reason why it is essential to approach the design and deployment of a complete, holistic solution from an architectural perspective.

Security architectures are multilayered and multifaceted, and, like all physical architectures, their components must be present and mutually supportive. The architecture itself must be consistent because experience has shown that a flaw will be exploited whenever it is discovered. Therefore, all programmed electronic responses, behavioral policies, procedures, and physical safeguards must be logically organized in a rational and coherent structure to ensure the virtual asset.

The atomic components of the solution are referred to as "security controls." Those are planned and programmed electronic, behavioral, and physical behaviors that are established and seamlessly integrated into the day-to-day operation, in order to ensure a sufficiently trusted level of operation. Four common-sense steps guide the development of that substantive cybersecurity architecture. These are:

1. Understand the context
2. Design for feasibility
3. Plan the coverage
4. Implement the priorities

Understanding – the critical first step in the process is to get a common understanding of the security requirements for the entire organization. All organizations vary in purpose and intent. Hence, they all have differing security needs. The steps that you take to achieve a proper understanding of those requirements imply the need for a comprehensive analytical process. The point of that process is to achieve complete and continuous alignment between the threats present in the threatscape and the specific organizational responses deployed to mitigate them.

Organizational complexity is the single point of failure for that process. Since cybersecurity is a desired state, not a concrete objective, obtaining a common understanding of the best way to attain and maintain effective cybersecurity will inevitably involve numerous conflicting points of view. That part of the process will be political in nature in any organizational undertaking. Accordingly, it is necessary to undertake an organization-wide agreement process among all legitimate stakeholders to analyze and agree on the assurance requirements. The outcome of that process is a formal statement of priorities.

Designs are important because they convey a clear understanding of how the organization will implement cybersecurity. Thus, the design process is built around a clear understanding of the organization's strategic goals and fundamental cybersecurity policies. That process produces a formal statement that enhances the acceptance of the resultant cybersecurity solution among a diverse set of organizational participants. The outcome of the agreement process is a substantive architectural design.

The architectural design must enable line managers to clearly understand how the proposed cybersecurity policies will be implemented through routine day-to-day practices. The general relationship between new cybersecurity activities and existing legacy functions must be clearly defined to a level of detail that provides the necessary understanding to underwrite integration. At a minimum, that design process involves the following:

- Identification and evaluation of the sensitivity of organizational information assets.
- Creation of plans to ensure deliberate control over every identified organizational asset.
- Development and implementation of training programs to enable and enforce the understanding and the use of proper security measures.

Planning – The plan brings the now well-defined requirements for assurance into a single, coherent, continuously evolving set of strategic actions. It probably goes without saying that the competitive position of the organization relies on its virtual assets. That is because the information that is stored in a company's computers comprises what that organization actually does. A formal planning process enables control over those assets ... the mandatory outcome of which is the substantive plan. That plan assures that all necessary players and resources are available to execute the process as visualized.

Every organization has strategic aims. Hence, the organizational policies for cybersecurity must flow naturally from the business's strategic imperatives. The actual process will differ because every organization is unique, and each one implements its processes differently. Nevertheless, all cybersecurity solutions are built on the same practical set of requirements ... which are that all digital assets of value are assured: correct, confidential, and available. In addition to these general responsibilities, holistic security demands that a well-defined control traceably mitigate all relevant threats.

The assigned security commitments for each role in the overall plan must be regulated by a substantive accountability and enforcement process. That process must also be present, and regular and systematic assessments must be done in order to ensure that those roles are performing correctly. Training and awareness are the standard methods for ensuring that all of the relevant roles in the security process understand the importance of their actions.

Implementation – The outcome of the planning process is always a substantive, organization-wide cybersecurity system, which balances the aims of policy with real-world conditions and constraints to produce adequate assurance of the virtual asset. In practice, organizations adopt and follow a systematic process that guarantees that every one of its security requirements has been identified and addressed by a substantive countermeasure.

The atomic-level components of a security architecture comprise an integrated set of electronic, behavioral, and physical controls designed and implemented to ensure a specific state of desired security. These should all be directly traceable to the policies that defined them. The ongoing assurance of appropriate alignment between strategic policies and day-to-day procedures ensures that the assurance system is effective in operational settings, as well as capable of evolving with the changing threatscape.

The security solution itself must be conventionally systematic. In essence, it must be reliable and repeatable in day-to-day operation. That reliability can be verified if the requisite set of organizational controls is in place and working as planned. That proof comes from measuring operational control performance against the outcomes that are specified in the plan.

Controls are implemented to regulate and secure certain aspects of the organization's cybersecurity operations. In effect, each control independently enforces some small aspect of the overall cybersecurity strategy. This is accomplished by ensuring the ability to guarantee the confidentiality, integrity, and availability of a designated element within the digital asset base. Finally, then, a properly developed control architecture ensures that uniform control is enforced from top to bottom across the entire organization.

The security perimeter marks the conceptual boundary of a security system. It is not difficult to build an effective defense if the boundaries of the problem are well known. But that understanding is rarely the case with virtual assets. Digital assets are abstract entities, and worse, the threats to them continually evolve. The fog of war hides these, so to speak. The problem is made even more complex because it is difficult to detect or even characterize attacks that target an abstract entity, such as a digital asset within a protected virtual space.

Hence, it is hard to say with any certainty whether the security perimeter is functioning effectively or even exists in any substantive way. Consequently, the next critical step in the process is to explicitly define a substantive perimeter that can be evaluated for effectiveness.

First, let's look at what a security perimeter is. A security perimeter is any potential point of access for any space that you plan to secure. The identification and characterization of that perimeter is difficult because all three attack surfaces must be factored into the control understanding. In essence, any harmful event that may occur on any of those attack surfaces must be recognized, characterized, and an effective mitigation strategy developed that is practically feasible.

We need to stop here and take a look at the feasibility. Feasibility is the likelihood that a task or purpose can be accomplished. In cybersecurity, this is typically based on whether the solution aligns with the organization's available resources and capabilities. Obviously, no matter how elegant the solution is, it is useless if it is not feasible. Many problems can be solved if you throw enough money at them. However, organizations operate within budgets, and some solutions require technologies that have yet to be invented. So, it is always a balancing act.

For example, sophisticated biometric technologies can be used for secure access control. However, biometric solutions might not fit within the budget of the average company. Thus, a biometric solution for a minor application is questionable because it does not fit financial constraints. That would be the case even if the biometric control itself worked properly and fulfilled its purpose in every other respect.

The decisions about feasibility might change if the protected space contains assets that are highly valuable or sensitive. That situation might justify the added cost and trouble of employing biometrics. However, if there are no apparent threats in the threat landscape, the price of a biometric solution might not be regarded as justified. The point being that practicality, in terms of both impact and cost-benefit, is always a consideration when developing a security perimeter.

Accordingly, a central tenet for implementing a holistic security system is that the threats against a given protection object must be evaluated and weighed against the availability of financial and staff resources. Factors that enter into this decision include such considerations as: What is the level of criticality for each of the information assets falling within the scope of the protection scheme, and what is the degree of assurance required for each?

In the worst case, a non-essential, low-risk resource might be left outside of the defensive perimeter due to a lack of resources. However, if that decision is based on precise knowledge about where that asset fits into the overall purposes and aims of the organization ... then that is an *informed risk*.

Decision-makers use a prioritization process to optimize the real-world elements of the cybersecurity protection scheme. As such, it is crucial to involve representatives from the organization, as well as relevant third parties, in the perimeter definition process.

This is particularly important in formulating a working cybersecurity system because virtual security boundaries are dynamic. Hence, the borders with information assets are subject to ongoing refinement as threats and resources evolve. Proper modifications to those controls are performed based on feedback from the operational units over time.

NOW, LET'S MEET THE ADVERSARY

> *If you know the enemy and know yourself, you need not fear the result of a hundred battles. If you know yourself but not the enemy, for every victory gained, you will also suffer a defeat. If you know neither the enemy nor yourself, you will succumb in every battle.*
>
> —**Sun Tzu**

We wouldn't be having this discussion before the advent of the World Wide Web. That is because the new adversary, the one we are concerned with here, is a creature of global connectivity. So now, it is necessary to factor the diverse capabilities and motivations of a wide range of threat actors into the question of how to create a knowledgeable and responsive defense. That understanding is necessary because any competent adversary will adopt the approach they need to defeat an existing countermeasure array – and that approach will not necessarily be addressable by electronic controls.

Instead, it might be a behavioral attack, such as social engineering, or even the outright theft of the physical device that contains the digital asset – whatever it takes to obtain the thing that the adversary wants to steal or corrupt. Each of the classic adversary typologies we will discuss here brings a distinct set of capabilities and motives to the table, and you must understand these if you want to develop a targeted defense.

Everybody's security problems were local in the 1980s and early 1990s. So, for regular people, a typical cyber-attack was a computer virus obtained from an infected floppy disk or a piece of pirated software. The individuals who attacked other users were often hobbyists or counterculture types who worked independently and on the fringes. Of course, that leaves out the tiny group of highly trained and organized nation-state actors working at places like the National Security Agency. But those are a different breed of cat. Those types of attackers were the ones who perpetrated mainframe network exploits that were limited to a small set of targets, mainly for financial or geopolitical gain.

The situation changed radically as soon as the internet became the primary communication medium for businesses. Now, instead of being threatened by simple things like disk infections or piracy, each of us is subject to new horrors, from financial ruin to potential cyberwar. Hence, the old-fashioned stereotype of a basement-dwelling loner living on Skittles, while engaging in 72-hour hacks to satisfy some weird ego need, has been replaced by a much more diverse and capable collection of adversarial typologies. Such typologies are well organized and much more focused on committing mischief for specific purposes. Knowing those purposes will help you shape your defensive concept.

There are 11 general types of adversaries in cyberspace, now. Each adversary is differentiated by their fundamental motives, intent, and outcomes. Hence, understanding each one's motive and intent will inform your protection strategy. It should be noted that although many of the behaviors in each of these categories are similar, the types of adversaries you might encounter in cyberspace are:

Script Kiddies are technologically inept and either random or trivial in intent. They use preprogrammed scripts to trespass in individual and organizational systems that they are familiar with, such as their school or a friend's. Their actions violate confidentiality. However, their motivation is typically recreational hacking or simple curiosity.

Nonetheless, more advanced kiddies might engage in targeted invasions of privacy, typically for ego reasons, like cracking a celebrity's system, and they can occasionally unleash accidentally destructive attacks such as Distributed Denial of Service (DDOS) worms. This happens because, although kiddies might be of any age, they are often technologically incapable; hence, their attacks are not novel or well targeted. Hence, script kiddie attacks are the ones that are most likely to be thwarted by a standard electronic defense, such as a firewall.

Cyberpunk Hackers represent the counterculture. Therefore, their intent is almost always to perform an exploit for a culturally driven impact. A cyberpunk is technologically proficient, but not typically superb, and their attacks most often have a behavioral focus, such as spoofing and/or spear fishing. Cyberpunk hacker groups like Anonymous are frequently responsible for code insertion, or application-layer attacks, that target establishment organizations and products, as well as massive numbers of social engineering ploys, particularly click-driven gambits aimed at installing malware.

The aim of a cyberpunk attack is, by definition, social/political, generally for peddling influence, or for the target's embarrassment. Hence, the exploit is most often information theft and/or disclosure for the purpose of influencing public opinion. An example of this is the personally embarrassing exploits that have occasionally surfaced in the political realm. The critical point to note is that cyberpunks will only engage in acts of information theft, disinformation, and sabotage on what they perceive as legitimate targets, such as political parties and/or culturally noteworthy corporations.

Code Warriors are the first of the more destructive adversaries. They are driven almost strictly by monetary gain. As such, they engage in acts of theft or sabotage aimed at some aspect of a corporate or geopolitical operation. Their attacks are built around code insertions, specifically application-layer attacks and Trojan horse insertions through social engineering. They are technologically superb and likely to design and execute a wide range of structured, coordinated exploits by manipulating the subject into installing a malicious code segment into their OS or application layer functioning.

As all of these attack types involve vulnerability exploitation or code insertion, including the exploitation of zero-day vulnerabilities and supply chain update attacks, the code warrior is likely to operate in a highly organized manner that features multiple probes for reconnaissance. That behavior can be utilized to spot a code warrior.

Cyberthieves are motivated by monetary gain. They profit either by stealing information of value through electronic or behavioral means, or by outright physical theft of the data, through direct contact with the machine, or by simply swiping the device. Their attacks will involve any set of actions that achieve their purpose, which is to acquire something valuable by theft. As such, individuals in this category who are attempting to attack you remotely will employ sophisticated network sniffing tools and social engineering exploits to insert Trojans and malware. They are also very adept at pulling classic con games, such as the grandmother scam, which aim to get their victim to do something that benefits the attacker, for instance, clicking on a poisoned link.

Cyberhucksters are the spammers and general purveyors of clickbait. Their motives are monetary gain, and their target is commercialization. They are adept at social engineering. They also use spoofing to obtain sensitive information, such as user details. This profile employs surreptitious methods, such as tracking cookies and spyware. They are even operators of legitimate data mines, which they then sell on to nefarious individuals and organizations. Cyberhucksters are not prosecuted as conscientiously as they should be, because their actions are viewed as more annoying and resource-wasting than criminal. However, the cyberhuckster will absolutely and utterly violate your personal privacy, which is a trespass in the criminal world.

The *Unhappy Insider* is perhaps the most dangerous adversary in this entire set. This adversary can easily steal information, set destructive logic bombs, or perform other malicious acts on the system because they are already inside the organization's defenses. The distinctive feature of this category is their unhappiness with the organization. They are invariably motivated by revenge or monetary gain, and they use their legitimate access to the organization's digital resources to execute direct betrayal, blackmail, or exposure of company secrets.

This is a management challenge, not an electronic one. Because insiders, by definition, are trusted and have all of the associated rights. Thus, behavioral monitoring and targeted awareness and training are your only viable protection strategy. The monitoring can be aided by electronic surveillance. However, big companies have a large number of employees, and it is challenging to predict which of them will choose to turn bad. More importantly, however, somebody has to manage the electronic monitoring, which makes those people prime candidates to be trusted. Thus, deep background checks are a vital countermeasure.

Ex-insider is the terminated former employee. They are motivated by extortion, revenge, sabotage, or disinformation. These individuals are focused on harming the organization that dismissed them. So, they might set logic bombs or lock-out passwords for all employees if they can see the dismissal coming, as was done in San Francisco several years ago. Otherwise, a terminated employee might steal insider information that they can gain while still having access rights, which can then be used to harm or discredit the company from the outside. The only protection from this type of malcontent is to carefully plan a dismissal that ensures the targeted individual cannot access the system. Finally, attacks on company vulnerabilities that were not public knowledge are a sure sign of the work of an ex-insider.

Cyberstalker is an individual who is motivated by some form of psychological dysfunction. The primary intent of this adversary is to invade privacy for the purpose of learning something that satisfies a specific personal need, such as jealousy. The primary tool of attackers in this category is the keylogger; however, more sophisticated cyberstalkers will use targeted Trojan horses to gain surreptitious access to their target. This profile is differentiated from the other adversary categories in that their exploits are driven by a particular psychological dysfunction, rather than a desire for monetary gain or to wreak havoc. Identification of the need will often suggest ways that the organization can thwart this type of attacker.

The *Conman* is an individual strictly motivated by monetary gain. The intent of this adversary is theft or some form of illicit commercialization. This adversary category is adept at social engineering and identity spoofing ... or in simple terms, old-fashioned con games. Members of this group run traditional swindles, as well as newer exploits like targeted catfishing. Due to the anonymity of the internet, this type of con artist can be difficult to identify once they have completed their particular scam. Since the con man depends on the victim's ignorance, the only real defense against this category of attacker is a dedicated awareness program, which is an entirely behavioral response.

The Mafia Soldier represents organized crime's entry into the field of cyber warfare. These individuals are differentiated from all other categories by their capability and the attacker's high level of organization, which is second only to that of the warfighter. Mafia soldiers are motivated by the same goals that typically inspire classic organized crime: monetary gain or the ability to influence the actions of others for personal gain. The objectives of the Mafia Soldier are achieved through classic criminal means, including theft, extortion, and, occasionally, the invasion of privacy for blackmail purposes. The classic type of Mafia soldier has all of the capabilities of the code warrior and the con man. They will always operate in well-funded, highly organized groups, often with the best technology that money can buy at their disposal.

The Warfighter is not an adversary when he is fighting on your side. Conversely, when the warfighter is on the other side, their actions can be extremely far-reaching and destructive. The warfighter is motivated strictly by cyberwar. Hence, they aim to provide strategic advantages for their country and to harm the enemy. These individuals are technologically proficient, making them extremely dangerous.

For instance, they can wreak havoc on the physical infrastructure by attacking SCADA control systems. Their attacks are most frequently carried out through application-layer attacks and Trojans are delivered surreptitiously over a prolonged period. DDOS is another form of attack that can literally bring a corporation or a country to its knees. Warfighters can spread disinformation. This might be done by targeted attacks on the print, or digital media, or through social engineering. Since this category of attackers primarily characterizes the members of any elite government agency, the best defense against a warfighter is another friendly set of warfighters, as there are too many attack surfaces to defend fully.

NOW, LET'S TALK ABOUT ATTACK SURFACES

Let your plans be dark and impenetrable as night, and when you move, fall like a thunderbolt.

—**Sun Tzu**

THE TECHNICAL ATTACK SURFACE

There are a limited number of attack points on the technical front. That is because access to protected space can only be through a permission-based technical endpoint, which is programmed and then maintained as part of a functioning computer system. Accordingly, technical attacks are limited to two general categories: the injection of a malicious object via nefarious means or through an attack that is specially targeted at a system vulnerability.

Excluding the script kiddies, any of the adversary types we have just discussed can successfully perform either of these two types of exploits. Nevertheless, since the approach is generally shaped by the intent, there are good logical reasons to assume that certain types of exploits are more closely associated with particular types of adversaries.

There are four generally recognized types of attack: viruses, logic bombs, Trojan horses, and malware. Each of these has a slightly different intent and execution method; therefore, each involves a different type of adversary.

Viruses are probably the most common types of electronic attack. Viruses are tiny code segments that attach themselves to host programs and then activate when the host program is executed. Digital viruses are, by definition, a non-targeted exploit, since it is impossible to predict in advance who the victim of a given virus might be. In most cases, virus distribution typically involves some form of behavioral exploit, such as getting the victim to click on a link. Viruses can involve every type of malicious exploit, from installing a simple tracking application to violate a person's privacy, to massive worldwide Distributed Denial of Service (DDoS) attacks.

Viruses are generally created for personal reasons, such as a cyberpunk defacement, rather than from a deliberate attempt to take over the world. So, in general, a simple virus is a mild example of a confidentiality violation or corruption exploit. On the other hand, worms, which are a specialized type of virus, might have features that would be associated with one of the more aggressive types of adversaries, such as the Warfighter, since they are responsible for DDOS.

When triggered, these types of viruses will perform propagation attacks on a company or a global network, potentially shutting down their availability. In that respect, DDOS viruses are an extremely costly form of attack. Worse, they don't require much technological competence. In fact, one of the most destructive viruses of all times, the "I Love You" DDOS virus was perpetrated by a script kiddie – albeit by accident. Therefore, the virus category is not a trivial consideration in planning a cybersecurity defense.

Because they are increasingly used for espionage, virus exploits now underwrite grave state-sponsored warfighting and criminal, extortion, and sabotage actions. The motivation behind these types of attacks is almost always destructive. Consequently, people who utilize these types of code exploits are more likely to have specific criminal or geopolitical motives, and the attacks themselves tend to be large-scale, both in terms of their impact and the damage they cause.

The tradecraft behind warfighting virus exploits is relatively arcane and unique, making it difficult to counter without a major intelligence gathering operation, which is why the National Security Agency has become so interested in intelligence analytics. Stuxnet is the oldest known, classic example of a geopolitical type of attack virus. That virus was purposely designed to target the programmable logic controllers (PLCs) for the gas centrifuges used to separate fissionable material for the nuclear programs of Iran, and it is believed to be responsible for causing substantial damage to that program.

Logic bombs, on the other hand, are a true example of a planned software-based exploit, dating back to the mainframe era. Logic bombs are passive, often even large-scale, programs that are set in a host machine and only activated based on parameters built into them by their programming. They are almost impossible to detect in the vast amount of code that an organization operates, and they are invariably damaging if they detonate, as they have been purposely set for a specific destructive purpose.

Logic bombs are a key tool for crimes, such as extortion, sabotage, and espionage. Their weakness is that close, or hands-on, access is almost mandatory to set a logic bomb, unless it is delivered by a Trojan horse. As such, logic bombs are nearly perfect examples of insider actions. They can be extremely dangerous because, if set by hand, it is possible to build a great deal of malicious functionality into a logic bomb's programming. That is because the code size is not limited by a network's delivery requirements. Since the delivery of logic bombs normally requires proximity. The adversary can be detected and countered just as he or she would for a physical crime.

Trojan horses are like their namesake. They are typically wrappers for malicious payloads attached to innocuous-looking programs. Because they are hard to detect, Trojan horses are the primary means of delivering a range of malicious objects via the internet. The Trojan Horse is most frequently deployed when an uninformed individual grants it permission by clicking on a poisoned link. Therefore, the most effective way to counter a Trojan horse is through simple education and awareness.

Since Trojan Horses are typically deployed by being invited into the system, the primary electronic means of countering them is a heuristic network intrusion detection system (NIDS) based on anomaly detection. These fall under the general rubric of artificial intelligence. Such systems identify items that do not fit into a baseline of "normal" behaviors and deny them or flag them for additional inspection. The challenging part in creating such a system is building the reference baseline, and defining what constitutes normal behavior within a large business setting can be subjective, to say the least.

Malware: Finally, there is the special case of malware. Malware is differentiated from viruses by its size and purpose. Malware is typically installed surreptitiously in the same way a normal application is installed. At the bottom end of the scale, personal malware can be transferred via a Trojan Horse when a user clicks on a link or visits a site where malicious cookies are set. Malware of this type can include seemingly innocuous applications such as data miners and adware.

The problem with building defenses in this category is that malware is most frequently delivered due to something the user does. So, clicking on a link that might seem innocuous can install all kinds of nasty functionality, including snooping software, identity hijackers, or even attach your computer to a Botnet. Hence, user awareness and training programs are the only really effective defense against acquiring this type of malware. The problem is that most organizations do not view user education as a protection measure that needs to be treated with the same seriousness as the firewall.

On the other end of the scale, strategic malware is often designed for specific purposes, such as theft, corruption, or outright sabotage. The technology underlying that particular exploit is relatively straightforward, but the method of delivery is almost always novel, in that the actions that characterize this type of attack simply utilize the longstanding body of knowledge and best practices in system management.

For instance, the actions required to embed the malware into SolarWinds update exhibited the kind of tradecraft typically seen at the Central Intelligence Agency (CIA). In other words, the SolarWinds hack was a long-term and highly strategic exploit conducted with the intention of compromising U.S. National Security. It was successful because nobody in system management had anticipated that the malware would be embedded in a humble operational update. So, none of the operational practices or automatic watchdog systems, which are programmed to see and/or counter malware, detected it. However, the damage caused by SolarWinds is the primary argument for strategic thinking in cyber defense planning.

The problem with protecting against any type of malware is that the malicious agent is merely the warhead of a delivery system that is typically embedded in a well-planned and strategic act of sabotage or espionage. Meaning that the most destructive malware attacks are launched through tradecraft sponsored by nation-states or large corporations. Since the victim is, by definition, the target of extensive reconnaissance prior to the attack, it is very difficult to anticipate and create active controls to prevent the outcomes that the adversary has so carefully planned.

The SolarWinds hack of 2020, which we referred to earlier, is a characteristic recent example of this sort of attack. SolarWinds was also the first instance of a code exploit built around the exploitation of a supply chain vulnerability. In it, the Russian Federal Security Service (FSB), under its guise of Cozy Bear, managed to inject a malicious item into a routine update of the SolarWinds network monitoring Orion software. As a result, they were able to successfully compromise 100 major companies and about a dozen government agencies, including the Cybersecurity and Infrastructure Security Agency, or CISA, at the Department of Homeland Security, whose job it is to protect federal computer networks from cyberattacks.

THE BEHAVIORAL AND PHYSICAL ATTACK SURFACES

The fact is that purely behavioral attacks are and have always been legitimate attack vectors. Thus, one primary justification for this book lies in the fact that cybersecurity attacks are rarely considered or addressed from a behavioral and physical control perspective. As we saw in the previous section, behavioral and physical controls, which are not typically considered part of everyday cybersecurity defense, address weaknesses that, in their impact, represent a significant portion of the problem.

The most obvious and long-standing of these is the insider attack. Insiders can cause all kinds of surreptitious mischief because they are by definition "trusted." Hence, they can send critical information to any external location without worrying about the firewall, as firewalls are designed to protect against incoming attacks. Worse, nobody knows the security system better than a person who has the best-use handbook already in hand. So, the blueprint for the attack is already in hand.

More importantly, if a formerly trusted person chooses to be an adversary, they can steal privileged information by simply loading it onto a memory stick and walking out the door. Edward Snowden is perhaps the most notable example of this type of behavioral threat. As a result, behavioral attacks have to be factored into the planning for the protection scheme. A holistic cybersecurity system demands that.

Fortunately, since these attacks center on human behavior, they can be studied, categorized, and controls can be developed and deployed to counter them. The important point to note here is that the really destructive behavioral attacks are just as carefully devised and executed as electronic ones. Therefore, they share common characteristics and requirements that can be profiled and then utilized as a means of establishing an effective array of controls. For instance, many companies already have a carefully planned dismissal protocol that they follow to mitigate the threat posed by an unhappy former employee.

Password attacks – The aim of a password hijack is to obtain a password. They are simple exploits designed to allow remote access to a user's system. Nonetheless, they can have serious consequences such as theft or corruption of virtual assets, or even ransom demands. Password attacks are enabled by technical methods, such as software-supported brute force attacks. However, passwords are most often obtained through password sharing, a procedural flaw, or social engineering exploits, including phishing. Passwords are also tricked out of a user through confidence scams or even routine work activities, such as the password-sharing problem. Passwords can also be guessed because users often use familiar passkeys, such as their birthday, as a means of remembering them.

In the past, the primary goal of most password attacks was to gain unauthorized access for a specific purpose, such as allowing the attacker to spy. However, password-enabled access can also lead to theft and sabotage. In both of these more serious cases, the attack has to be planned and executed. Consequently, a password attack is invariably classifiable as a serious breach of security.

Password attacks are typically social engineering exploits, but they can also originate from Trojan horses, network sniffing, or specific application-based assaults, such as dictionary attacks. If the attack is electronic in origin, for instance, from the Internet and very little harm is done, then the hacker will tend to be a script kiddie or a cyberpunk. If the aim is sabotage, extortion, or theft, then the capabilities of a code warrior, cyberthief, or even a warfighter will most often be required.

Even so, given the reliance on social engineering, which involves manipulating people to trick them out of sensitive information such as passwords, the most likely method of attack is through person-to-person contact, whether remotely or face-to-face. Social engineering-based password attacks account for up to 90% of the total number of such attacks. Consequently, the best countermeasure is an extensive awareness and training program that targets users specifically, making them aware of typical threats to their password security and providing basic behaviors to avoid them.

Snooping attacks are carried out to obtain specific information about an individual. Snooping itself is passive, so it only serves to provide information, such as passwords and account data. The primary objective in most cases is to gain a competitive advantage by obtaining information that the individual considers confidential, for whatever eventual purpose.

Snooping is primarily designed to steal something, such as a password. Another purpose might be to acquire an account or social security information, which can underwrite theft and sabotage of the individual. If it is to satisfy a personal need, such as learning something private about another person, then snooping is generally nothing more than a social engineering con, or it might even be a physical attempt to learn something the user has written down, like a password. Those types of attacks can be perpetrated in any workplace and are best addressed by practicing appropriate security hygiene, like not leaving a workstation unattended. If subsequent exploits are performed using information gained from a snoop, they may be of an electronic or behavioral nature. If the aim of the snoop is to underwrite theft or sabotage, then there is normally a follow-on exploit to carry out the real purpose.

Finally, in addition to the types of adversarial behavior we have discussed, snoopers also use snooping exploits for the purpose of invading privacy. These are almost always motivated in the same way as other types of personal crimes against individuals. The aim of this behavior is to gain some form of advantage or control over the victim by securing knowledge that is either private or personal. In cases such as this, the adversary will almost always have some form of direct relationship to the victim. Thus, security discipline is the primary factor and that has to be motivated and enforced by a well-defined organizational best practice policy.

Spoofing is another example of a planned and coordinated type of behavioral attack. The steps required to convince others that the sender of an Internet packet or message is legitimate usually involve careful planning and execution. These are con games that are carefully crafted to appear authentic. Therefore, behavioral measures such as awareness and training are almost the only way for individuals to avoid being spoofed. Oddly enough, electronic spoofing is the easiest to counter because the computer can perform preprogrammed analyses of such things as packet headers or electronic messages that will detect bogus transmissions.

Because spoofing has become something of a business enterprise in both the U.S. and various third-world countries, the spoofer is almost always part of a large and well-organized group of adversarial participants. Unlike snooping, spoofing of this type is carried out in order to perpetrate a more destructive kind of attack, such as massive theft or a major act of sabotage. At the technological level, this exploit is typically characterized by Internet Protocol (IP) spoofing, which involves modifying the packet header information. At the behavioral or social engineering level, spoofing can entail simple or elaborate phishing scams or spamming using recognizable addresses.

Spoofing is almost always done for the purpose of gaining access to the individual user or corporation for the sake of profit. Thus, spoofing is a common technique employed by all categories of adversaries. Nonetheless, behavioral spoofing is the primary technique employed by cyberthieves, cyberhucksters, and electronic con artists. At the geopolitical level, this is the trademark of the Cyberwarrior.

For the spoof to work properly, the victim must be tricked into believing something that is not true. One of the interesting aspects of this method is that, due to IP spoofing, the computer itself is just as likely to be the target as any human dupe. Therefore, measures to validate IP information are a primary feature on the electronic attack surface.

The likeliest type of individual to employ IP spoofing is the cyberthief or code warrior. The more powerfully malicious categories, such as the mafia soldier and the warfighter, also employ this technique, but compared to the other categories, there are relatively few of the latter types in the game. The common thread for all of these types, however, is their technical proficiency. As such, compiling the list of suspects in an IP spoofing incident is fairly easy compared to identifying the practitioners of behavioral spoofing.

Individuals who engage in behavioral spoofing are akin to the old-fashioned con men of literary fame. In fact, many of these spoofing exploits bear the same time-worn names, like the Nigerian Scam, the Lottery Scam, and the ever-popular Pigeon Drop. In a behavioral exploit of this type, the victim is unknown to the criminal until they respond to the spoof. The spoof itself is typically a "mass-mailing" exploit targeting a large number of unknown but potentially vulnerable victims. Because the behavioral spoof does not specifically target a victim, the victim's actual behavior is the vulnerability that needs to be addressed and mitigated.

Social engineering is a strictly behavioral exploit. It is also a very common form of attack. Social engineering scams can vary in sophistication, ranging from dumpster diving to running short- and long-term con games and stings. These are always well-planned, almost systematic forms of attack, and they almost perfectly fit the attributes of the more sophisticated types of adversary.

Social engineering attacks are typically used to steal sensitive information, such as passwords or account details. However, they are also used for a wide range of purposes, including information warfare, strategic objectives, and disinformation. Since social engineering gambits are behavioral, they can generally be classified based on the intent of the exploit.

CHAPTER SUMMARY: THE HOLISTIC APPROACH

The premise of this chapter is that cybersecurity is a state, not an operational element of the organization. Therefore, people and organizations must take active steps to achieve and maintain that state. This implies that you are not secure if you have not taken every step necessary to achieve it. The primary problem is that virtual information is susceptible to three distinct types of attack: *Electronic*, *Behavioral*, and *Physical*. Therefore, a cybersecurity solution must embody a set of well-planned and effective responses to every valid threat in each of those domains. The problem is that the present field of cybersecurity is fatally stovepiped.

That's because the current approach to protecting digital resources tends to focus strictly on the electronic attack surface. This is due to the logical fact that the protected resource itself is electronic. And that kind of thinking might have even made sense before the advent of advanced behavioral and other non-electronic exploits. However, the significant losses we sustain as a result of non-electronic attacks, such as insider theft, supply chain hacks, and simple confidence games, do not involve anything strictly electronic.

Hence, it ought to be obvious that the scope of the general approach to cybersecurity needs to be expanded to ensure that all feasible attack vectors from every valid source are identified and mitigated. In essence, the only effective cyber defense is a comprehensive one. Thus, the profession of cybersecurity needs to modify its vision to realistically incorporate and protect the complete set of elements that impact virtual security.

The catch-all term for this approach is "Holistic." A holistic cyber defense is a single unified system of electronic, behavioral, and physical controls that enforces continuous security across all common attack surfaces. Hence, holistic defenses will embody discrete, well-defined, and rational actions explicitly targeted to address every meaningful threat. And in that respect, the end product of a holistic security process comprises an integrated, appropriately tailored set of electronic, human, and physical security protections.

Logically, every control element within that holistic protection scheme should have a purpose, and each should contribute measurable value to the ultimate outcome. So, the development of a sustainable protection scheme requires a carefully coordinated classic architectural design activity. Hence, it is important to approach the design and deployment of a holistic solution from an architectural perspective.

Security architectures are multilayered and multifaceted, and, like all physical architectures, their components must be present in a rational and coherent structure. The architecture itself must be coherent because experience has shown that a flaw will be exploited whenever it is discovered. Therefore, all programmed electronic responses, behavioral policies, procedures, and physical safeguards must be logically aligned to ensure the virtual asset.

The problem is that the advent of the global internet has created a broad range of adversaries, all with differing motivations and capabilities. It is essential to comprehend the diverse capabilities and motivations of the broad range of threat actors in order to effectively respond to the diverse array of attacks on the three legitimate attack surfaces.

The fact is that the adversary only wants to get at your stuff. Therefore, any competent adversary will adopt the most effective approach, such as social engineering, subverting an insider, or even stealing the device if an electronic attack isn't possible. Every one of the characteristic groups we just discussed brings a different set of aims and capabilities to the party. Therefore, it is essential that you understand the unique characteristics of each adversary and respond accordingly, rather than simply listing the usual suspects and hoping it works. This is best accomplished by adopting the holistic approach, which will be discussed in Chapter 2.

Chapter 2

Attack and defense

Building a holistic protection

Figure 2.1 A detailed pencil drawing of a chessboard where a human hand is carefully moving a chess piece forward, with other pieces – pawns and a queen – standing nearby. Symbolism: The expert "moves" the enemy through foresight and positioning, not force.

BUILDING A HOLISTIC PROTECTION

Thus, the expert in battle moves the enemy and is not moved by him.
—Sun Tzu

DOI: 10.1201/9781003603412-2

Just like any other complex system or structure, cybersecurity systems are developed through an organizationally sanctioned strategic planning process. The process aims to implement well-defined and widely accepted best practices as a comprehensive, fully operational cyber defense architecture. The process itself must be long-term focused across the entire organization to ensure the sustainability of the protection. Consequently, that architecture is built and then maintained through a rational "lifecycle" methodology that provides a continuous and consistently effective holistic cyber defense posture.

This chapter will detail and explain the substantive steps and building blocks that comprise the holistic security development process. We will focus on describing how each step in the lifecycle's progression contributes to the value of the final, holistic solution. The discussion will include the role and purpose of each building block, as well as the practical development procedures that support it. In addition, we will examine how each lifecycle step logically interacts with all the other stages within the process to ensure a systematic and synergistic cybersecurity solution.

It is essential to understand that the rationale for adopting a lifecycle approach is to create a pragmatic organizational system that encompasses all critical interactions among a diverse and disparate array of components. Those must then operate together as a unified and synergistic end product. Since each component is engineered to add something crucial to the overall purpose and outcome of security, the impact of a holistic cybersecurity system will be greater than the sum of its individual components. In that respect, all constituent components must be fine-tuned to function effectively within the specific cybersecurity solution tailored to that organization.

Holistic systems are created through a logical, well-defined, top-down process that ensures that the resultant cybersecurity architecture is comprehensive in scope and correctly implemented. As a result, holistic system architectures are developed within a practical three-domain meta-process, which aims to ensure that no gaps exist in security protection, for the pragmatic reason that adversaries are always seeking to find the killer gap.

Hence, the first section of this chapter will detail the rationale behind adopting a lifecycle approach. Then it will justify the steps that the organization must follow to ensure that the cybersecurity solution is appropriately complete and comprehensive, e.g., without any significant exploitable vulnerabilities and correctly implemented.

As we demonstrated in our little parable about the elephant, the disciplines that comprise cybersecurity must secure three separate, dissimilar, and distinct attack surfaces: electronic, behavioral, and physical. The overall purpose of the controls set on each of these surfaces is to ensure a key aspect of routine organizational functioning, as well as to monitor the security status of each component. Therefore, the lifecycle elements that we will present here encompass all the principal steps necessary to ensure a viable state of security control. Nevertheless, this discussion will not focus on any current countermeasure tools. That is because the shape of those products will change constantly as the technology evolves.

As we have said several times before, the holistic process assumes that the role and responsibility of the cybersecurity function is to secure every organizational asset from any viable electronic, behavioral, and physical form of attack. As a consequence, the resulting process must provably protect every asset of value in whatever form it might exist and on whatever attack surface is relevant to its compromise. This further assumes that the tangible outcome of a holistic cybersecurity development process is a stable operational cybersecurity assurance operation, where all necessary controls are present and are functioning properly at all times.

The holistic lifecycle comprises three separate sequential domains: analysis, response, and countermeasures. The process itself is illustrated in Figure 2.2.

STEP ONE: THE DOMAIN OF ANALYSIS

> *If you know your enemy and you know yourself, you need not fear the result of a hundred battles ...*
>
> —**Sun Tzu**

The domain of analysis is the first domain in the holistic lifecycle model. Digital assets are abstract. So, logically, the first step in protecting them is to ensure that all virtual, as well as tangible, objects that might fall within the protected space are identified and precisely categorized. That is for the practical reason that you can't protect something that you don't know exists.

Consequently, the domain of analysis represents the primary point of entry for a meta-process aimed at developing a comprehensive architecture of security controls. That is because one must identify and characterize each feasible risk associated with every virtual asset to make informed decisions about real-world protection.

First, and perhaps most importantly, the objects that the organization wishes to protect must be identified by the appropriate formal process. That identification is based on the business purpose of each object. Those assets deemed worth protecting are then organized into a practical set of objects that will reside within a secure space. The justification for this initial step is the same as it would be for drawing up a blueprint before building a structure. Meaning you have to understand and describe the way that all of the components fit together before you can do the actual work.

Once the potential protection objects have all been identified, and there will be a lot of those, the next step in constructing a cyberdefense architecture is to inventory and characterize the exact form and behavior of the

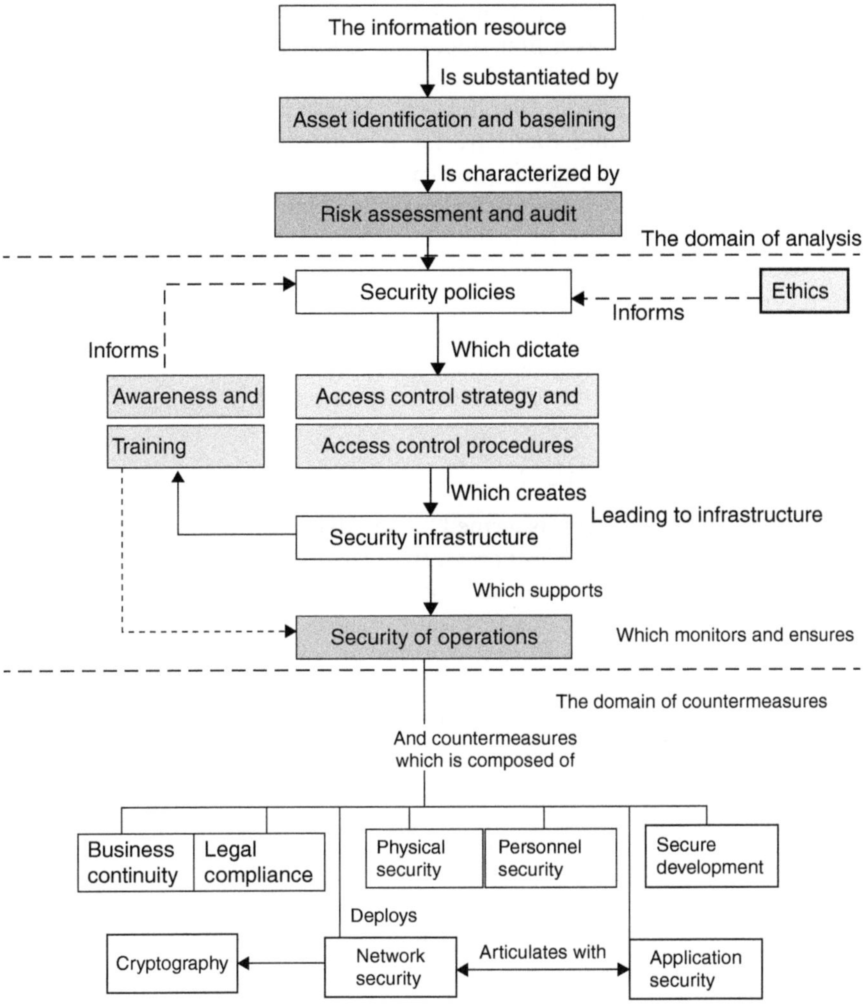

Figure 2.2 Diagram titled "Figure One: The Information Assurance Lifecycle." It shows a top-down flow beginning with "The Information Resource," which is substantiated by "Asset Identification and Baselining," then characterized by "Risk Assessment and Audit." These feed into "Security Policies" within the Domain of Analysis, informed by Ethics as well as Awareness and Training. Security Policies dictate "Access Control Strategy and Procedures," which create "Security Infrastructure." The infrastructure supports "Security of Operations," which monitors and ensures protections. Below, in the Domain of Countermeasures, Security of Operations is composed of multiple areas: Business Continuity, Legal Compliance, Physical Security, Personnel Security, Secure Development, Application Security, Network Security, and Cryptography, with arrows indicating how network security deploys cryptography and articulates with application security.

significant threats to each of those objects. The context in which those as yet unidentified and unnamed threats exist is typically referred to as the "threatscape." Hence, as a first step, each legitimate threat within a given threat context must be made real to plan how to counter it.

This is a logical first step because the threats to each protection object are infinitely varied, and there are far too many to deal with effectively within the resources the organization can invest. Therefore, the most critical threats must be identified by order of priority. That prioritization will allow top-level decision-makers to make an informed choice about how much they want to spend to safeguard their organization, or, using our parable about the bear, what will it take to outrun the other hikers?

Hence, the primary aim of the actions in the domain of analysis is to accurately identify and fully document every meaningful risk to each protection object, and then make a business decision based on it.

ASSET IDENTIFICATION

The first step in this process is termed "asset identification." Asset identification encompasses all activities necessary to ensure that all items of value are identified and their characteristics fully understood before a plan to protect them is developed. The characterization of potential protection objects is operationalized through a formal description and labeling process. As we just said, you can't protect what you don't know about. So, this first stage is the only way to identify and describe all of the organizational assets that could potentially be placed within a secured space. That is, this step must precisely document the shape of the security perimeter, as well as the secure space it encloses.

The actual identification and subsequent recording of the protection objects is nothing more than an inventory process. Anything of value that might be stored or processed by the system is identified and assigned a unique identifier, known as a "label." That object is then placed into a "baseline" of related objects that will serve as a tangible record of the contents of the asset as a whole. In essence, the asset baseline describes all the objects of value that the organization has chosen to protect ... documented as a commonsense collection of things.

The baseline record is considered to be tangible by definition. In that it is the only concrete representation of the organization's complete set of virtual and physical assets of value. The potential protection objects, meaning the labeled components related to each other by the baseline, must then be unified into a provably complete and logically related set of well-defined entities, which, in essence, fully describe the asset as a tangible organizational element.

Practically, a baseline is nothing more than an assembly of appropriately related objects that represent a coherent inventory of the things that the organization has chosen to protect. There will always be more objects of value needing protection than resources available to protect them, so a decision must be made that justifies the asset value with the resources the business is willing to commit to protect it.

The industry term for the result of this cost-benefit analysis is "protected space." Protected space is defined by a virtual, yet well-defined and commonly understood boundary, known as a "security perimeter." The security perimeter delineates the operational boundary between protected and unprotected space, and it is the primary location where the access controls are typically placed. If, as is standard practice, the protection scheme is built around increasingly rigorous concentric zones of access control, it is termed a "defense in depth," or DiD, and it embodies increasingly powerful access controls.

RISK UNDERSTANDING AND PRIORITIZATION

Once every asset of value is identified, baselined, and placed within a protected space, all attacks that could conceivably impact the organization's desired level of security must be identified, analyzed, and the precise set of risks must be enumerated, characterized, and assessed for likelihood and impact. In essence, a formal threat and risk analysis, e.g., TARA, is performed at this point. A TARA aims to specifically characterize the level of risk that each threat represents in relation to a given protection object in the baseline. A TARA must be done for each of the three attack surfaces and threats of all types and must be rolled into a single "threat picture," or "threatscape," for a given baseline application. Relating threats to the objects that they impact is the essential next step, since a specific understanding of all legitimate risks is a precondition for establishing a targeted set of cybersecurity controls.

In the classic sense, risk assessments identify vulnerabilities that might potentially be exploited, as well as each attack deemed likely to cause that exploitation. To ensure against exploitable gaps – e.g., vulnerabilities – the assessment must consider the entire set of legitimate business and technical threats across all three attack surfaces. The aim is to identify, evaluate, and manage only those threats that could cause meaningful harm. The actual degree of damage requiring a response is a choice made on a priority scale by the decision-makers in the organization, and nobody else. Since this is not a technical decision, it is a financial tradeoff between the resource expenditures to mitigate harm and the actual business impact.

Accordingly, the first step in the risk analysis stage is to triage the potential set of protected objects down to just those assets that cost justifiably fall within the scope of protected space. In the most basic sense, this is a simple cost-benefit analysis, and the outcome must be accurate because the cost of mitigation must never exceed the value of the asset being protected. Or in simple business terms, you don't want to waste precious resources protecting something that doesn't require protection, or whose value is less than the cost of mitigating it. So, the formal threat and risk understanding and evaluation process requires the organization to weigh three critical and highly integrated factors:

- The relationship between all assets
- The specific threats to each asset
- The business and technological vulnerabilities associated with those threats

Classic risk assessment operates under the assumption that appropriate controls can be developed if every likely and impactful threat is identified and correctly described. Hence, the risk assessment itself is arguably the most critical element in the formulation of a holistic security response. That is because it:

- Identifies the potential threats
- Assesses the harm that might ensue from each
- Analyzes and categorizes options for response.

To create and implement a reliable set of controls, the risk assessment must consider every relevant real-world attack that can be associated with each protection object. Risk assessments involve evaluating the likelihood of potential threats and assessing the degree of possible loss or harm that would result if those threats were to occur, thereby determining their likely organizational impact. Hence, in practical terms, the risk assessment poses the common-sense questions of ...

- What could go wrong?
- How likely is it to occur?
- What are the consequences if it does?

Risk assessments ensure the long-term sustainment of the organizational asset base; therefore, they must be an ongoing organizational function. Risk assessment is continuous because new threats are constantly emerging. Finally, and most importantly, the evaluation of what is required to mitigate a potential threat is conducted for all three attack surfaces. That is because a missing related control on any of those surfaces creates an exploitable gap.

Gaps are typically identified by comparing an "ideal" model of best practice to the organization's current mode of operation. Preferably, the gap analysis process is based on a well-defined and commonly accepted statement of formal best practice, such as an ISO or a NIST standard. These models have been painstakingly created to address every consideration of every attack surface. Therefore, they provide a useful template to ensure that nothing is missed.

The point of holistic security is to ensure that exploitable gaps do not exist. But organizations are big and complex. Therefore, an industry- or government-sponsored strategic framework of best practices, such as ISO 27000 or FIPS 200/NIST 800-53, provides a structured basis for identifying and then considering the various issues that the eventual security solution must address. Any best practice gaps identified will represent a specific vulnerability, which may then require a substantive control to mitigate it.

Because a particular threat may not necessarily cause measurable harm, all identified risk exposures must be evaluated to isolate those weaknesses whose exploitation would create specific and undesirable vulnerabilities. To determine the impactful vulnerabilities, the potential damage of each identified vulnerability must be carefully analyzed in comparison with the particular business requirements. The significant vulnerabilities are prioritized in descending order, so that those with the most critical organizational impacts are addressed first.

The simple valuation of the assets themselves is the hardest part of the prioritization process. That is the case because, in the real world, there are never enough resources to secure every protected object in the information asset baseline. Even worse, since the baseline will be overwhelmingly composed of abstract entities, the value of each asset will also be abstract, meaning not substantively known. That lack of a commonly agreed-upon price tag can turn this entire aspect of the process into a political mess. Hence, every organization needs to adopt a formal, commonly agreed-on method of valuation and then use that method to evaluate and prioritize the information assets systematically. The primary objective should be to safeguard the most critical assets first.

The product of the asset prioritization phase is a concrete set of protected objects. Those objects are then fitted within a formally documented security perimeter. Identifying an optimal set of protected objects is a crucial aspect of this process, as there is a direct relationship between the resources required to establish the desired level of security and the extent of the territory that can feasibly be protected. Operational factors that influence this decision include the level of criticality of each unique information asset and the specific degree of resource commitment required to ensure each item.

It may seem self-evident that the primary reason to undertake a cybersecurity exercise is to protect the business's assets. But that fundamental reason-to-be is sometimes lost in the profound challenge of conceptualizing and then implementing a holistic cybersecurity system. Hence, it must be understood that the critical success factors for cybersecurity originate at the business level, and no other place – e.g., cybersecurity is never an end in itself, and that any form of operational asset valuation must be rooted in and reflect the vision, strategies, and purposes of the parent business. The benefit of rooting any protection decisions in business asset valuation is that the organization will know with certainty that its most critical assets are adequately secured.

Additionally, the performance of the valuation process will provide evidence to the organization's members and any relevant outsiders that due diligence was conducted in defining the shape of the control architecture. Or, in essence, the actual prioritization process is a fundamental aspect of best practice. Thus, it is an element of strategic planning. Accordingly, evidence of a carefully considered and precisely targeted value tradeoff will allow the organization to act with the assurance that they are basing their resource commitments on the realities of the situation.

THE DOMAIN OF RESPONSE

> *The general who wins the battle makes many calculations in his temple before the battle is fought. The general who loses makes but few.*
>
> —**Sun Tzu**

The Domain of Response is the second domain in this model. The purpose of this phase is to create a sustainable, holistic architecture. This domain designs the tangible security system and then works to maintain that system as correct and relevant over time. The subsequent state of security protection must be demonstrably viable as a long-term operation. The aim is to establish trust in the security solution, both internally and externally. The requirement for sustainability of the practical architecture also implies the need for a concrete and repeatable management process to ensure that the evolving cybersecurity system is always maintained in alignment with every priority threat in the threatscape.

There are six general areas of consideration in this domain. Three of these are sequential: *Security Policy*, *Security Infrastructure Design*, and *Security of Operations, Deployment, and Sustainment*. These are the practical stages in the long-term development and operation of a holistic cybersecurity system. However, other considerations inform these three stages, which shape the actual security architecture. Those are: *Access Control*, *Human Factors,* and *Societal Security/Ethics*. These latter two areas of consideration go directly to the establishment of a holistic culture and will be discussed later. The logical consequence of the decisions made during the risk analysis portion of the lifecycle must be translated into substantive policies to guide the day-to-day operation of the cybersecurity system. Hence, the development of a complete and correct set of security governance policies is the next phase in the lifecycle.

SECURITY POLICY/GOVERNANCE

Total assurance requires a unified and coherent set of strategic governance policies, which first implement and then sustain a comprehensive and coordinated infrastructure of controls, the correctness and reliability of which can be objectively demonstrated. Hence, the organization must adopt a complete and consistent set of policies to guide the cybersecurity assurance process properly. Each policy should address a priority risk identified by the threat and risk assessment. The outcome of the policy formulation phase is a rational governance model that ensures holistic, continuously evolving protection, addressing inevitable changes in the threatscape.

We have already said that cybersecurity is a state that is maintained as a continuous operational process. Therefore, the policies for ensuring that the state is systematic and effectively embedded in the organization as a whole must be in place. We have already touched on the simple fact that electronic protection alone is insufficient to ensure security, as there are two other viable attack surfaces available for exploitation. Hence, cybersecurity policy formulation must consider and incorporate all relevant control measures, including electronic, human-centered, and physical, to be fully effective. That array of controls must then be integrated into a fully unified organizational system.

Cybersecurity policies address all relevant attack surfaces, not just the ones that are convenient or interesting, and that solution must then be rationally evolved to meet the changing characteristics of the threat environment. The policies must ensure a reliable long-term assurance capability that addresses all likely threats and responds appropriately to all incidents. That final set of policy guidelines must be systematic and maintainable for the foreseeable future. Finally, and most relevantly, the cybersecurity response must directly support and be traceable to the requirements of the business case since competitive advantage is the only practical justification for creating and maintaining a cybersecurity system.

Once the complete set of cybersecurity policies is agreed upon and documented for the entire organization, those policies are substantiated by well-documented and commonly understood actions, known as "controls." The final set of approved controls is integrated into a single best-practice operational infrastructure that provides unambiguous marching orders for executing the cybersecurity process.

INFRASTRUCTURE DESIGN: PROCEDURE AND PRACTICE

Any given set of organizational policies is implemented through a practical, operational infrastructure that comprises a concrete and detailed statement of the substantive actions to be taken. To create that infrastructure, the organization must design, implement, and enforce a logical and consistent set of well-defined best practices, which allows all stakeholders to benchmark their performance. Coordination and control of complex work will always require standard and coherent procedures put in place to standardize the actions to be taken. It probably goes without saying that those procedures must be directly traceable to the business policies that they implement.

In actual business practice, an infrastructure of operational best practices is typically referred to as a governance framework. In applied terms, the primary aim of creating a well-defined governance framework is to avoid a piecemeal solution, e.g., one that is full of gaps. Therefore, the governance framework for that particular organization will encompass all the actions necessary to ensure a comprehensive and reliable state of cybersecurity protection. It is always unique to the individual organization, because it characterizes that organization's specific business strategies and approach.

An engineered governance framework prevents the organization from adopting a piecemeal solution – e.g., one that contains easily exploitable gaps. The confounding fact is that every enterprise is secured by some set of practices that it considers its cybersecurity operation. These practices are typically based on an individual unit or manager's idea about the proper way to secure something, and they tend to become embedded in the organization over time, without any particular logic.

Typically, cybersecurity solutions have evolved in this manner. They develop incrementally as the situation arises, rather than as a comprehensive, rationally planned, and managed structure. The outcome of this meandering approach is an unknown, but usually substantial, number of exploitable gaps in the protection scheme. Hence, it is not difficult to see why there are so many successful exploitations. Because, logically, a proper cybersecurity solution must encompass all the necessary controls to address every feasible attack vector.

By contrast, holistic cybersecurity governance solutions encompass a well-documented and comprehensive infrastructure of protection practices explicitly designed to optimize the overall effectiveness of the security situation. As with any complex construction process, this infrastructure can only be operationalized by a rational and explicit framework of procedures that are directly traceable to the policies that they implement. The practical management term for such a framework is a security governance infrastructure.

A security governance infrastructure underwrites and provides tangible proof of due diligence in protecting the organization's information assets. Security governance implies a rational and deliberately designed configuration of organizational behaviors and relationships that operate as a system to control access to digital assets strictly. Hence, security infrastructures represent the tangible link between the cybersecurity function and the overall business.

The organization builds a holistic cybersecurity system by adopting practices to ensure against a known set of threats. The outcome of the threat identification and prioritization process is a coherent and fully integrated holistic security response. Nonetheless, this is not a one-size-fits-all approach. Instead, the determination of each element of the system must be driven by targeted decision-making. The factor that underlies the need for that decision-making is that all situations are different.

Thus, a correctly developed holistic infrastructure is always precisely tailored to the particular requirements of the circumstances in which it is applied. The result of the tailoring is that the controls embodied in the final system design comprise a complete and tightly integrated solution which, when properly configured and operated, will produce an acceptable state of cybersecurity. Nine commonly recognized factors are instrumental to the overall success of the holistic security process. These are:

1. The existence of a formally documented set of security policies
2. An implementation approach that fits with organizational culture
3. Visible support and commitment from management
4. Organization-wide understanding of security requirements
5. Effective marketing of security to all managers and employees
6. Appropriate training and education
7. A comprehensive system of measurement
8. The provision for feedback and suggestions for improvement

Therefore, the organization must formulate policies to fulfill its aims and purposes and then embody them through procedures that comprise a tangible and coherent structure of carefully selected behaviors – e.g., security controls. As a unified set, those controls apply throughout the cybersecurity system lifecycle.

Security controls are atomic-level actions implemented to identify, counter, or mitigate a specific adverse action that may occur on the electronic, behavioral, or physical attack surface. They can be as simple as a password control or as complex as an organization-wide training and awareness program. Security controls protect the electronic elements of the system – both hardware and software. They also ensure against purely human-centered actions, such as clicking on unknown links, or human resource violations, such as insider attacks. Physical security controls can be as simple as traditional top guards, locks, and gates. But they can also include biometrics, intrusion detection, and security surveillance cameras. All of these controls must be explicitly documented, as they would be of no benefit if they were not widely understood and enforced.

Each security infrastructure control and control process must be designed, integrated, and implemented into a substantive protection scheme. The substantiation and documentation of that scheme is based on the concept of "tailoring." In essence, the general control actions specified in a selected best practice framework, such as ISO 27000 or FIPS 200/NIST 800-53, are individually tailored to the specific requirements of a given protection situation. This is necessary because every threatscape is different, and the impacts of a given threat on a particular attack surface can vary with time and circumstance.

Additionally, a formal assessment procedure must be specified to determine whether an organization's security controls have been implemented correctly and are functioning as intended. This is a continuous day-to-day responsibility. The assessment ensures that the control set is producing the desired control outcome and that it continues to meet the business case requirements. Ongoing assessment will ensure that the control set evolves in line with the threat picture.

SECURITY OF OPERATIONS

The security of operations function is conceptually orthogonal to the lifecycle. Security of operations is a day-to-day operational matter rather than a strategic process. Security of operations ensures the reliable day-to-day security performance of the control framework, as established in the policy and procedure stages, throughout the system's long-term operation. In its most basic form, the security of operations function is incident monitoring and incident response. It ensures the continuous and proper execution of all defined cybersecurity controls in the governance framework across all three attack surfaces, and it responds to any anomalies that may arise in day-to-day operations.

In effect, the security of operations is the glue that holds the entire process together. Without an adequate security of operations function, the organization would be unable to guarantee the long-term viability of its holistic capabilities. Consequently, this humble monitoring and correction function may be the most critical part of the holistic cybersecurity lifecycle, since it ensures the integrity and performance of the organization's security practice on a routine, everyday basis.

Security of operations confirms that policies and procedures are consistently followed. It monitors and evaluates the execution of the continuity, compliance, physical security, and personnel security aspects of the processes. It ensures that all necessary technical countermeasures are in place and functioning correctly. Ultimately, when problems are detected, the security of operations function is responsible for coordinating corrective action.

Security of operations involves pragmatic organizational activities, such as ensuring that current operating practices are appropriately aligned with security policies, monitoring the performance of routine security practices to confirm they correspond to proper procedures, and utilizing standard operational testing strategies to validate that the overall cybersecurity function continues to operate correctly.

As the name implies, security of operations is less involved with strategy than it is with underwriting dependable day-to-day performance. The role of security of operations is to maintain correct alignment between the organization's security policies and its security practices. Nonetheless, the overall security environment is constantly evolving, and therefore, policies and procedures must change accordingly. Thus, the security of operations also monitors the execution of each of the other processes to ensure alignment.

The focus of this monitoring activity is on detecting meaningful deviations from correct practice. Typically, this is accomplished by:

- Identifying and recording problems as they occur
- Analyzing each problem to develop effective countermeasures
- Taking the appropriate corrective, adaptive, perfective, or preventive action
- Validating the integrity of the change

Furthermore, because the security environment and the organization itself are constantly evolving, confidence in the integrity of the security response must be continuously assured. Therefore, the security of operations will also periodically verify and, in some cases, certify the effectiveness of the security solution. In that respect, the security of operations function will routinely review, inspect, test, and audit the performance of each element that constitutes the overall security response.

Where problems are encountered, the security of operations function is responsible for planning and coordinating problem resolution. As such, the security of operations and intrusion detection functions might be considered two seamless aspects of the same larger purpose, which is to ensure that every feasible threat is promptly identified and appropriately responded to.

ACCESS CONTROL

The primary objective of access control is to ensure the access rights of legitimate users while denying access to unauthorized individuals. Hence, in that respect, regulating access is the primary purpose of any protection scheme. The principle of selective access encompasses whatever operational steps the organization must take to enable control over its assets. In effect, then, a cybersecurity system is no more than a particular organization's practical form of access control.

Access control is more of a required state than it is a substantive area of assurance. To perform their jobs properly, all operational processes must establish the specific access rights of each person and process seeking to cross the protection perimeter into the secure space. Similarly, just as a bank authenticates your identity before you can withdraw money, every entity seeking access to it must be authenticated, and its privileges must be determined before it is allowed to make a withdrawal.

The concept of access refers to a subject's ability to interact with a specific object. The definition of what constitutes a proper subject can be extensive. In essence, the subject can be any person or a process. If it is the latter, it can be either a process running on a computer or an organizational one. At the same time, the object that the subject is accessing can be anything of value that the subject might legitimately touch. That could be everything from physical space to a file or a hardware device.

A security perimeter separates subjects and objects. In essence, that perimeter encapsulates the objects in a protected space. Access controls allow trusted subjects, or processes, to cross that boundary. The concept of protected space denotes the generic security principle of separation, or segmentation. The ability to precisely gauge what access controls are necessary to achieve a required functional state of separation is a critical element of the process.

The concept of protected space describes a logical set of resources that are grouped for control. These resources are encapsulated in a well-defined, secure space. That is referred to as a "security domain." Each domain represents a level of assurance that shares

- Common security properties
- A single security policy
- A single source of governance control.

Thus, the contents of a security domain comprise a logical set of subjects that might be appropriately grouped and that share a common protection perimeter. Security domains are differentiated by the level of requisite trust that is assigned to each.

A security domain aims to isolate similar subjects and objects into logical categories of value, thereby imposing a well-defined and appropriate degree of control. The operational term for the requisite level of trust needed to gain access is typically characterized as a "clearance," or sensitivity level. Security domains are generally grouped hierarchically based on the levels of security that they implement. Each level has a set of formal rules that specifically determine objects that a subject can access within a given domain – this is colloquially termed the "privileges."

Logically, then, access to the assets in a domain requires that the subject have the appropriate level of "privilege." Then those privileges have to be strictly enforced. That requires the access control process to validate the identity of the subject, or process, which is seeking entry into the domain, and then assign the proper set of access privileges. This is similar to our bank analogy. The bank manager will have different access privileges than an individual who wanders in off the street. However, those privileges must be officially granted, and both individuals must understand the rules.

Identification

Access to any protected object always begins with identification. The assignment of privileges is based on the individual characteristics of the individual or the process that is seeking access. The identification process validates those unique properties. Therefore, it is clear that no other person can share those characteristics. The subsequent assignment of privilege is typically based on the subject's preassigned membership in a well-defined security category, such as, in its simplest sense, trusted versus untrusted. The confirmation is then used to authorize the data or system resources that the subject is permitted to access.

The practical outcome of the identification process is accountability. Accurate identifications enable the system to differentiate and track the activities of individuals within a secure space, as well as hold them accountable for their actions. Consequently, identifications are issued and maintained through a formal process. Unique tokens are typically issued for practical access control purposes. The most common example of an identity token is a password. Hence, traditionally, most identification processes boil down to good password management. That happens because passwords are still the most straightforward and most economical means of identifying an individual subject to the system. They are also relatively easy to maintain, and if good security hygiene is followed, they can be effective, which is the reason why password sharing is verboten.

Authentication

Identifications uniquely identify the individual user or system objects to the system. However, that is only one side of the access equation. The other side is the authentication process, which is the practical verification of the subject as a valid user. The validation requirement implements the Saltzer and Schroeder principle of failsafe defaults. Or in simple terms, all accesses are based on permission granted rather than defined exclusions. That principle must always be followed for a cybersecurity scheme to function correctly.

The role of authentication is to verify the trustworthiness of the user seeking access based on an authentication token. Logically, only trusted users are granted access. Authentication ensures that the proper identity information is communicated to the access control device, which allows a decision to be made on whether to permit or deny an access request. Identify tokens, which are assigned by the Identification function, are validated to determine those access rights.

As we said earlier ... the most common token is the password, e.g., "what you know." But it can also be "something you have," e.g., a swipe card, or even something you are, e.g., "biometrics." Those tokens are typically combined into a multifactor identification process – e.g., both something you know and something you have, like an ATM withdrawal that requires the password and the bank card. Doubling the access requirements increases the security exponentially.

Authorization

Permission to access a given set of objects is granted once the system has authenticated the subject seeking access. That specific assignment of privileges is the function of authorization. Authorization grants the individual privileges of the user vis-à-vis the virtual resource that they are seeking to access. Saltzer and Schroeder called that decision "least privilege." In essence, every user or process must be given access to only those virtual assets necessary to do their job. The spy novels refer to that as "need to know." The term "authorization" can describe either the process of granting those rights or the subsequent capability to access a given resource. In actual practice, authorization is the on-the-fly determination that a particular subject has the necessary level of clearance to access the target resource. Consequently, authorization is also sometimes referred to as "permission" or "privilege."

Authorization is based on the principle of "trust." Subjects are allowed access to a specified set of services based on both their level of assigned trust and their need to know. Untrusted or unknown subjects are not granted access because they are not authenticated. In practice, authorization also refers to the management feature that grants users their specific privileges. In highly secure applications, there may even be authorizations that specifically identify the resources the user can access during that session. In modern operations, authorization is characterized by four generic methods:

- Policy-based access control – privileges granted based on organizational policies
- Discretionary access control – privileges granted based on an organizational need
- Mandatory access control – privileges granted based on an assigned level of trust
- Role-based access control – privileges granted based on organizational role

THE DOMAIN OF COUNTERMEASURES

One need not destroy one's enemy. One only needs to destroy his willingness to engage.

—Sun Tzu

All the explicit countermeasures in a holistic solution are deployed and overseen by the functions established in the second phase, e.g., policy, procedure, and operations. Those functions specify and maintain the specific countermeasure actions needed to secure all assets of value from all threats identified in the first phase. That implies the need to create, deploy, and maintain a robust set of concrete countermeasures.

Countermeasures are what people think of when they hear the term "cybersecurity." A countermeasure, or at least its outcomes, can be observed and evaluated, which makes it the only tangible representation of the cybersecurity system. Countermeasures are discrete behaviors designed and implemented to counter a specifically identified threat, action, or actor. Hence, the domain of countermeasures is where the organization's real-world security requirements are operationalized.

Since three legitimate attack surfaces need to be secured, the protection scheme requires accurate placement of each measure. That entails the precise placement of a myriad of distinctive, logically related countermeasures. Given the intricacy of the threat environment, this requires a design and implementation process that is no less complex than the planning that goes into creating any complex piece of software.

A rationally developed control array will typically address eight specific countermeasure areas. Those are organized into two subdomains. The first subdomain encompasses all of the traditional technical countermeasure areas. These are primarily focused on securing the electronic attack surface, and they comprise the usual list of suspects ... network and software security, along with encryption.

The second subdomain is less traditional and well-known, but essential, nonetheless. These are the chiefly managerial/behavioral measures that ensure organizational control over the cybersecurity function. These also directly address threats on the human and physical attack surfaces. Both the technical and behavioral domains must be designed to interact rationally for the protection scheme to be holistically correct and synergistic.

TECHNICAL SECURITY

Traditional electronic countermeasures reside in the subdomain of technical security. It should be noted that for many people, this domain comprises the only set of actions that are considered actual cybersecurity. The general areas in this domain are.

Network security

Network security is a crucial aspect of cybersecurity, and for many organizations, the cybersecurity process ends there. The countermeasures in this domain ensure secure network access to electronic assets. To accomplish this, the network security function establishes and oversees both network access control and network monitoring. Network security:

- Identifies and distinguishes trusted users (identity management)
- Authenticates users to the system (identity tokens)
- Authorizes and assigns privileges to authenticated users based on their degree of trust
- Monitors and regulates access during use

Network security also involves the elements necessary to ensure the secure operation and sustainment of the network and associated network architectures.

Encryption

Encryption is a necessary foundational requirement for electronic security. It is not precisely an organizational function but rather the basis for secure message transfer. Due to the adversary's proven ability to hijack plaintext files, obfuscation of data through encryption must be viewed as a vital countermeasure. Encryption encompasses all the technical requirements and actions necessary to convert plaintext into an encrypted representation. Encryption also ensures non-repudiation of origin for remote transactions. The general area of encryption encompasses all asymmetric and symmetric encryption methodologies, as well as the key structures that underlie the business data communication process.

Application and operating system security

This area of technical security ensures the continuing security and integrity of the computer itself. It secures all applications and system code running in a given information technology context, and in that respect, it is the most fundamental form of computer security. Activities in this area include securely installing and maintaining application and system software, analyzing operating system security performance, including load balancing, reporting, and resolving defects in code or in its operation. This area also ensures the secure performance of all software within the system's operational environment. This includes resolving anomalies and conflicts in both application and operating system performance.

BEHAVIORAL SECURITY

The countermeasure in this area constitutes the subdomain of behavioral security. These are the commonly accepted policy and procedural actions that the organization takes to ensure long-term security performance and sustain the effectiveness of the overall response over time. In many respects, these areas are performed by the organization in some form in all instances. But they are rarely systematically coordinated, which is the source of serious compromises. The general areas that make up this domain are.

Continuity: Business continuity and disaster planning

This area develops and maintains a comprehensive strategy to ensure the long-term sustainability of asset value. It involves explicit practices to ensure that the business will continue to operate if its information assets are lost or harmed. This typically involves real-time mirroring of those assets in redundant backup sites, or the cloud, as well as strategic activities such as contingency development and formal disaster and recovery planning.

These are relatively high-level activities compared to the nuts-and-bolts focus of functions such as network security. Nonetheless, the organization's long-term viability hinges on its ability to mitigate disasters. So, you might not want to pay for car insurance, but you will undoubtedly live to regret it if you're involved in an accident. That is how continuity planning works for every organization that depends on its technology.

Compliance: Legal and regulatory

This area encompasses all mechanisms used to ensure compliance. It fills the conventional organizational role of assuring that the stipulations of all contracts for technology and services are properly satisfied, as well as ensuring that all relevant laws and regulations are correctly adhered to. Compliance also ensures that due diligence is exercised in meeting all the stipulated obligations that regulatory or legal entities may impose. Hence, compliance primarily involves the formal audit and documentation activities necessary to demonstrate due care.

Due to the litigious nature of the environment and the regulatory demands that are a fact of life in doing business in the twenty-first century, this might be one of the most critical areas of assurance among the entire set of countermeasures. That is because the harm that might be done by violating a contract, or proven negligence, or a direct regulatory infringement can cost the organization a very concrete fortune. As a result, the legal and regulatory countermeasure areas are usually a high priority in even the most electronically oriented cybersecurity operations.

Physical security: The domain of things

The purpose of physical security is to ensure control over all of the organization's tangible assets of value. This includes both the equipment and any data that may reside within individual data storage devices. Physical security establishes a realistic physical asset management scheme for the defined protected space. It creates a protection perimeter around the physical boundaries of secure spaces, such as server rooms and any other defined secure areas. It monitors and controls all physical assets of value.

Physical security is often the stepchild of the cybersecurity process. However, physical losses, such as theft of or damage to processing equipment and storage devices, as well as simple human error, account for up to one-third of the total loss in value for any given year. Because many businesses don't see the connection between a physical incident and loss of virtual asset value, physical losses are often not included on cybersecurity's scorecard. However, the loss of data because it was hacked off the internet, or if the device that it was on was stolen, is a loss nonetheless. That is a fact.

Physical protection is established based on a realistic physical protection scheme that incorporates all of the necessary real-world practices to ensure the integrity of physical resources within a well-defined protection perimeter, including barriers, patrols, sensor technology, and monitoring cameras. The physical protection scheme is continuously updated based on feedback from all of those sources.

Personnel security: The domain of people

This is the classic human security function. Operationally, it is based around employee screening and the assignment of roles and access privileges. However, a much larger control obligation is implied by the fact that trusted individuals have legitimate access to the assets they are authorized to access. Since humans are unpredictable at best, there is no way the organization can assume that somebody they have chosen to trust will not sell them out or make a simple mistake that will empty the vault.

The lack of predictability is probably the reason why conventional cybersecurity operations consider insider threats to be somebody else's problem, even though the exploits associated with purely human-centered attacks, such as social engineering, account for another third of the value lost every year. So, the fact remains that a sophisticated and expensive intrusion detection system is operated by a human being who could be influenced to turn it off for the right price. Therefore, behavioral countermeasures are a vital part of the protection scheme, whether information technology personnel want to deal with them or not.

Personnel security encompasses a comprehensive set of management procedures to ensure employee compliance with security policies. It then systematically monitors the ongoing security activities of employees to ensure compliance. It conducts intelligence gathering and threat analysis to identify any behavioral trends that may adversely impact the workforce. Most vitally and importantly, personnel security maintains a security culture through comprehensive and well-targeted employee awareness and training programs that are built on and ensure current best practice in security behavior.

Software assurance: The domain of software security

This focuses on ensuring code quality. This area is not a technical process. It primarily ensures validation and verification of both the specification of requirements and the code itself. It is a necessary addition to the holistic security function because organizations are increasingly dependent on software.

The area encompasses all methods and best practices to ensure that secure coding procedures are embedded in all development, acquisition, and maintenance work. That requires staying up-to-date with trends and new processes for technical work. It also operates and oversees walkthrough reviews, inspections, and audits to ensure that security functionality is integrated into all products during development. These purely managerial functions are essential because code vulnerabilities are the primary source of exploitation on the electronic interface. Therefore, the entire process must be well-defined and conducted in accordance with best practices, even though its execution is part of the technical work involved in software development.

SECURITY CULTURE

There are two final aspects of the holistic assurance process. Like access control, these do not fit specifically within the lifecycle model. Instead, they are higher-level areas that establish the necessary "security culture" of the organization. Although they are peripheral to the day-to-day process of establishing and sustaining a holistic security system, they are critical to its long-term success, as they contribute to the enforcement of organizational norms.

Human factors: Maintaining capability

Human factors is a process that is orthogonal to the holistic security development process. Meaning, rather than being a specific developmental step, the consideration of human factors dictates the policies and practices that ensure the actions of the people who work in the organization. Its primary purpose is to underwrite awareness and motivation and enforce discipline. It achieves that by ensuring that all necessary security policies and procedures are understood and adhered to in a disciplined fashion.

Human factors determine and then define the specific actions that each individual must perform to achieve a satisfactory level of assurance for the organization. The functions that are studied and addressed are classified into three generic categories: routine functions, operational duties, and management responsibilities. It is necessary to have an adequate definition and a required set of actions for each of these areas to ensure adequate holistic protection.

Routine functions safeguard the virtual asset from threats that may arise from day-to-day operations. These can involve such humble activities as safe housekeeping procedures, which are designed to protect computer equipment or media against petty theft. They can also involve technical duties like ensuring that the operating system and network is appropriately configured.

Operational duties, as the name implies, underwrite the day-to-day functioning of the system. This is not a matter of preventative maintenance. It entails tasks such as monitoring staff activities to ensure that secure work practices are being followed, as well as the continuous monitoring system functioning to prevent misuse.

Finally, there is the requirement that the security operation must be managed appropriately. Practices can include taking steps to ensure that each business unit follows the required security procedures. However, they can also include such complex tasks as strategic planning to secure an organization's information function.

The rule of thumb is that specific accountability is assigned to every individual involved in the creation, handling, or use of virtual assets. Every person who falls under that mandate must be trained and knowledgeable in all aspects of personnel security requirements. The goal is to ensure a comprehensive understanding of all security functions within the organization, including management control processes.

Two critical factors drive this process. The first is the specific knowledge and skill of the people responsible for performing the assurance functions. The second is the willingness of all employees to carry out their security duties in a systematic and disciplined way. Hence, the security responsibilities of all individuals must be stipulated, and it is also essential to ensure that every individual knows their role and function.

Accordingly, the first step in establishing control over the human aspect is the development of a personnel security policy. There are two categories of human threats: outsiders and insiders. Hackers or cybercriminals are the best examples of an outsider threat. Generally, however, most serious threats to information stem from the actions of insiders. That is because everyone in the organization is trusted to some extent. So, there is always the potential for such adverse acts as internal fraud, misuse of the asset, theft, or human error.

The most critical aspect of human behavioral control is establishing an optimal perimeter. People constantly come and go across the security perimeter. It would be both unrealistic and economically infeasible to attempt to control their actions after they extend beyond a logical point.

For instance, every employee commutes to work. There are many places in the trip where controlling that employee would be meaningless or irrelevant ... for example, when the employee is in their own driveway. However, there are essential places on the protection perimeter where that employee's access must be monitored and controlled ... for instance, at the front gate. The determination of the location and type of control required will dictate where to place the countermeasures.

So, a guard shack would probably be sufficient to regulate access if the employee were driving back and forth to work. However, a very different and more complex response would be required if employees were working remotely. Hence, the crucial factor in perimeter setting is characterizing exactly how each employee gains access to controlled information. That determination has resource implications and, to some extent, will dictate how personnel policies will be set. For instance, the organization might decide that it did not have the resources to ensure teleworkers, which would result in a policy to ban that activity.

The elements and boundaries of personnel security are always a matter of perception rather than fact. That is because personnel security involves people. Therefore, every organization must make a conscious decision about the threats associated with user behavior to secure itself properly. The protection scheme has to embody the degree of security that is considered acceptable by the people within the user community. This is always a problem because people have different ideas about what constitutes a threat and the level of protection that would be necessary. This is particularly true when it comes to regulating their own actions.

Societal security: Maintaining an effective workplace culture

Societal security focuses on aspects of the holistic lifecycle that broadly impact society as a whole for better or for worse. The policies that shape proper societal behavior are formulated in light of an understanding of the organization's values. Or, in practical terms, the way an organization approaches its overall commitment to security is encapsulated in the statement of best practice. So, that point of view must be both expressed and clearly understood.

The ability of individuals to distinguish proper from improper is an essential factor in the holistic universe. Therefore, law, ethics, policy, privacy, and their interrelationship are key concepts in this area, as compliance with laws, ethics, and policies is crucial for safeguarding the security of corporate and government secrets and assets, as well as for protecting individual privacy and identity.

Obviously, none of the other assurance factors in this discussion would be of any use if it were not for the overall requirement that people behave properly. Proper behavior is characterized by performing a collective set of actions that essentially represent the proper way to act in a given circumstance. A coherent set of these actions is called "best practice," or more commonly a code of conduct. A code of conduct is a detailed statement of the organization's expectations about acceptable behavior. It defines the:

- Accepted values and principles of its particular domain.
- It dictates the duties and obligations of individuals in reference to the group norms.
- It provides the ability to manage the proper security behavior of that specific group.

Thus, a code of conduct outlines the appropriate choices for individuals in relation to the overall norms of the group. In a practical sense, a defined code of conduct helps an organization decide when an individual is not behaving correctly.

Codes of conduct serve as the concrete point of reference to judge every eventuality. They enable members of the profession to make informed choices and exhibit proper behavior in any given situation. The practical value of a code of conduct lies in its formalization of the principles governing acceptable use and behavior within the group. It also provides the group's decision-makers with an effective yardstick to evaluate the conduct of individual employees.

The goal of a formal code of conduct is to guide members of the organization in making informed, day-to-day decisions. Any choice about behavior must balance what is suitable for the individual or the group against the greater good of society, and that balancing act is dynamic; there is no absolutely correct answer.

In a discussion about something as abstract as best use, it is essential to provide clear definitions of the terms. This is especially true, as a documented statement of best use underwrites the organization's and individuals' tangible understanding of proper behavior. Although it is intangible, best use is a critical concept in the holistic security process because it underwrites trust and trustworthiness. Therefore, a system that centers on the description of commonly accepted principles for best practices and practical rules of thumb for applying them is an essential overall control feature in any holistic security process.

Finally, holistic security requires the codification of the necessary level of capability to perform an organizational task. This is called a standard level of professional competency. It describes the degree of proficiency that a reasonable person may expect from a professional under a given set of circumstances. Standards of competency are always required in the professions where public trust must be guaranteed. For instance, in the case of a doctor, the minimum standard level would be the probability that a medical condition would receive the proper diagnosis and treatment. Their medical license attests to that.

The problem is that the same degree of capability cannot be assumed for cybersecurity professionals. That is, at present, people working in cybersecurity are not subject to formal licensing requirements. Thus, although there are certifications based on representative common bodies of knowledge, there is no single system to guarantee the professional competence of practitioners.

Consequently, there is extreme variability in skills and competencies within the profession. That has a potentially profound effect on the type and degree of protection that can be expected, and the potential for misunderstanding and miscommunication should be obvious. Consequently, although the public believes that there is a minimum standard for cybersecurity practitioners, there is actually no guarantee that this is the case.

CHAPTER SUMMARY

The holistic security lifecycle is a logical process for deploying and maintaining an effective holistic security response. The various lifecycle activities ensure that all of the necessary elements of assurance are considered at the right time. Hence, the process also ensures that the assurance will be dynamically relevant to the threat environment. At its core, this system provides a defined set of rational responses to changing threats as they evolve, or changes in the business case that must be addressed to maintain effective security practices.

Any system that follows this lifecycle approach will respond quickly and appropriately to any relevant change in environmental conditions, as rational processes of analysis and design ensure the long-term relevance and sustainability are maintained.

Chapter 3

Implementing holistic architecture

Figure 3.1 Pencil drawing of four armored warriors in close combat, facing each other with crossed swords and raised shields. The figures wear helmets and medieval-style armor, their blades intersecting at the center of the image, conveying tension, struggle, and direct confrontation in battle.

DOI: 10.1201/9781003603412-3

SECURING THE ENTERPRISE

> *Victorious warriors win first, and then go to war, while defeated warriors go to war first, and then seek to win.*
>
> —Sun Tzu

The last chapter presented the concept of the holistic security lifecycle. The salient point of that discussion was that holistic security is a comprehensive and continuous, strategic process, not an everyday operational activity. Thus, holistic security implementation involves a set of large-scale, high-level design activities. Therefore, it is now time to turn our attention to the practical issue of translating an abstract concept, such as "holistic," into a comprehensive, real-world solution that ensures the integrity and confidentiality of an organization's day-to-day business operations. That is the topic we will discuss in this chapter.

Organizational systems are composed of technology, people, and process, and they are highly complex. In that respect, it is nearly impossible to properly interrelate all the components of a large, often geographically dispersed, organization-wide virtual system without undertaking some form of formal design activity. The pragmatic aim of such a process is to ensure that all components and the inherent interrelationships of the end-product function as required and are correctly aligned as a synergistic, systematic structure, thereby accomplishing the organization's intended purpose.

Every creation, be it a child's Lego castle, a commercial skyscraper, or a virtual system, must be assembled into precisely the right combination of logically related parts to function correctly. The process that is employed to develop such a tangible structure is commonly termed "architectural design." The emphasis of that particular design activity is to produce a complete and fully coherent structure. In that respect, then, a comprehensive, thoroughly planned, and formally instituted architectural design process ensures that all of the elements and associations of a virtual entity, such as an organization's cybersecurity solution, are accurately described and implemented.

Architectures themselves are pragmatic in that a well-defined and commonly accepted set of best practice principles is utilized to design and achieve a tangible organizational system, which meets the goals of the project. In turn, the architectural design process itself is underwritten by and based on a formal, structured methodology that guides the definition and organization of all of the required system elements into a rational, concrete, real-world framework of interrelated actions.

The term "enterprise architecture" is used in everyday practice to describe the practical design outcome and the subsequent tangible implementation of any abstract concept, such as holistic security. The architecture process itself entails the identification and detailed description of every aspect of the solution, as well as the associated interactions that must occur to achieve a specific operational purpose. In essence, architectural design involves the precise specification of a system's requisite components and interfaces. Hence, the architectural process substantiates both the tangible, primarily technical, elements and the practical behaviors required to achieve the enterprise's stated purpose.

WHAT IS AN ENTERPRISE

Precise and well-documented boundaries characterize enterprises. Those boundaries encompass all of the elements needed to achieve a specific organizational goal. In effect, the entities within the organizational boundary comprise a dedicated set of people, processes, and technologies that the business is committed to achieving a fundamental purpose. The boundaries themselves can be broad, or narrow, complex, or simple. But the single distinguishing characteristic of all enterprise boundaries is that they are commonly understood and accepted as separating controlled space from uncontrolled space.

Logically, the explicitly identified and labeled assets contained within a controlled space are placed there to achieve a commonly understood organizational objective. In that respect, then, the architecture is a tangible realization of the practical aim of ensuring the secure state of an identified set of objects that exist within a given boundary. That assurance is achieved through the combined actions of an optimal configuration of control behaviors that the organization has implemented to ensure the confidentiality and integrity of the objects in the protected space.

The critical set of resources that the organization has provided to underwrite a given business purpose, and which are uniquely attached to the protection requirements of that organizational instance, operate strictly within the protected space. The tangible realization comes in the form of a specific set of electronic, human, and physical security controls that are allocated, by design, to ensure the desired level of protection. This unique set of actions constitutes the enterprise's security architecture. Thus, in effect, the enterprise architectural design process, which we are discussing here, formalizes and then embeds the organization's specific security solution into a corporation's overall operation.

For that reason, the specific process that achieves those tangible ends must address all of the realities of the business environment within the specific set of resources that have been committed to achieve the organization's particular strategic aims. Three factors dictate the ultimate shape of a holistic solution as well as the everyday conduct of the real-world management process that oversees it. These are architectural design, practical implementation control, and long-term sustainment. The first of these is the generic architectural design process, which we will discuss next.

THE ARCHITECTURAL DESIGN PROCESS

The supreme art of war is to subdue the enemy without fighting.

—Sun Tzu

The generic architectural design process involves two pragmatic activities. The first is the abstraction and documentation of the design. The second is the precise specification of how each element in that design will interoperate. Or in simple terms, these elements are the design and implementation phases of the organization's specific holistic architectural development process.

The architectural design process is methodological, involving hierarchical, top-down decomposition of the problem space. In essence, the entire system is decomposed into a distinct set of logically consistent layers. These layers represent the subsystems of the solution. Then, once a discrete set of layers is defined ... and that will typically involve several iterations. The architect makes decisions about the components that populate each level and their appropriate relationships to one another. This is usually based on best practice guidance and driven by the business purposes of the protection scheme.

The decomposition process will proceed all the way down until the technical components and behavioral aspects of the business operation are individually identified and fully described. Thus, the outcome of the decomposition process is a unitary and rational architectural model that documents all of the tangible control actions and associations that enable a complete and correct security solution within the day-to-day operation of the conventional business. Essentially, the development of effective architecture involves performing three primary planning functions:

- *System Decomposition*: The decomposition process begins with the top-level system description. As we said, the representation of the component architecture is then layered at a logically consistent level of abstraction. Each level describes the requisite components and relationships necessary to enable the required functionality at that particular level. For example, all the constituent actions essential to achieve the functional purpose of a given component are specified and related. That design schematic can either be visual, or textual, or both.
- *Best Practice Methodologies*: These are the methodological approaches that underwrite the many design decisions required to achieve a satisfactory solution, which is appropriately adapted to the specific organizational business purpose and environment. The outcome may be achieved by techniques, tools, principles, standards, and common best practices. The final product of the methodological

phase is a set of unambiguously specified and logically related components that enable a particular business purpose, as well as the unique inputs required to ensure a predictable outcome.
- *Implementation plans* are the back end of the process. They provide formal guidance on how the design and implementation process will be embedded and sustained within the overall business operation. Those plans serve as both the basis for the practical development process and ensure the proper installation and sustainment of the long-term solution.

IMPLEMENTING A PRACTICAL ARCHITECTURAL SOLUTION

Strategy without tactics is the slowest route to victory. Tactics without strategy is the noise before defeat.

—Sun Tzu

The second element, practical implementation, is the engine that drives the process. Cybersecurity is critically important because businesses rely heavily on their technology, and with that reliance comes the increased need to ensure that every aspect of that technology is adequately protected. The real-world business implication of the requirement for across-the-board protection is that the company must deploy a complete and correct operational cybersecurity protection scheme. Thus, as business organizations grow and diversify, increasingly powerful implementation strategies are required.

As we have seen, the value of adopting a single, unitary understanding of the problem space's boundaries is that it avoids creating vulnerable gaps in the protection scheme, which can lead to exploitation. However, designers must see and understand the entire elephant to ensure a comprehensive, seamless, and gap-free security scheme. In this respect, the design of operations for a holistic cybersecurity system is especially challenging because virtual work is conducted in multi-layered, multi-vendor, and even multicultural team settings, where all players and eventualities must be adequately understood and controlled.

The adage about too many cooks spoiling the broth should help you understand why coordination and control of complex work require a single, common perspective to both manage and benchmark performance. That point of reference is the unitary security architecture that a given organization creates to embody a particular cybersecurity vision. The problem is that this development process is often anything but planned and well-coordinated.

Typically, most cybersecurity architectures are cobbled together piecemeal. In other words, security control actions are developed and applied incrementally in specific areas as needed, rather than as a comprehensive, fully designed, and implemented solution. The result is that exploitable gaps will exist in the security architecture, and the only challenge for the hacker will be to "find the gap."

The alternative to a piecemeal solution is a complete, top-down architecture that embodies a unified and formally defined set of security best practices, specifically designed to optimize the effectiveness of a particular set of protection objects. As with any complex deployment, this infrastructure is best understood and substantiated through a strategic development process.

To begin with, there are larger contextual factors that need to be identified and settled before you can get down to the work of substantive design. Specifically, that is the overarching requirement that the solution be developed and managed as a single, coordinated, organization-wide activity. Thus, the need for coordination of the solution effectively locates the responsibility for cybersecurity assurance at the top of the corporate ladder.

It is placed there because no system exists in a vacuum. Every functional business system interacts with other organizational systems to achieve that particular organization's goals. Therefore, logically, the only entity with the authority and vision required to integrate and manage a wide array of functions seamlessly must be located at the top. Consequently, strong top-level executive sponsorship is a critical prerequisite for the success of any holistic cybersecurity solution.

Furthermore, the implementation of the security process will almost always represent a radical change in the way the organization does business, and the natural human urge to resist any alteration of a comfortable routine represents a significant barrier to instituting a new and often unfamiliar set of security practices. Accordingly, the only way to overcome that resistance is for the company's executive management to directly sponsor and oversee the installation of a capable, well-defined, and consistent set of security best practices.

The location of responsibility at the very top is a controversial idea. Most corporations create a hybrid C-level technical manager and then hand them the cybersecurity assurance portfolio. However, as we have seen, given the requirement that the solution must systematically mitigate every relevant threat across three uniquely different attack surfaces, delegating to a centralized information technology manager will never be an effective solution. Thus, one essential requirement is that the effort to ensure cybersecurity protection must be viewed as an integral part of the organization's business operations.

Nevertheless, it isn't easy to convince actual decision-makers – the CEOs, presidents, and members of the board – that they should be held accountable for the safety and security of the corporation's information assets in precisely the same way that they would be for its financial assets. Therefore, we should probably spend some time explaining the practical reasons why top-level executive sponsorship for the design, implementation, and sustainment of the cybersecurity function is a nonnegotiable requirement.

It all comes down to the legal term due diligence. Due diligence refers to the organization's obligation to take all reasonable steps to prevent harm to any person who places their trust in the corporation's products or services. Specifically, each organization is obligated to ensure that the personal information of their customers and clients is maintained confidential, available, and free of alteration.

The only logical way to ensure a proper level of assurance is to establish a tangible, overarching system of rational best practices that clearly links the cybersecurity solution to the business's goals and purposes. The provable effectiveness of the architecture is a crucial requirement because, in this litigious society, negligence in the handling of individual data can lead to severe consequences for both the corporation and individuals.

Therefore, to be held harmless in any subsequent litigation, the business must demonstrate that it has adopted a coherent set of strategic actions that prove that due care has been exercised. That includes being able to show audited proof that all necessary management roles, organizational behaviors, strategic policies, and security objectives have been satisfactorily designed, tested, and implemented.

These necessary protective requirements involve much more than the implementation of a purely electronic response, which is what information technology typically provides. Additionally, the solution must incorporate all provably relevant behavioral and physical controls to demonstrate proper due diligence. That requires the type of strategic vision that you only get at the top, which is why a comprehensive, organization-wide architecture must be sponsored by and overseen by the individuals responsible for the organization as a whole.

Specifically, there are five sequential tasks that top-level implementers must account for to ensure a holistically designed and organization-wide holistic security solution. These are:

1. Fully delimit the *scope* of the protection scheme.
2. *Analyze* and effectively understand the threat environment.
3. *Design and develop* applicable real-world controls to address priority problems.
4. Seamlessly *integrate* the finalized solution into the everyday business operation.
5. *Sustain and operate* the solution as a standard function of the business.

SCOPE

The first of these tasks is scope. That term describes the deliberate establishment of an unambiguous distinction between the protected objects within the boundaries of the cybersecurity solution – e.g., a protected space – and the rest of the universe. In some respects, this is the most critical step of all, as the dimensions of the access control perimeter, which define the scope, will then determine the form and extent of the rest of the process, and more relevantly in the real world, which implies a conscious balancing act between need and resources.

The scope must always address protection issues in light of resource constraints. In the worst case, that might involve leaving a non-essential or low-risk protection object outside of the boundaries of the defense. However, if that decision is made based on precise knowledge about the cost/benefit derived from including a given object within the established perimeter, this is an informed risk. In the hands of a capable decision maker, the principle of scope maximizes resource utilization and provides the foundation for the rest of the process.

The underlying issue that the scope-setting process addresses is ... "How does the organization get the most assurance out of what it has to spend?" In day-to-day practice, this means that it must be possible to make an informed decision about the level of risk that can be accepted, given the available resources. Obviously, anything can be secured if enough money is thrown at it. However, no organization has the funds to put a cop on every street corner. So, a deliberate process has to be undertaken that balances deployment of the response against the likelihood and material consequences of the threat.

Factors that might enter into this process include considerations such as the following. What is the level of criticality of each potentially safeguarded asset, and what is the degree of assurance required for each? Other factors that may influence decision-making include market or regulatory conditions. That determination can be captured on a ten-point asset classification rating scale, which ranges from "not needed" at one end to "the business would close without this" at the other end. Once all assets have been identified and their criticality prioritized, actual design work can begin.

Effective design requires a sufficient understanding of the threat/risk environment. The actual risk assessment process is carried out using best practice organizational evaluation principles. That allows us to note that the process of establishing a security system is always dynamic. In the case of scope, this means that the boundaries of the system are subject to ongoing refinement based on information fed back from other organizational activities, particularly the assessment of the changing risk environment. In essence, although the first step in the process is to define the system scope, the boundaries of that scope are never fixed. They are always subject to change as the realities of the environmental circumstances dictate.

ANALYSIS

Analysis is the second task. Analysis is a primary player in any system development process because it is essential to understand the problem conditions and the state of the system as it evolves. Analysis is systematic and methodological, based on best practice protocols. It aims to determine the current status of a given concern. In the case of security system design, that question revolves around identifying threats within the system's operating environment. Those threats must be prioritized because it is never possible to mitigate every threat to a given system. Thus, decisions have to be made. Those decisions are based on data derived from assessing the threats, specifically the probability of occurrence and impact.

This analysis process is usually based on and structured by commonly accepted best practices, which have been developed to inform and guide the security response. In essence, the current operational practices of the organization are compared to a standard reference model for best practice, which is typically expressed in the form of a national or international standard such as ISO 27000, NIST 800-53, COBIT, or any other commonly recognized industry framework.

In essence, the organization evaluates whether the controls it has deployed comply with and satisfy the best practice specifications of the reference model it has selected. If all of the commonly accepted requirements for best practice in a given instance have been met, that establishes that the requirement for due diligence has been satisfied.

Depending on the outcome of the assessment process, there might be a long period of trade-offs and refinement before an eventual decision about the practical shape of the protection scheme is reached. Those concerns are evaluated for their level of impact and probability by a formal risk assessment. A particular threat may not have a significant effect within a given organization's operating environment. So, the entire set of identified concerns is analyzed to differentiate only those that would create specific and undesirable impacts. These impacts are then carefully prioritized in terms of their resource implications. These ratings are recorded and implemented so that those with the most critical impacts are addressed first.

However, it is given that the controls represented in the final implementation of the solution must address all the vulnerabilities and threats identified during the assessment – e.g., a missing control is considered an exploitable weakness. Accordingly, the end product will always comprise a concrete and coherent set of control behaviors that are compliant with and enforce the best practice recommendations of the standard model adopted as the template for developing and deploying the best practice solution.

Once the problem space has been sufficiently understood, explicit control behaviors are tailored to the specific setting. These might be nothing more than a simple statement of expectations in a best practice handbook, or extensive training and education programs might reinforce them. Whatever the control approach specified, the outcome is typically a set of detailed descriptions of a routine collection of across-the-board security behaviors, which will represent that organization's interpretation of everyday best practice.

DESIGN AND DEVELOPMENT

Design is the next stage in the process. The outcome of the design phase is a tangible, real-world architecture that addresses all known constraints and concretely mitigates each issue identified in the risk assessment. It should be noted that designs are not necessarily technical. In the case of a business model, the design might be a strategic plan or a policy and procedure manual. Design is always a creative and conceptual endeavor, in the sense that it translates an abstract understanding of situational conditions into a tangible, real-world solution.

All designs exhibit common characteristics. They are complete in the sense that they encompass the entire problem space. They are correct in that all elements of the solution that logically should be present are there. They are understandable in that they unambiguously communicate the precise form of the solution, and they are conventionally pragmatic in that all of the elements in the design are traceable back to a business purpose.

The design document must build the quantitative foundation for the evaluation function. In addition, the design also explicitly embodies the elements necessary to make a qualitative judgment – one that will allow decision-makers to evaluate the overall solution. Thus, they are based on stated criteria. These criteria are used to assess the effectiveness of the system itself.

For instance, the specification that the system must be "reliable" is a typical qualitative element. Of course, reliability is important, but it is always in the eye of the beholder. Accordingly, there is no way to judge reliability until the organization establishes a commonly accepted definition of what reliable means. Thus, every qualitative criterion has to be accompanied by a statement of the real-world basis for judging it. Such as, "reliability is established as being greater than 98.6% up time." That is a criterion that can be measured and evaluated.

In addition to the architectural aspect, the design must provide a clear direction for integrating the security system into the existing organizational process. Technical elements of a new system must be programmed at their interfaces to ensure appropriate interaction between components. The business elements, such as management responsibility, have the same requirement for precise specification of interactions. This means that, from a strategic standpoint, all necessary relationships between system elements of every type must be identified and documented in the design.

Also, as the name implies, there is always some planning outcome that accompanies the design. The planning outcome actively and deliberately aligns the system operation with the organization's specific situational needs. Because that plan provides the explicit direction for the integration process, it is the essential product of this phase.

In the case of a small business, the planning might produce a relatively trivial documentation item, such as a memo of agreement. However, where the security solution is large or complex, an implicit element of long-range strategy is involved, and the result of that activity is always a detailed strategic plan. In that case, the organization performs all of the activities associated with strategic planning. This includes rationalizing the solution against business goals and objectives, as well as formulating a delivery schedule and contract.

INTEGRATION

Integration is the most critical principle in terms of the actual time spent performing the process. Integration might be just as fittingly termed "realization," or "implementation," because its end product is the substantive solution. In the context of general security goals, the aim is to regulate access and ensure that a proper set of controls accompanies the processing and storage of data. The first goal is typically achieved by satisfying the five common attributes of a secure system.

1. *Authentication*: whereby an individual, an organization, or a computer can prove its identity.
2. *Authorization*: the ability, once identity is verified, to control access to specific resources.
3. *Confidentiality*: the ability to maintain the privacy of the interaction between authorized parties.
4. *Integrity*: the capability to ensure the correctness of transmissions and data.
5. *Non-repudiation*: assurance of the identity of the sender and contents of a transmission.

All data of value has to be protected by deliberate measures to ensure strict access control. From the standpoint of electronic security ... that is the role of the generic firewall, or the operating system's reference monitor, if you want to be more specific. The purpose of those two is to protect the system from unauthorized external access by granting or denying permission based on criteria that they are set up to enforce.

A firewall fulfills Saltzer and Schroeder's principles of "fail-safe default" and "complete mediation." Commercial applications that do this, such as Internet firewall products, are considered to be sufficient in the popular imagination. But installing an effective firewall is like buying the most secure front door but not ensuring that the door is locked. Or in more prosaic terms, a firewall can't protect a business from dishonest employees, which violates the Saltzer and Schroeder principle of complete mediation. Therefore, other threat types must be factored into an effective solution.

To fully understand and address the requirement for complete mediation, the implementation process is divided into eight stages. These eight stages compel the organization to thoroughly examine all the intricate details of its security situation, ensuring that the solution is both optimally resource-efficient and continually improving.

Step One: Identification of Protection Objects – The first step in the process, logically, involves gathering all the necessary information to identify every item that requires protection. Essentially, this involves distinguishing, labeling, and valuing each of the organization's cyber assets, and subsequently formulating these into a comprehensive baseline of potential protection objects.

In many respects, this part of the process resembles the generic identification activity that would drive any fiscal accounting or physical inventory process. In that sense, then, all of the organization's objects of potential value are differentiated and accounted for in a permanent record. That record is typically kept in a digital repository, quaintly labeled "The Baseline Ledger." Because it is the only tangible outcome of the identification process, that baseline ledger is kept current and secure under the dictates of rigorous, classic configuration management.

Step Two: Risk Assessment – After all the organization's information assets have been identified and organized into a coherent baseline of protection objects, the next step is to determine their status. The purpose of the status assessment is to understand and document the exact security needs of each individual item in the baseline. This involves using the risk assessment process to characterize all direct threats, vulnerabilities, and weaknesses for each baseline item. The outcome of the risk assessment activity is that all of the factors that might impact security are understood and factored into the security response.

Once the entire set of information assets and their related controls has been identified, the organization's decision-makers undertake a rational impact analysis to establish the criticality of each protection item. This step weighs the implications of all relevant threats against the actions required to address them. In pragmatic terms, this means that the potential business impacts of the threat are assessed, and a level of significance is assigned to each. This activity applies to all potential protection objects with respect to any identified threats, including any substantive legal, contractual, compliance, and/or business issues.

The working principle here is that the probability of the problem actually occurring must be balanced against the resources required to mitigate it. The subsequent outcome is a sliding-scale interpretation, known as a risk reduction decision – e.g., a range of partial solutions. Potential choices will range from not addressing the threat at all to deploying the necessary resources to eliminate it. The final set of substantive decisions is then aggregated into an aggregate picture of the security requirements for the entire baseline set of items.

This leads to a decision about the resources that will be committed to implement each item, as well as the overall response itself. It should be noted that this is not a simple matter of plugging holes, as the assessment is likely to uncover many more threats than the organization would ever have the resources to address. Instead, decision-makers perform a triage activity as a means to prioritize the entire set of security concerns. The goal of this activity is to ensure that the organization's critical functions are adequately protected within the resources available.

Implementation: The following three steps are really aspects of the same process, which is the concrete implementation of the system. Once all of the elements of risk and resources are understood, it is time to array the initial set of controls into a tangible blueprint for implementation. This involves an iterative testing, evaluation, and functional enhancement process. Over time, the organization fine-tunes the controls that it identifies as the most effective. Any necessary alterations to the final control set are based on feedback from stakeholders, and this typically occurs over a significant period of time. Once the final set is implemented and working, the documentation of the protection items and their associated controls is kept in a final security baseline configuration ledger.

MONITORING AND SUSTAINING THE SOLUTION

> *Victory comes from finding opportunities in problems.*
>
> —**Sun Tzu**

Monitoring and sustainment are the final concepts. A robust measurement and evaluation program operationalizes both of these critical aspects. Measurement is essential to the sustainment process because high-level architectural designs are abstract things. Thus, the conceptual objects of the architecture must be made tangible to inform decisions about their current status and how they can be best maintained in a proper state of day-to-day functioning. Thus, measurement and evaluation are the fundamental elements of long-term management control.

Quantitative assessment helps decision-makers evaluate ongoing performance and assign accountability. Accordingly, every sustainment scheme must be accompanied by a description of the measurement program. The measurement program itself ensures that quantitative data establishes confidence in a given security solution. In that respect, then, measurement provides the consistent monitoring function required to ensure that the appropriate controls are in place and functioning correctly.

The formal measurement process is based on the execution of regular reviews of the organization's operational elements at pre-planned and mutually agreed-upon intervals. Measurement programs are typically founded on a range of business-specific metrics. These enable managers to assess performance at any given point in time, regardless of the situation. Correctly set up and maintained, the measurement program will monitor the security control operation and bring any deviations to management's attention. Hence, an essential component of any security implementation plan is the explicit schedule for conducting verification activities.

There are no universally recognized standard measures for assessing security performance. Instead, individual organizations choose the measures that they feel best fit their particular situation. The rule for this is straightforward: whatever metrics are selected, they must be uniformly and consistently applied throughout the system assessment process. In particular, since security operations are focused on preventing breaches, there is a need for a uniform definition of what constitutes a security breach. This requires the organization to delineate the attributes that it considers evidence of a security violation. These are typically expressed in terms of level of criticality.

For instance, although most people know that unauthorized access is an undesirable action, password sharing is often not understood in the same way, even though it can have similar impacts. This is not a black-and-white proposition. Therefore, whether a particular organization considers sharing to be a breach must be expressly stated. That formal clarification process must be documented for every known security concern to ensure that the data produced by the assessment is accurate and meaningful.

The express clarification of the characteristics of specific violations is necessary to ensure accurate and meaningful interpretations of the raw measurement data. That requires the organization to prepare and disseminate a standard classification and definition of all security violation characteristics. Moreover, new threats will likely be identified during the process of breach characterization. These will force the organization to make cause-and-effect decisions about the latest threat actors and the methods they use to create and exploit specific breaches.

Using that approach, it is possible to achieve a consistent and measurement-based control over the assurance architecture of a particular organization. The organization can engineer, or at least consider, the effectiveness of its security solution by following the complete set of activities discussed earlier. The result of the painstaking execution of these tasks is a coherent and fully integrated security response. Nevertheless, this process does not produce one-size-fits-all solutions. Instead, the determination of each element of the system must be based on managerial decision-making, which takes into account factors such as the degree of assurance required within a particular business setting and the resources available in that specific instance.

Best practice templates

The question is, “How do you determine best practice?” That comes from commonly acknowledged best practice standards that can be used as templates. The rule is that all situations are different; thus, an appropriately developed infrastructure is always precisely tailored from the larger set of practices to correspond to the specific requirements of the organizational circumstance in which it applies.

In practice, there are security responses that ensure different levels of the operation, and they are meaningful to various groups within it. The result of that state of affairs is that the practical purpose and precise application of the particular solution have to be documented and understood in detail – that is ... if the solution is going to be properly operated. Therefore, all stakeholders must be adequately identified and addressed.

Group understanding is usually leveraged by the generic best practice standard that has been adopted for that particular organizational instance. The recommendations embodied in a best practice standard are intended to encompass a broad range of managerial functions and are publicly available. Therefore, their recommendations can be considered widely accepted. Nonetheless, it is also worth noting that the current crop of best practice standards aims to produce a holistic system. In this respect, the recommendations of a best practice standard are not standalone elements. They substantiate every facet of the security function, which, taken together, constitute an aggregation of recommended best practices.

THE TAIL DOES NOT WAG THE DOG

> *Those who are victorious plan effectively and make decisive changes. They are like a great river that maintains its course but adjusts its flow.*
>
> —**Sun Tzu**

As we have seen, the primary purpose of creating a holistic enterprise architecture is to make the organization’s cybersecurity response concrete and comprehensible. That is an essential condition if you want to implement and operate a practical, real-world solution. That understandability is achieved by decomposing the components of the general problem into abstract, rational chunks, each chunk embodying a well-defined element of functionality, until all the essential chunks are laid out on the workbench. Then the actions required to adequately protect each component can be thought through and decided upon.

Given what has just been said about aligning resource commitments, the question at hand is, "How does the business ensure that the cybersecurity function, as represented by the particular architecture that it developed, effectively and directly achieves the organization's business aims?" Or in simple terms, how does the business make sure that the expenditures for cybersecurity serve the purposes of the business ... no more, no less.

That may seem like another nonsense question. I mean, isn't the point of the protection system to keep a company's assets safe? That is true, on the surface. However, the nature of the threats in the broader risk environment and the volatility of the situation tend to blur the connection between the shape of the implemented solution and the business's needs and purpose. That is why a formal, long-term strategic alignment process is a necessary element in ensuring an effective cybersecurity solution in any organization.

The term "alignment" refers to the degree to which an implemented cybersecurity solution directly supports a given business's overall purpose. The goal of the alignment is to achieve and then maintain consistently effective collaboration between the business operation and its attendant cybersecurity functionality. The outcome of properly executing the alignment process is effective interoperability between the holistic cybersecurity architecture and the business purpose.

The success of an alignment is measured by how well the organization's cybersecurity operations facilitate and assist the business in achieving its long-term business objectives. In effect, the cybersecurity process must enhance the organizational purpose provably, rather than operate independently of it. Therefore, the outlay of resources for the cybersecurity function must be directly justifiable by the business value it provides in terms of protection. Which, in straightforward terms, makes alignment a sustainable business role, not a technical security function.

Thus, it can be assumed that the alignment process must become an essential part of the organization's generic strategic planning, which further illustrates the degree to which the organization's cybersecurity operation must be deliberately shaped to underwrite business success. The objective of a formal alignment process is to achieve and then maintain a consistent functional relationship between a well-defined set of cybersecurity actions – e.g., controls ... and the business purpose that they have been specifically defined and resourced to support. Hence, the assurance that the business and the cybersecurity architectures are, and remain, properly aligned is a critical outcome of the overall business strategic planning function.

Business strategies and cybersecurity strategies are interdependent, since the cybersecurity process is derived from the explicit goals and strategies of the business operation itself. It is also worth noting that well-planned investment in the cybersecurity function will enable the business to adopt new business models. Consequently, both aspects of the relationship must be adequately considered when formulating an alignment plan for cybersecurity.

As we mentioned earlier, the problem with cybersecurity is that people within the organization only see the part of the elephant that they are touching. Therefore, solutions are hopelessly stovepiped. That is, managers tend to focus on how their particular areas of concern align with the overall solution, to the exclusion of other interdependent facets of the organization. Nevertheless, if the planning is done from an individual unit standpoint, the eventual solution will almost certainly be dysfunctional. That's because the goals of the production operation will differ significantly from those of finance or HR. As a result, exploitable gaps will almost certainly be created in the overall security architecture.

Hence, the real focus of the alignment process must be to ensure the priority security requirements of every functional area are addressed by a proper set of security controls that have been integrated into a single, dynamic, and seamless organization-wide solution. Eight explicit conditions must be met for the process to work correctly. The business must:

1. Recognize that capital spending for cybersecurity is a strategic investment
2. Recognize that the protection strategy must enhance business value
3. Focus all control alignment decisions at the functional level
4. Ensure seamless interoperation between business purpose and protection scheme
5. Be careful not to create silos
6. Prioritize the protection targets
7. Utilize metrics and data to support decision-making
8. Ensure complete transparency during implementation and sustainment

Recognize that capital spending for cybersecurity is a business investment. If the cybersecurity solution has been implemented to support the business, then all decisions about how that solution is resourced and subsequently operated must evolve from and be aligned with overall business planning. Thus, cybersecurity system development, deployment, and sustainment decisions are a top-level executive responsibility driven by the overall goal of protecting the organization's virtual assets.

This requirement stipulates that the resources required to enable the creation and operation of a cybersecurity function, at a given level of rigor, must be treated as evolving business expenditures. This is actually a common-sense condition, in that the protection requirements for the enterprise will vary based on factors such as the threat environment, the sensitivity of the assets, and the business purpose. Nonetheless, the modifying condition is that the investment in the cybersecurity architecture should not exceed the identified impact levels. That's the Goldilocks principle, not too much – not too little – just right! Therefore, this principle requires a cost-benefit analysis to be conducted before any concrete implementation decisions are made.

Recognize that the protection strategy must serve to enhance business value. In conjunction with the need to align resource commitments with the appropriate level and type of protection required, it is also essential that any decisions about the long-term conduct of the cybersecurity process are tied directly to prospective business plans. Organizational leadership should never have to guess about the tradeoff between the cost of protection and business value when making decisions about the investment in a new line of business. Therefore, the organization must adopt a comprehensive risk analysis and alignment strategy as an integral part of its overall long-term business planning.

Again, this argues that all strategic decision-making about the system should be permanently located at the top of the organization. That is because it is necessary, perhaps even required, to have a deep understanding of the business and its goals to ensure effective alignment with the cybersecurity function.

That requires a formal and tightly facilitated communication process between the people making the strategic decisions about the organization and the managers of the cybersecurity operation. And it is not an "Oh, by the way kind of obligation." These conversations must be formally integrated into the cybersecurity process planning, in the form of schedules and protocols for conducting the discussions.

Focus all alignment considerations at the functional level – ultimately. The devil is in the details. Or, in simple terms, alignment can only succeed at the functional level. Therefore, all relevant threats to day-to-day business operations must be identified, and the appropriate mitigations must be developed and implemented as part of a comprehensive system. That level of focus is far below the C-suite and entirely outside the realm of the information technology operation. Accordingly, a dedicated function must be established to ensure that the process is logically consistent throughout the decomposition ladder, running from the organization as a whole down to the individual solution element level.

That doesn't mean that a new layer of bureaucracy has to be created. In fact, this is best done by the line managers who are already in place, functioning as a tiger team. That approach is also an effective basis for ensuring interoperability because everybody relevant is in the room. The aim is to establish the most effective alignment between the actual cybersecurity controls deployed for each operational area and the business needs of that unit.

The confounding issue is that the existing design typically creates a situation where the control requirements far exceed the available resources to implement them. That, then, leads to the prioritization process we have already discussed. Thus, top-level management has to steer the ship. The presence of top-level decision-makers is required because prioritization decisions must be driven by the business's long-term goals and purpose. The aim is to facilitate alignment in a way that keeps the organization ahead of the curve, adaptive to change, and responsive to resource constraints.

The problem is that this process is political. Line managers with identified security needs will consider it their duty to argue for full protection of their particular function and its resources. However, the fact is that some low-impact or low-probability-of-occurrence protection candidates will have to be excluded from the final cybersecurity solution. The business's strategic managers are the only people who can make that decision, so they have to be included in the alignment process during this phase.

In fact, it is probably best for top-level decision-makers to regularly engage with the managers of functional and product areas throughout this stage of the process. This can be achieved through monthly or quarterly business reviews, as well as during strategic planning sessions. The point is that somebody with the corporate decision-making mandate must be engaged in the alignment process from its outset.

The aim is seamless interaction between business purpose and asset security – The security function isn't something that is strapped onto a business operation. There are too many moving parts in a standard, everyday business function to add security measures as an afterthought. That will create gaps because things will be missed in the subsequent design process. Thus, the controls to ensure a persistent and reliable state of security must be developed in conjunction with the associated business activities.

Baking security into a business operation demands a deliberate commitment to understand the essential activities of a given aspect of the operation and its specific threat environment. Obviously, this implies mutual cooperative work between representatives of both the security function and the business operation that the organization plans to protect. That can only be achieved by integrating the two, business functionality and security protection needs, into a single, tailored solution that enables a total understanding of the purpose and protection needs. In the simplest terms, the two functions must work together in the planning stage to jointly develop business behaviors in conjunction with any associated best practice security requirements.

There are several benefits to that approach. First and foremost, the protection requirements will evolve directly from the planning for the business process itself, ensuring the most effective alignment between purpose and protection. But equally as necessary, the business and security aspects of the operation will be fully knowledgeable about the other side's thinking, and that builds trust.

Finally, it also leverages the clarity that is essential to ensure top-level sanctioning and leadership. Security functions require up-front investment. It's like buying car insurance. You invest money to protect against potentially catastrophic expenditures that might happen down the road. Practically speaking ... Cybersecurity does not directly contribute to the bottom line. In fact, the extra rigamarole associated with measures like two-factor authentication and other purely assurance-oriented actions looks like time-wasting to the non-technical workers who comprise the majority of the business operation. Plus, technology is "mysterious" to everybody who is not a part of the IT function.

That lack of understanding encourages stakeholders to distrust the organization's actual cybersecurity operation and its associated strategies and fosters the blame game among units if any hitches occur. However, a shared process of joint development opens the communication channels, allowing both businesspeople and technologists to understand each other's viewpoints and perspectives. This transparency gives both the top-level business leaders and middle managers confidence in what might still be to them "the arcane" concepts and practices of the cybersecurity function.

Be careful not to create silos – Ideally, alignment ensures the efficient utilization of resources to achieve a particular business purpose. In conjunction with that justification ... alignment ensures that there are no gaps in the protection scheme. That is the ideal, of course. However, effective strategic alignment necessitates processes and activities that fall outside the primary business purpose, which is to grow and sustain the organization.

Therefore, as we have said several times, there has to be a dedicated, quasi-formal effort to reduce the natural tendency toward self-aggrandizement among the various functions that are standard parts of the routine operation, like finance, production, human resources, logistics, and also ... even the conventional information technology part of the operation.

For instance, there are a range of organizational aspects that might justifiably be included in the business alignment planning effort. Information technology and/or the formal electronic cybersecurity operation are obvious functions. But human resources is an essential aspect of identity management. In other words, the employee must be onboarded to be identified by the system. Additionally, organizational roles and responsibilities are managed through a combination of management and human resources planning. Finally, every aspect of physical security will fall under the purview of the Director of Physical Security and their staff. Proper alignment will consider all of these necessary factors because any chink in the armor, whether electronic, human-centered, or physical, is a potential disaster waiting to happen.

You get a silo if any, or all, of these functions operate independently from each other. To illustrate, the escalation of privilege is a typical security problem because it allows individuals to accumulate unauthorized levels of access that violate the principles of separation of duties and least privilege, as outlined by Saltzer and Schroeder. Privilege escalation occurs because individuals in an organization are assigned access rights for a given role, and when/if they change roles, they are then given a different set of privileges. Suppose the changes are not monitored by Human Resources and passed along to the privilege setting function in the IT operation, to adjust the attendant access rights. In that case, the individual will accumulate an inappropriate set of privileges by combining their past role and their present one. That stacking of privileges could conceivably lead to a serious security occurrence.

That is only one example of many potential vulnerabilities in a siloed organization. All of these risks stem from a lack of formally organized and sanctioned coordination between units that are not necessarily aligned with each other, either in terms of function or culture. And that is the result of the organization's inability or unwillingness to specifically address the natural problem of insularity among its business functions; essentially, it comes down to the age-old battle for turf.

Therefore, one of the primary requirements of the strategic alignment planning process is to bring all potential actors together in one room to ensure total interoperability between planned business initiatives and the attendant requirements for logical security assurance. In other words, to ensure a secure process, everyone involved in that process must communicate effectively and rationally. That includes specifying what they do and the accountabilities they will face if they do not do it properly.

The advantage of this kind of formal communication process is that there will be more proactive protection, with less ad-hoc firefighting occurring. The latter, which in most businesses is referred to as incident response, is the standard way businesses handle attacks and security breaches. The dilemma is that once the fire is put out, the house will already have been damaged or perhaps destroyed. Thus, alignment focuses specifically on preserving value through proactive means, rather than on putting out fires. It establishes silo-free transparency, collaboration, and unified work for long-term benefit. Nevertheless, that requires planning, organization, cooperation, and in many cases putting aside monumental egos in the service of overall business success.

Prioritize the solution – Prioritization is essential if your goal is to create a comprehensive, seamless security response. That is because it is inevitable that security needs will always exceed the resources required to mitigate them fully. The annual budgeting process is the mechanism that is used to fund the constituent functions of any business. But that is a zero-sum game. In other words, if one business unit receives additional funding, then another business unit loses an equal amount. This creates the potential for turf wars that can only be resolved through strategic policy-making and enforcement from the top during the budget planning process.

The best way to ensure close alignment is to start at a high level, such as with a statement of overall business goals and key performance indicators. Then planners drill down by decomposing the organization into the units that are responsible for achieving those results. That is then further broken down into the practical functions within each unit that are responsible for achieving those results. Those functions are then formally described and mapped to the requisite performance and response requirements for achieving each outcome. Then each of those functions and their associated behaviors are evaluated for their business value – e.g., contributions to the larger purposes of the organization. That process is conventionally known as asset valuation.

Asset valuation is the analytical process for determining the actual value of a discrete element of a business. Thus, asset valuations are often used to make informed decisions about specific activities, such as business expansion, cost-benefit analysis, or mergers and acquisitions of an entire business. But the asset evaluation process is also perfectly appropriate for prioritizing business assets for protection. In simple terms, asset valuation determines the economic value of a specific business process or business unit, enabling the prioritization of its security.

Triage is the essential basis for creating defense in depth. At a minimum, defense in depth involves ensuring that the highest-priority elements in the protection scheme are situated behind the most robust possible defenses. Then items of lesser priority are grouped into less robust zones of protection, ranging from "important but not vital" to "should be protected but not important." In that respect, then, a formal asset valuation can be used to understand the importance of a given asset to the business as a whole and then assign its priority.

Knowing the value of each potentially protected asset is an excellent way to objectively assess the degree and level of investment required to protect it. Depending on its purpose, an individual asset can be valued in numerous ways. However, each approach must provide an empirical basis for assessing the criticality of the asset to assign substantive protection measures. Thus, the asset evaluation needs to evaluate the asset's individual value to predict the impact and consequences of any damage. The process for doing that embodies a lot of what we have talked about so far:

Identify all potential protection objects and classify them in functional groups – e.g., electronic, human, physical, and process/service-centered assets.

Identify repositories and classify them by the criticality of the data they contain. Map all information assets, such as data, to every repository that contains it. Then, utilize audits to determine the criticality and value of each container. This is generally expressed in the form of a numeric or sliding scale, ranging from the most crucial/essential assets to the least critical/significant assets.

Perform a quantitative estimate of the likelihood and impact of each threat for each asset. The following formula determines the quantitative measurement of threat impact: Potential loss/damage times the statistical probability of occurrence equals the risk Impact score. Using that score, it is possible to conduct a cost-benefit analysis to determine the investment necessary to mitigate a given threat.

Decide on protected objects – once the identification, valuation, and categorization of the cost-benefit of threat mitigation are fully understood, the organization is now ready to develop a holistic solution based on a prioritized set of protected objects. Those objects are contained within a security perimeter that delimits the scope of the solution and controls access to the protected space. Every access to that space falls under Saltzer and Schroeder's Complete Mediation principle and, in every respect, represents the implemented cybersecurity solution.

Design the real-world system – the resultant cybersecurity solution is nothing more than an integrated and mutually supporting collection of controls deployed to mitigate all identified threats to the protected space. To accomplish this in a pragmatic, business sense, it is necessary to estimate the price of implementing the control versus the cost/impact of not implementing it. This final decision-making process is needed because the cost of a fully implemented set of risk management controls would be prohibitively expensive in the real world. If the risk is considered acceptable based on the cost-benefit analysis of mitigation, then no further action is required. But if the risk is not acceptable, it must be controlled through five separate prevention options and/or mitigation measures:

1. Fully control the risk
2. Do not fully control the risk, but set controls to reduce the impact
3. Do not fully control the risk, but set controls to reduce the likelihood
4. Transfer the risk to a third party – e.g., insurance
5. Avoid the risk – e.g., separate the risk away from the asset by either changing the nature of the asset, or placing it in a separate location in the organization

Identify any existing controls and perform a gap analysis – the actual control set is developed from a commonly accepted best model. In most organizations, there is usually some form of cybersecurity solution in place. Therefore, it is necessary to identify and characterize any existing controls, as well as map their application and interdependencies. Once the existing inventory of formally instituted controls is mapped, there will almost certainly be additional controls required to make the solution holistic – e.g., comprehensively addressing all recognized threats. This can be formally understood and implemented by using a strategic best practice model, such as ISO 27000 or NIST 800-53, to organize existing and new controls into a single, coherent, and comprehensive structured solution.

Ensure complete transparency during the implementation and sustainment process – transparency in both the design and execution of the security function is arguably the most critical success element of the entire process. As we said earlier, there is nothing attractive about the organization's cybersecurity operation. Any action taken for the purposes of enhancing cybersecurity can be reasonably classed as overhead; staff and equipment add nothing to the bottom line, nor will the additional steps that the process imposes on the workforce seem like anything but a burden. That is ... unless they are seen for what they are, necessary protection measures in a world that is overrun by threats.

Hence, full stakeholder involvement and transparency in the design and sustainment process of the cybersecurity solution are the best ways to guarantee its adoption and subsequent acceptance. An organization that fosters transparency will benefit from several things. First and foremost, comprehensive stakeholder involvement is the most effective way to ensure alignment between business purpose and strategies, and it holds all stakeholders accountable for adhering to all specified best practices. Second, full transparency requires everyone in the organization to understand what the specific goals of the business are and how they will be measured. Finally, transparency helps stakeholders understand the *why* behind key decisions. That builds trust.

Understanding the reason why the system is built and operates the way it does leverages better acceptance of a potentially burdensome new process, which is being introduced to organizational stakeholders. This ensures that shareholders, employees, and the general public can assess the performance of both the standard, everyday cybersecurity activities and the capabilities of those in charge of managing them.

The cybersecurity process always yields measurable outcomes, such as the number of attacks and losses prevented. That data can be used to assess performance and to guard against any possible failure or malpractice by workers or bosses. This ensures a state of accountability for the actions of every party responsible for practical cybersecurity work. Nevertheless, the chief advantage of a fully transparent approach to cybersecurity is that the organization as a whole can evolve its cybersecurity response in tandem with broader environmental changes.

In most of these situations, the focus is on the correct implementation of new processes and the attendant evaluation of outcomes. The problem is that the technology environment is inherently volatile. Changes in the environmental context of the organization manifest themselves in many forms – new policies, organizational rebranding of programs, or the introduction of new business initiatives. All of these factors have the potential to disrupt a well-established operational routine. That is why the assurance of transparency during the process – from the C-suite downward to direct reports, and laterally among peers – is the lifeblood of building alignment at all levels in the organization. And that relies on ensuring proper understanding through communication. The practical fact is that alignment involves securing buy-in from everyone who is involved in, or affected by, the process. Therefore, a formal process of training and awareness is necessary to convey the message effectively.

MANAGING THE HUMAN FACTOR: INJECTING CAPABILITY MATURITY INTO THE RESPONSE

If you know the enemy and know yourself, your victory will not stand in doubt.

—Sun Tzu

Threats to corporate information arise at various levels and appear in a variety of forms. These range from penetrations of the network by technically sophisticated "hackers," all the way down to petty thefts perpetrated by people who knowingly, or even unknowingly, harm something of value. All the same, each of these threats has to be countered by a substantive response to ensure an effective security solution.

This means that a valid and appropriate array of practices has to be in place and consistently followed throughout the security assurance process. Obviously, proper procedure and the relevant technology are essential aspects of any protection scheme. However, these factors alone cannot assure reliable security performance. To ensure a consistent state of security, individuals within the system need to adopt and consistently observe highly disciplined security practices.

Therefore, human factors themselves are also essential and substantive contributors to the success of the security enterprise. Logically, no matter how robust the access control and how stringent the policies are, the workers who operate the system are the ones who violate security for the sake of convenience and who are susceptible to every conceivable form of social engineering. As a result, the human factor is easily the weakest link in the system.

Because of that fact, human behavior cannot be left to chance when developing a fully aligned holistic protection solution. In essence, the human factor must be addressed by a tangible set of practical controls, designed to eliminate the adverse impacts of routine human behavior, which is the chief vulnerability in any properly designed and implemented solution. Realistically, a dependable day-to-day security solution will always implicitly rely on the people who use the technology and execute the routine tasks. Because of that fact, human behavior cannot be left to chance. It has to be addressed by a tangible set of practical controls.

Where people are involved, it is almost impossible to ensure consistent security performance. The root cause lies in the fact that the protected asset is highly abstract, making it difficult for those who utilize a system to comprehend all the ways it can be threatened or compromised. That is the reason for implementing standard operating procedures. Nonetheless, those procedures must be consistently followed to be effective. Consequently, the successful execution of any cybersecurity process entails addressing human factors, such as understanding and acceptance.

Those two affective factors influence security performance because they dictate how rigorously procedures are followed and how consistently prescribed actions are taken. Thus, adequate holistic assurance requires that all individuals in the organization understand their precise roles and responsibilities within the security process. Most work depends on the condition that all of the participants have an adequate understanding of what is required of them. So, formally acknowledged or not, it is the organization's duty to ensure a satisfactory level of experience and acceptance for every participant.

This means that every member of the business has to precisely understand what is expected, as well as the consequences of non-compliance. This can only be ensured through a planned and organized awareness and training process that ensures that everybody has mastery of their specific security responsibilities. Hence, it is the organization's duty to establish a formal awareness and training program as part of its overall security response.

The point of a formal process is to establish security discipline organization-wide. The term "discipline" denotes nothing more than the reliable exercise of a required method of practice. Cybersecurity requires disciplined practice because standard procedures must be consistently executed by all participants at all times to ensure complete protection. Inconsistent performance can lead to security breakdowns and harm to the resource. Therefore, disciplined practice is one of the first conditions for instituting a properly aligned, holistic cybersecurity solution.

The bedrock of the entire solution is implementing and maintaining a disciplined set of practices for all participants. That is because this ensures that the protection system is consistently reliable. The problem that this creates is that rules tend to impose additional requirements, and people tend to resist any substantive change in current practice. Thus, they must be motivated to do so.

Motivation is the other important human factor in the cybersecurity process. Motivation is the aspect of human behavior that initiates, directs, and sustains all forms of interaction among people. It is the driver that maintains a person's willingness to carry out a given task or achieve a set goal. In a broader sense, motivation also determines the degree, direction, and persistence of any given effort over a specified period of time.

Even so, motivation is only possible if there are sufficient incentives. Those incentives are enforced through an accountability system that rewards correct actions and discourages improper ones. It is impossible to establish accountability if the explicit rules of behavior are not formally understood. Therefore, the organization must also ensure that all employees understand the consequences of noncompliance. For that reason, the second critical aspect of the process is to ensure that every member of the organization understands all accountabilities.

It should be apparent from this discussion that human behavior must be controlled to ensure proper cybersecurity alignment. It should also be evident from this discussion that establishing a proper understanding requires properly defining and training stakeholders about the fundamental levels of security competence required. The clarification of what's expected serves as the point of reference for establishing the desired level of assurance within the organization.

A properly designed and functioning model of this type would allow an organization or individual practitioner to build their overall understanding of what's required of them individually. Adequate understanding of individual responsibility is achieved by moving the individual worker through a logical path of increasingly rigorous levels of security knowledge. This is the only practical approach since nobody instantly gains all of the knowledge they need. There are four discrete levels of knowledge associated with such an approach:

1. Recognition – the organization recognizes the need for security
2. Awareness – the organization has informal security practices
3. Understanding – the security practices are planned and monitored
4. Control – decisions about security practices are based on measurement and data

Stage one: Recognition

The most fundamental of these levels is simple *recognition*. Here, the majority of individuals recognize that security is a necessary and valid concept. Until that recognition is achieved, the organization is essentially undefended. Once adequate recognition is established, individual workers begin to understand that security is a concern. This may not necessarily be done in a consciously active fashion. But it does involve a persistent underlying acceptance that secure behavior is necessary.

Two conditions must be met for an organization to satisfy the requirements of the recognition level. The first of these is that security issues are publicized. This can be done through simple mechanisms such as posters, handouts, or reference cards. But the specific outcome must be that the members of the organization are aware of and informally discuss topics related to security.. Although this level provides very little substantive protection, it creates the potential that some adverse events will be detected.

Stage two: Awareness

At the next level, *awareness*, participants become more conscious of security practices in their day-to-day work. All members of the organization are aware that security is a concern, and they follow basic procedures in response to this awareness. However, these procedures are not sufficiently thought through or organized to ensure proper institutionalization of security. That happens in the next level of understanding.

Awareness introduces basic planning and coordination practices. Therefore, awareness programs should consistently reach everybody in the organization. They should alert the membership to hazards that are particular to that individual environment. As such, there needs to be some analytical work done to understand and characterize the specific risks that are inherent in that organizational setting. This analysis is necessary because awareness has to be planned, and the adequate level of awareness will vary depending on the line of business.

Another requirement of a correctly functioning awareness program is widespread knowledge and acceptance. That is, there must be an intuitive understanding among every member of the organization of the fundamental need for uniform security practices. This does not necessarily imply a rule book. Nor does it demand that everybody in the organization march in formation. What it does require, though, is a basic consistency in execution.

Establishing awareness is a programmatic function. That is, it is the outcome of a formal knowledge acquisition process that must be tailored to the specific needs of the individual situation. Accordingly, awareness programs are designed based on a situational understanding, which is then deliberately resourced, planned, and deployed. Second, there has to be a formally constituted and organized effort to develop and publicize all best practices. These are typically promoted in the form of adages, such as "always back up your files," rather than being explained in depth. The primary value of awareness is that it enables the organization to establish a basic level of security assurance with a minimal commitment of time and resources.

Stage three: Understanding

The third stage, *understanding*, is the first level where a consciously planned and formally established holistic solution exists. At this stage, each individual in the organization understands and acts on a mutually acknowledged need for formal security. The response may not be extensively organized, and it is often dependent on individual willingness; however, it is recognizable in that security procedures are documented and commonly accepted. This level represents a considerable advance over the awareness level. It begins to establish security functioning as a consciously delivered and continuous process. It enables a company to address its most pressing needs, and it typically provides a solution to fundamental security issues.

The understanding stage is the first truly institutionalized response. To ensure a minimum level of disciplined security practice, this stage is underwritten by formal training programs. A conscious and organized effort, designed to instill the proper skills, is the only way to establish a formal understanding. As such, this level is embodied through the identification of the specific requirements of the organizational setting, which are then referenced to a formal response that comprises the specifically tailored instructional content.

Two absolute conditions must be met to attain this level. The first of these is that the organization's security requirements are unambiguously defined and documented in a location where everyone can see and understand them. The second is that these practices must be represented as a formally acknowledged and commonly accepted set of behaviors, which are implemented by clear procedures.

The design of a training program is always supported by an understanding of the current needs of the organization, which can be effectively targeted through individually focused training exercises. One of the primary differences between this level and the next is that training is not formally institutionalized as a process. Instead, it is often left up to the initiative of individual managers and process owners within the business. The result is that, although some goals are achieved, others are left by the wayside because they were either not recognized as necessary or the functional area was too preoccupied with other tasks.

Stage four: Control

The fourth stage, deliberate *control*, is typical of a well-organized security operation. It entails an institutionalized security response that is built around a tailored set of procedures. These are derived and managed based on a precise understanding of the situation's requirements. Accordingly, this level is frequently supported by quantitative measurement and defined accountability. It is operated under the complete control of the organization's management team. At this level of functioning, the organization can be considered both safe from common threats and actively practicing the necessary steps to maintain that requisite level of security.

The controlled level is where the holistic solution resides. It is comprehensive, coherent, and institutionalized as part of the ongoing organizational planning and decision-making function. This can only be achieved through a formal planning and deployment process. This level is managed and accountable. The level of understanding is embodied through risk assessment and planning, which leads to the implementation of a specifically tailored security program.

This requires that three conditions must be met. The first of these is that the roles for security are assigned and understood among all of the organization's staff and management. It also requires a complete and correct set of best practices and control objectives, which are implemented by a clear set of procedures. These must be unambiguously defined, documented, and precisely tailored to encompass the entire range of known security requirements of the organization. A valid and quantitative set of performance measures and metrics must accompany them. This level is also fully supported by a systematic risk assessment process.

The resulting response is assumed to be a mix of procedures, technologies, and methods, which are integrated by design into a complete organizational system. The requirements for properly executing that system are reinforced through the comprehensive education program. This process is programmatic in the sense that it functions as an established institution within the organization's operating structure.

The advantage gained by an effective organization-wide control system cannot be overstated. As we have said, security is a complex and multidisciplinary challenge that is rooted much more in individual behavior than in technology. As such, it is essential to both carry the message and reinforce the behavior. A properly aligned system of controls does this. It both provides the individual worker with the necessary knowledge to do their job right because it conveys the proper set of best practices. And it reinforces the cultural and behavioral norms associated with the security operation.

CHAPTER SUMMARY

Logically, the specifically identified and labeled assets contained within a controlled space have been placed there to achieve a commonly understood organizational objective. In that respect, the architecture is a tangible representation of the practical solution proposed to ensure the secure status of an identified set of objects within the protection scheme's boundaries. That assurance is attained through the actions of an optimal configuration of people and equipment that the organization has allocated to ensure the integrity of protected space.

In essence, the critical set of resources that underwrite a given business purpose and which are uniquely attached to the protection requirements of that organizational instance operate strictly within a well-defined space. Then a tangible set of electronic, human, and physical security controls is allocated, by design, to ensure the desired level of protection. This constitutes the enterprise's security architecture. So, in effect, the enterprise architectural design process that we are discussing here formalizes and then embeds the organization's specific protection solution into a corporation's overall operation.

For this reason, the actual process that realizes those tangible outcomes must consider all the realities of the business environment, as well as the specific resources that can be committed to achieving the organization's strategic aims. Three factors dictate the ultimate shape of a holistic solution as well as the routine conduct of the real-world management process that oversees it. These are architectural design, practical implementation, and long-term sustainment.

The generic architectural design process entails two pragmatic elements. The first is the abstraction and documentation of the design. The second is the precise specification of how each element in the design will interoperate in everyday practice. Or in simple terms, these elements are the design and implementation phases of the holistic architecture process.

The architectural design phase is methodological, involving a hierarchical, top-down decomposition of the problem space. In essence, the entire system is decomposed into a defined set of logically consistent layers, such as the subsystems of the solution. Then, once a rational set of layers is defined ... and that will typically involve several iterations. The architect makes decisions about the components that populate each level and their proper relationship to one another, based on best practice guidance regarding the system's purposes.

The second element, practical implementation, is the engine that drives the process. Holistic solutions are essential because businesses rely on their technology, and with that reliance comes the increased need to ensure that every necessary aspect of that technology is appropriately protected. The real-world business implications of the requirement for across-the-board protection are that the company must deploy a complete and correct operational cybersecurity protection scheme. Thus, as business organizations grow and diversify ... increasingly powerful implementation strategies are required.

A carefully implemented, top-down architecture that embodies a unified, comprehensive, and formally defined set of security best practices, specifically aimed at optimizing the assurance of a particular set of protection objects, is an alternative to a piecemeal solution. As with any complex deployment, this infrastructure is best understood and substantiated through a rational and explicit design and development process.

The location of responsibility at the very top is a controversial idea. Most corporations create a hybrid C-level technical manager and then hand them the cybersecurity assurance portfolio. But, as we have seen … given the requirement that the solution must systematically mitigate every relevant threat across three uniquely different attack surfaces, kicking the can down to IT will never work. However, it is challenging to convince actual decision-makers – the CEOs, Presidents, and members of the board – that they should be held accountable for the safety and security of the corporation's information assets in the same way that they would be for its financial assets. Thus, one essential requirement is that the effort to ensure cybersecurity protection is viewed as an integral part of the organization's business operations.

As we have shown, the only logical way to ensure a proper level of assurance is to establish a tangible, overarching architecture of rational best practices that comprises a provably effective link between the cybersecurity response and the business operation's goals and purposes. The provable effectiveness of the architecture is a crucial requirement because, in this litigious society, negligence in the handling of individual data can lead to severe consequences for both the corporation and individuals.

Therefore, to be held harmless in any subsequent litigation, the business must demonstrate that it has adopted a coherent set of strategic actions, proving that due care has been exercised. That includes being able to show audited proof that all necessary management roles, organizational behaviors, strategic policies, and security objectives have been satisfactorily designed, tested, and implemented.

To achieve a holistic security solution, top-level implementers must address five sequential tasks. These are:

1. Fully delimit the *scope* of the protection scheme.
2. *Analyze* and effectively understand the threat environment.
3. *Design and develop* applicable real-world controls to address priority problems.
4. Seamlessly *integrate* the finalized solution into the everyday business operation.
5. *Sustain and operate* the solution as a standard function of the business.

Chapter 4

A methodology for holistic security

Figure 4.1 Pencil drawing of a weary armored soldier in profile, wearing a helmet and shoulder armor, wiping sweat from his brow with his fist. Drops of sweat run down his face, and a shield is visible at his side, conveying exhaustion, strain, and the human cost of battle.

DOI: 10.1201/9781003603412-4

ENTERPRISE ASSURANCE: CYBERSECURITY BY DESIGN

Sweat more during peace: bleed less during war.

—Sun Tzu

The last chapter discussed holistic enterprise architecture. The salient point is that holistic architectures are developed top-down through the functional decomposition process, and they must map directly to the business's goals and objectives. That implies the need for a single, comprehensive strategic planning and design approach that progresses through a set of discrete stages. Thus, the following three fundamental stages comprise a structured approach to the creation and maintenance of a holistic, enterprise-wide control architecture:

1. *Classify and design* a fully converged and integrated unitary organizational control response
2. *Implement* a real-world system of control elements traceable to business purposes and goals
3. *Manage* the long-term effectiveness of the system through quantitative decision support

The rest of this book will be devoted to fleshing out these three stages. The overall goal is to demonstrate how to build practical, holistic, and architectural frameworks that address all meaningful cybersecurity threats across all three legitimate attack surfaces. The aim here is to illustrate how traditional technology and business-related factors, as well as the specific needs of the stakeholder community, can be integrated into a comprehensive, holistic solution that ensures a provable level of protection for each of the organization's priority business assets.

The first phase of this process involves identifying and classifying all applicable risks and developing a strategic response to address all meaningful threats. This stage is a precondition for the conceptual design of the enterprise's cybersecurity architecture. Consequently, this chapter will focus on the initial steps of the enterprise architectural development process – classification and design.

The goal of this phase is to identify all threat conditions that might impact the organization and then document, based on that understanding, a rational design that ensures holistic protection for all assets of value within the organization. Therefore, in essence, this chapter will show you how to gather the necessary information and then formulate a blueprint for an effective real-world cybersecurity process.

Logically, the chapter that follows this will examine the practical implementation concerns of the process, specifically how to map and ensure comprehensive and appropriate day-to-day control over the organizational threat space as it evolves. Following that, the next chapter will discuss the means of guaranteeing practical alignment with the business purpose as the organization operates its holistic cybersecurity system. Or in simple terms, that chapter will demonstrate how to maintain the protection scheme so that it demonstrably supports the goals and objectives of the overall business purpose. Some might refer to the outcome of this final chapter as the generic cybersecurity process.

The final chapter of this book presents an applied example of a standard best practice enterprise security model. It will illustrate how the profession as a whole views the architectural design and implementation process. As we mentioned, the threat environment is continually evolving, with new and increasingly dynamic threats emerging daily. Therefore, a disciplined, best practice-based framework model is the most effective practical mechanism for addressing dynamic changes in the business context. The underlying principles and assumptions, as well as the adaptation of that general process to develop a pragmatic cybersecurity solution, will be discussed there.

WHY IS A HOLISTIC APPROACH NECESSARY?

> *There are not more than five musical notes, yet the combinations of these five give rise to more melodies than can ever be heard.*
>
> —**Sun Tzu**

As we mentioned, enterprise architecture is essentially a conceptual framework that provides the necessary perspective for rational organizational control. Specifically, the framework serves as the point of reference that underpins disciplined management. It lets stakeholders understand and subsequently manage complexity. It is an absolute necessity to have a concrete, central point of reference for this, because the threat environment is purely virtual, and the assets being protected are, in most cases, invisible. Thus, there must be a concrete basis to document the tangible shape of the organizational solution being implemented.

Practically speaking, every cybersecurity operation needs an explicit roadmap to implement and then maintain a seamless, holistic, organization-wide cybersecurity solution. That's because most businesses are complex, and their operations will inevitably become increasingly intricate as the organization's size and scope increase. Hence, functional decomposition of the organizational problem space into increasingly finer-grained and less intricate modules is the only feasible basis for accurately documenting the problem.

The fully decomposed view of the problem space must capture and characterize the fundamental understanding of the business process. Therefore, the final set of decomposed modules must encapsulate all of the problem's explicit individual components and represent them with clearly defined interfaces that fully describe their business purpose. The specific threats to each element, along with the necessary mitigations, can then be expressed in concrete architectural terms. That blueprint then serves as the means for designing and concretely developing the most practical set of threat mitigations.

As we have frequently stated, most cybersecurity responses are exclusively focused on ensuring the electronic aspect of the threat space. Hence, the current process isn't directly responsible for developing a targeted set of mutually aligned controls for the human element. The argument is that there are other parts of the organization that are specifically accountable for ensuring people's good behavior, such as managers and the human resources function. At the same time, physical security doesn't see a clear relationship between its mandate and an abstraction like cyberspace. Consequently, most organizations are limited to a tangible cybersecurity approach that will reliably address precisely one-third of the problem space.

I hear you asking, "What are the consequences of this limited view of the problem?" Well ... Is it never a good idea to leave obvious points of access unguarded, particularly in the face of known threats? As a consequence, the world loses an estimated $6 to $10 trillion annually to cyberattacks. One might think that the business world would view this as a big problem – and if so ... you would be wrong. In fact, not a single sector in the critical infrastructure has published a sector-wide strategy for comprehensive cybersecurity. There is no consistent agreement about what constitutes a critical breach. So, even with the clear evidence that very bad things are currently occurring, you could reasonably characterize the overall executive attitude toward cybersecurity as disconnected.

It should go without saying that an effective cyber defense must address every potential electronic, human, and physical hazard. Viewing the problem from any other angle is dangerous due to an indisputable fact: cyber exploits target three attack surfaces, not just one. Therefore, a proper cyber defense requires a unified array of controls that addresses all three access points.

The primary issue with the current approach is that the adversary doesn't adhere to the rules. For ordinary people ... the only legitimate type of attack is purely electronic, including hacking, malware, and other creative forms of electronic penetration. But the practical reality is that those attacks don't cause the majority of the problem. The remaining damage, approximately seventy percent, is attributable to human exploits, such as social engineering and insider threats, along with real-world abuses, including the physical theft of virtual devices like computers and thumb drives, as well as the simple loss of vital data due to accidents.

As we said in Chapter 1, the adversary's goal is to break into your system by any means possible. So, the adversary will employ "anything that works." Consequently, any gap in the protection scheme, whether electronic, behavioral, or physical, represents a point of exploitation. It is essential to keep in mind that any electronic, human, or physical flaw that permits unauthorized access essentially negates the rest of the defensive perimeter, regardless of which attack surface is exploited.

Accordingly, since the adversary will exploit any available point of entry, the organization's defensive perimeter must incorporate all necessary controls to ensure reliable protection. Accordingly, a complete, well-defined, and managed array of countermeasures is essential. Moreover, these controls must work together across all three attack surfaces to prevent compromises through the exploitation of interdependencies. That is why a comprehensive set of interoperable control behaviors is the only acceptable solution.

THE VITAL NEED FOR A CONVERGED PERSPECTIVE

Concentrate your energy and hoard your strength.

—Sun Tzu

The term used to describe an all-inclusive and unified solution is "converged." Convergence creates the unitary point of understanding and control that is always required to deploy and oversee a complex, rational, organization-wide cybersecurity protection scheme. Convergence merges all relevant security factors into a single strategic solution.

The steps necessary to achieve a converged state are just as complex as the general system design process itself. A single individual mechanism must be designed and practically implemented that continually senses and analyzes the organizational threat environment to identify every potential form of attack.

A single mechanism is necessary because every organization contains cross-functional processes. For instance, financial accounting is entirely dependent on the IT function. Hence, any IT compromise will directly impact the organization's finances. Therefore, to be fiscally responsible, a single organizational entity must be made accountable to unify the oversight and control of all of the organization's cybersecurity protection processes. Moreover, due to cross-functional requirements, that entity also must have the authority to reach across the organization to develop and coordinate all the concrete elements of its cybersecurity architecture. There are four standard functions that this function must ensure. These are:

1. Assurance of the accuracy and integrity of the asset inventory
2. Asset status accounting
3. Assurance of an appropriate protection scheme
4. Maintenance of protection

ESTABLISHING A UNITARY POINT OF CONTROL

The height of strategy is to attack your opponent's strategy.

—Sun Tzu

By its nature, holistic security must cross unit boundaries. That implies the need for a formally authorized and fully integrated approach that enforces the protection strategy's required practices at the appropriate points on the organization's three attack surfaces. In conjunction with this, the organization must also identify and secure all interdependencies among control elements. That is necessary because control interdependencies are points of covert access. But if the interdependency is unknown, then it is not controlled. Even so, those interdependencies are difficult to identify because they usually involve unanticipated interactions with other elements of the business. Therefore, a unified approach to understanding the problem ensures optimal situational awareness of both the protection scheme and all points of access and interdependencies.

As we have emphasized, only top-level managers have the authority to initiate and enforce the design, development, installation, and long-term operation of a comprehensive package of protection controls. Logically, the individual operations of the development and oversight process must be consistent across all attack surfaces to gain a complete understanding of the picture. Therefore, proper organizational placement is the key to achieving a converged perspective. The information technology, which is the conventional unit responsible for cybersecurity, is too low in the hierarchy to do this effectively.

ASSURING THE ASSET INVENTORY AND STATUS ACCOUNTING

Asset assurance formulates a baseline inventory of all of the organization's virtual business assets and then places them under an appropriate level of organizational change control. The four generic steps that comprise best practice for this area include:

1. Build a baseline of uniquely labeled information assets and controls
2. Create a classification scheme to describe where the item fits within the business process
3. Relate each asset within the classification scheme
4. Maintain consistent and reliable asset baselines?

The process starts with the classification of all relevant business components and factors. This is, in effect, a standard inventory process involving three related activities: *asset identification*, *asset baselining*, and *asset change control*.

Asset identification – generic cybersecurity design decisions require an unambiguous understanding of the status of every item of value. Or in practical terms, you can't make an intelligent decision if you don't know what all of the parts of the problem are and how they relate. Hence, the exact form of all items that will be placed within the protection perimeter of the system must be explicitly defined and documented. This requires a detailed inventory of the business assets to differentiate and then explicitly describe the entire set of contents.

The process of identification and labeling creates a tangible picture of the exact form of all potential protection objects. That picture then becomes the specific point of reference for the deployment and management of the holistic security function. The documentation artifact that makes the complete asset picture tangible is called a baseline.

The term "baseline" refers to the current understanding of the status of a documented entity. This, in turn, serves as a basis for measurement or control. In simple terms, the baseline documentation is the official specification of the asset's structure, and it provides the basis for designing and establishing the security protection scheme.

Asset baselining – so, why go through all of this identifying and documenting? The business assets that fall under the protection scheme are primarily intangible, including virtual files and databases. Hence, it is necessary to make them tangible. The baseline provides the required visibility by explicitly describing and documenting those items. This is crucial for two reasons. First, and most obviously, the baseline becomes, in effect, the asset itself. Second, and more importantly, the specific countermeasures and controls that you will develop and deploy are created and directly referenced to the protection objects maintained in that baseline. Thus, baseline documentation essentially serves to define the form of the operational security system.

There are two separate steps involved in creating a business asset baseline. First, the criteria that will be used to characterize the asset's form and value must be agreed on and made clear for all participants in the decision process. This includes an explicit itemization of all the decision criteria used to define the value of the asset. For instance, statements like ... "The protected item must contribute X amount of value to a business process ..." might serve as a basis for deciding whether an information item is worth protecting.

This is essentially a documentation process, and, as we said, it is always associated with the business case. The formal description of the asset item, which, in effect, documents a business component of a particular real-world function, includes a precise description of its purpose and general use. That description is formally recorded and placed in the baseline.

The asset baseline begins the process. The baseline itself is more descriptive than detailed. As the decomposition of constituent baselines progresses from layer to layer, all of the items that comprise the higher-level baseline are itemized in detail. Then, each of those lower-level baselines is broken down until a satisfactory level of understanding of the original item being decomposed is reached. To gain practical buy-in, the baseline items are always described in terms that users and managers can understand.

Each component in a given baseline is individually identified and uniquely labeled. That action is based on and guided by the components in the baseline that are directly above the current layer in the decomposition process. For instance, the items at the second level of decomposition might be labeled 2.x, and the next level items, which comprise the higher-level entity, would be labeled 2.xx.

The outcome of each pass is a detailed representation at a specific level of abstraction of the information assets that constitute a given real-world business process. These are uniquely labeled based on their position in the hierarchy. The decomposition process continues down to a level of description and understanding that provides a workable basis for the threat analysis and control development.

Change control is a process that applies to the entire range of assets within the organizational baseline. Baselines are dynamic because businesses own a constantly changing collection of resources. Therefore, all baselines will evolve as the form of the asset base changes. The management of the documentation of that baseline must be conducted in a controlled fashion, utilizing formal change management.

A considerable degree of discipline is necessary in executing this task due to the fluid nature of the information resource itself. The form of the information resource will likely be lost without a disciplined procedure to ensure that changes to the asset base are correctly represented and up to date. For this reason, these two processes – identification and change control – form the basis of the asset identification scheme.

An effective change control process offers two primary advantages. First, it ensures the integrity of the documentation of the related set of protected business objects. Second, it informs the organization and continuously updates the status of those objects. It also allows the organization's managers and policymakers to have direct input into the formulation of the security process by involving them in concrete decision-making about the business assets that will be protected within the scheme.

Practically, the rules of the baseline change control scheme are established during the holistic security architectural planning process, not after the assets have been identified. This process involves itemizing all specific procedures to be followed, ensuring that all assets have been identified, and outlining how to maintain the integrity of the asset identification and documentation outcomes. In that respect, then, all organizational roles, responsibilities, and inter-relationships must be explicitly defined and assigned by this plan.

The end product of this process is a formal, fully documented, and organizationally authorized approach to documenting all assets of value to the organization. That scheme must ensure that every asset that is considered worth managing and protecting has been identified and characterized. That description is subsequently used in every other aspect of the architectural development process. Therefore, the process itself is always guided by the business case.

As we have said, due to the level of detail required and the number of assets that must be protected, there are never enough resources to secure everything. Therefore, the practical decisions about which asset is inside the protection scheme and which asset has to be left outside are always guided by an explicit understanding of risk, which is the critical next stage.

ASSESSING THE RISKS

Generally, the requirement for risk analysis is a vital part of the overall protection process. That is because risk analysis underwrites the development of explicit and meaningful controls to address each credible threat. A risk is any threat that can exploit a specific vulnerability. Practically, however, the concept only applies to those threats that could cause harm to the organization's information assets. The systematic process by which threats are identified and decisions made about whether, or how, they should be countered is termed "risk analysis."

A risk assessment aims to identify, evaluate, and manage cybersecurity risks. To do this, the scope of the evaluation must encompass the entire set of business issues. In essence, the risks associated with a given organizational asset are itemized in terms of the specific vulnerabilities and attendant threats they represent to the actual business case. Hence, it is crucial first to identify the precise aspects of the business purpose that will guide the definition of the protection scheme.

It is then necessary to identify and prioritize these threats that are most critical to the business. This involves a purely subjective decision that stakeholders must make based on the available data. This activity aims to secure the assets with the highest priority with controls that will assure the most reliable degree of certainty. Hence, the risk assessment process itself requires the exact specification of three critical and highly integrated factors

1. The relationship between all assets
2. The specific threats to each asset
3. The business and technological vulnerabilities that relate to those threats

To develop a reliable set of controls, the risk assessment must consider every relevant issue that impacts each of these factors. In the classic sense, risk assessments are done to identify operational vulnerabilities that might be exploited, as well as all relevant threats that might take advantage of them. The process evaluates the possibility that any given threat might occur and assesses the degree of potential loss or harm that would result. As such, in practical terms, the risk assessment answers the common-sense questions of … "What could go wrong? How likely is it to occur? What are the consequences if it does? And finally, what steps can I take to mitigate the threat given the known circumstances?

Risk assessment processes operate under the assumption that, as threats are identified, the appropriate countermeasures will be developed and subsequently implemented to prevent the adverse event they are designed to address, or to mitigate the damage if it does. Hence, risk assessments entail an ongoing assessment process that is performed to ensure the long-term security of the organization's asset base.

A continuous approach to risk assessment is required because threats are constantly emerging. Accordingly, organizations must develop and maintain precise knowledge of all significant threats that could affect them. This is necessary to ensure timely protection. The process itself encompasses two general stages.

The first stage involves classifying the risk, a process that is analytical in nature. The second involves recommendations for risk mitigation or management, which is a management control process. The term "risk assessment" is sometimes used interchangeably with "risk management." That is not correct, since these are not the same processes.

Risk assessments seek to obtain an understanding of the nature of all feasible risks. They identify and evaluate each relevant threat, determine its potential impact, and itemize the safeguards that will be deployed to counter them. At the same time, risk assessments delineate both the strategy to reduce the likelihood of the risk occurring (preventative measures) and the measures to respond effectively if a risk becomes a direct threat (reactive measures). The risk management process then maintains the deployed countermeasures once they have been implemented. Risk management typically ensures effective and up-to-date alignment between known threats and measures deployed to mitigate them. This is a regular part of daily operations for the cybersecurity function.

Risk assessments should always answer two distinct but highly related questions. The first is: … "What is the certainty of the risk?" This is typically expressed as likelihood. The second is: … "What is the anticipated impact?" That is usually conveyed as an estimate of the loss, harm, failure, or danger if the event does happen. Ideally, both of these questions can be answered in easily understandable and believable terms. Understandability and credibility are key factors in risk assessment. That is because the results of a risk assessment typically guide traditional decision-makers in the deployment and management of the security solution, and those decision-makers must be able to trust the data on which they are basing their decisions.

There are risks in every field of endeavor. However, in the context of cybersecurity, the concept of risk specifically pertains to threats that could compromise the organization's information assets. Hence, all risk assessments provide two specific pieces of information – the probability of occurrence and an associated estimate of the consequences. These are independent but highly related factors, which, to a certain extent, dictate the security measures that will be required. However, there is an implicit order to how these two issues should be approached.

Practically speaking, the first consideration is always the likelihood. That is because there is never enough money to secure against every conceivable risk. So, in a world where time is money, an improbable event might not be worth the cost of further consideration, no matter how much impact it might have. Even so, the estimate of those consequences is the factor that truly shapes the form of the response. Therefore, the potential harm that each risk represents must always be balanced against the likelihood of its occurrence.

For instance, an event that might cause catastrophic loss will sometimes justify consideration, even if it is improbable. As a far-out example of this, the cataclysmic consequences of the Earth colliding with an asteroid justify spending considerable money to track the movement of such objects even though the odds of an asteroid striking the Earth are negligible.

Hence, the primary objective of the risk assessment process is to optimize operational deployment and resource utilization of the control solution. Risk assessment supports this by identifying those risks with the highest probability of occurrence and that will cause the most significant degree of harm. The options that these represent for the organization are then arrayed in descending order of priority and addressed based on the available resources. Since all of the decisions about the tangible form of the security system will depend on getting these priorities absolutely correct, it should be easy to see why a rigorous and accurate risk assessment process is so critical to the overall success of any security system.

It is easy to establish confidence in an estimate that is based on tangible things, such as an engineering problem. However, that confidence will diminish quickly if the forecast is based on an asset as complex and challenging to visualize as "information." As a consequence, cybersecurity risk assessments are always built around tangible evidence. That evidence is usually obtained by conducting interviews and documenting observations of both organizational and human behavior, as well as auditing system logs and examining any other relevant technical or managerial records.

Because the sources of data about risk are diverse, the collection process must be systematic and well-coordinated. As a consequence, every risk assessment should incorporate a commonly accepted and repeatable methodology that produces concrete evidence that can be independently verified. The gathering, compilation, analysis, and verification of all data related to risk can be a time-consuming and resource-intensive process. To ensure the effectiveness and accuracy of any particular risk assessment, the practical scope of the inquiry must be precisely defined, focusing only on a specific real-world problem that the organization plans to mitigate.

Operationally, it is perfectly acceptable to approach risk assessment in a compartmentalized fashion, as long as the organization understands that the results of any particular risk assessment characterize only the problem it is focused on. In essence, the need to paint a detailed and accurate picture of all conceivable threats almost always implies a series of targeted, highly integrated risk assessments that occur over a defined period, rather than a single, monolithic effort to capture risks for the organization as a whole.

Therefore, risk assessments typically target the various standard areas of threat – electronic, human, and physical. The insights gained from each focused assessment are then aggregated into a single, inclusive understanding of the entire threat environment. This then serves as the basis for determining how each threat will be addressed.

Risk assessments are meant to identify specific vulnerabilities and the threats that could exploit them. That explicit understanding is referred to as a threat picture. However, because threats are constantly appearing, that picture has to be continuously updated. As a consequence, risk assessment is always an ongoing process. That process must maintain continuous knowledge of three critical factors:

1. The existence and inter-relationships among all of the organization's information assets
2. The specific threats to each asset
3. The precise business, financial, and technological issues associated with each threat

These factors are separate considerations, in the sense that conditions for any one of them can change independently. However, they are also highly interdependent in the sense that changes to one of these factors will most likely alter the circumstances of the other two. The risk assessment process itself has two general components. The first is risk classification. The second is risk response.

Risk classification involves two practical procedures, risk identification and risk estimation. Because these activities both entail assessment of risks that are as abstract as the information itself, they tend to be more qualitative than quantitative. Nevertheless, these processes should both produce plausible evidence to support decision-making about the particular circumstance.

Risk identification

Risk identification is typically performed first and can occur without a subsequent risk estimation activity. Risk identification involves determining which events, among all the potential events that could happen, are most likely to do the most significant harm. Then, the organization describes and documents the precise characteristics of each event.

This is a simple classification activity that requires the ability to identify and evaluate the information assets that might be impacted, understand and communicate the actual form of the threat to the appropriate decision-makers, as well as determine all the potential adverse effects that would occur should the threat materialize. Each consequence should be characterized in terms of the real-world impacts and harms of the occurrence.

Risk identification is a simple range-finding activity. It is the most common form of risk classification. As a consequence, a gap analysis is an ideal method for identifying risks. As we mentioned earlier, a particular threat may not have a significant impact within a given circumstance or situation. Therefore, each deviation from what is considered ideal practice must be evaluated to distinguish those variations that could create dangerous vulnerabilities.

Risk identification then documents the characteristics of every one of the identified vulnerabilities. This includes itemizing a list of all of the threats that could exploit it. In practice, risk identifications ought to unambiguously differentiate and describe the precise area of threat, as well as identify the virtual assets that would be impacted.

Accurate risk identifications typically require exhaustive detective work. This may include extensive interviews with participants, detailed analysis of technical processes, and, in some cases, strategic business process analysis. Moreover, the same careful investigative process needs to be followed to identify and then track all known vulnerabilities. That is because of the potential for a latent threat to become active.

This is an essential footnote because latent threats might not have immediate consequences. Since the conditions that would make them harmful are not present yet. Therefore, latent threats are often disregarded in the real-world process of developing the security strategy. That is understandable, since logically, the organization's scarce resources must be concentrated on the threats that are known to cause significant harm.

Nevertheless, a latent threat can become an active one if one of the conditions changes. Therefore, all latent threats that could potentially cause harm should be identified and tracked. For example, a problem like insider theft might not be an immediate possibility if the organization is small and every employee is long-term and known to be trustworthy.

However, if the organization hires a large number of subcontractors for a new project, the potential for insider theft becomes significantly higher.

Thus, explicit countermeasures would be immediately required. Therefore, it is crucial that the conditions and circumstances that could transform a latent threat into an active one be identified and clearly outlined during the risk identification phase, and that all recommended mitigations be highlighted.

Risk estimation

The risk estimation process is a lot more quantitative and systematic than risk identification. It involves the actual evaluation of the circumstances of the potential threat. Thus, risk estimations measure and quantitatively describe each potential risk, unlike risk identification, which is a simple classification activity; risk estimation is a data-driven process. As such, risk estimation is the mechanism that provides the substantive data that will serve as the basis for the risk analysis. Hence, information from the risk estimation must be reported in as timely a fashion as possible.

Risk estimation determines the probability and impact of all identified threats. It provides the data for the analysis and decision-making about the form of the response. That is, any number of countermeasures might be appropriate to any given vulnerability. However, in the operational world, it is always necessary to deploy the fewest measures essential to contain the threat. That decision is guided by the information that is developed through the risk estimation process.

Quantitative factors that might be included in the risk estimation include such things as: *assets affected*, the *potential duration of the threat*, and the *severity of adverse impact*. Severity is typically expressed in standard quantitative terms, such as money or time lost.

Because likelihood is essential, risk estimations must also state both the probability of occurrence and any known cause-and-effect linkages. This is the part of the process that directly links the risk assessment to the organization's management control system. Thus, it must be based on quantitative data. For example, a threat might be objectively described as:

- Affecting all of the items in the information baseline.
- For the duration of the time that the system is operated.
- Involving the loss of integrity of those items.
- That estimation might be based on the fact that the system can be penetrated.
- And that the probability of that event occurring is in the range of 99%.

The decisions that risk assessment data have political and resource implications. That is because a detailed report would also provide an index of the degree to which management should respond and the substantive controls that would need to be developed.

There are four typical areas where the risk assessment process should be part of standard operating procedure. These are:

1. Operational threat assessments
2. Operational threat management
3. Long-term assurance of control capability
4. Audit

In order to maintain an understanding of potential threats, vulnerabilities, and weaknesses, the organization must define the best explicit practice procedures for the ongoing assessment of operational security risks. To ensure adequate identification and containment of those risks, the organization should:

- Establish a standard operational risk assessment procedure
- Install operational risk assessment as a fundamental element of strategic planning
- Perform operational risk assessments on an ongoing basis
- Sustain a systematic operational risk assessment process

To ensure adequate risk analysis has been undertaken, the organization should:

- Perform operational risk assessments as a fundamental element of basic management practice
- Ensure that the results of all risk assessments are documented in a formal risk analysis report
- Ensure that the organization employs a formal procedure to ensure that the risk analysis report is distributed to the appropriate decision makers

To underwrite proper risk analysis, the organization should:

- Ensure that all current operations, as well as prospective projects, are evaluated using a standard risk assessment procedure
- Ensure that the results of all operational risk assessments are reported to the appropriate decision-makers for corrective action

The aim is to identify any potential threats, vulnerabilities, and weaknesses associated with the work, thereby ensuring effective operational risk management.

Operational risk management

The organization must then undertake a range of formal, best practice-based risk management activities. These activities should be deployed and managed based on the type of operation being performed. The organization should ask and answer the following nine questions to assess whether this has been appropriately defined and implemented. Has the process:

1. Explicitly identified and classified all known risks as to the potential threat, vulnerability, and weakness that they represent.
2. Identified and quantitatively measured the impacts?
3. Developed a best practice-based risk assessment and control plan for each protection object?
4. Employed a standard methodology to determine if known risks are effectively ameliorated?
5. Formulated an explicit set of safeguards that are referenced to each identified risk?
6. Designated specific funding and resources to carry out systematic risk assessment?
7. Demonstrated that it has established an appropriate set of internal controls based on the results of the risk analysis?
8. Performed periodic scheduled reviews and tests to ensure the timely response and proper operation of internal controls.
9. Regularly audited and reported on the adequacy and distribution of internal controls.

In addition, to formally establish the risk management process in everyday organizational management, the organization should:

- Employ a standard risk assessment approach across its collective areas of operation.
- Adopt a risk acceptance policy that will ensure that the lowest level of acceptable risk will be determined for any situation.
- Conduct risk assessments and analyses before undertaking prospective business ventures.

CREATING THE SUBSTANTIVE RESPONSE TO RISK

If your enemy is secure at all points, be prepared for him.

—Sun Tzu

As we have mentioned, security solutions are multifaceted and multilayered, and all components must be present to establish a comprehensive and coherent response. The approach must be coherent because experience has shown that, if a flaw is found, it will be exploited. Therefore, all policies, procedures, and physical safeguards must be implemented and operated to ensure the security of the information asset. These are referred to as security countermeasures or controls in the cybersecurity industry. To provide a trustworthy level of protection, they must always be established and seamlessly embedded in day-to-day operations.

Step one: Understanding the threat space

The critical first step is to develop a standard specification of the requirements for security throughout the entire organization. This top-to-bottom understanding is difficult to maintain. It requires a continuous and disciplined effort to ensure it. That is because the complexity of the business process is the single point of failure in forming a protection system.

Concrete cyber assurance is an intangible condition that you create and maintain, not a concrete state. Moreover, reaching an agreement on the correct approach to ensuring it involves numerous conflicting points of view. Therefore, it is necessary to develop a common understanding through a formal process, which will let all participants examine and discuss the assurance situation. The outcome of this discussion is a holistic design.

Step two: Policy-based holistic design

Designs are important because they communicate the organization's understanding of how it will implement the holistic process. Holistic design should be built around and embody an unambiguous statement of the basic business policies and procedures. The design must help managers understand how to implement the operational relationships necessary to translate policies into day-to-day practices. Undertaking this process will also enhance acceptance of the end product among all stakeholders and participants.

An organization-wide awareness of security policies also establishes an adequate level of consistent performance required to support proper and consistent practice. At a minimum, that design process involves the following three steps:

1. Identification and evaluation of the sensitivity of organizational systems and data
2. Creation of plans to ensure security and control of every identified protection target
3. Development and implementation of training programs to enable and enforce the understanding and the use of proper security practices

Every organization has strategic aims. Organizational policies for holistic assurance should naturally flow from these business imperatives. Since the competitive position of an organization relies on its ability to control its data and information assets, the plan and the planning process must achieve beneficial business ends. The plan ensures that the necessary players and resources are in place to implement the policy effectively. It also brings these things into a single, coherent, continuously evolving response.

Nevertheless, every organization is unique and implements security measures differently. The actual process and its outcome will differ. However, all holistic security solutions share the same generic goal: to ensure that the virtual assets of the organization are fully and reliably protected.

The success or failure of the security effort can be judged based on the fulfillment of the following ten requirements for a properly functioning holistic solution. Does the system ensure that each identified and prioritized protection is:

1. Correct.
2. Confidential.
3. Available.
4. That all relevant security controls are represented in the solution.
5. That the responsibility for security is explicitly assigned.
6. That accountability and enforcement of those responsibilities is understood.
7. That regular and systematic assessments of security performance are done.
8. That security functions conform with and ensure applicable legal requirements.
9. That security cost is proportionate to impact and likelihood of known risk.
10. That the security function is ethically conducted.

In practice, organizations follow the same systematic methodology to address these requirements. The outcome of that methodology is a concrete, organization-wide protection scheme that balances the aims of the security solution with real-world conditions and constraints.

Step three: Implementation

At the most basic level of representation, the components of the plan are described as a set of substantive actions that meet the specified criteria. These actions must be traceable directly back to the business policies that defined them. The ongoing alignment of security best practices with the business policies they implement must ensure the security solution's real-world effectiveness in functional settings.

As we have mentioned many times, the strategic planning process is responsible for implementing the design. The correctness of the design is verified by evaluating whether a set of tangible, properly documented organizational behaviors, generally termed "controls," is in place. These controls are designed to regulate a specific aspect of the design. Taken as a whole, the complete set of controls represents the holistic security system.

The system must substantiate business policy by establishing tangible assurance of the protected objects sitting within the defined protection perimeter. A properly developed holistic solution ensures that a uniform structure of rationally interacting security controls has been implemented from top to bottom in the organization's everyday operations.

It is not difficult to build an adequate cyber defense if the boundaries of the problem are known. But as we have said, that is rarely the case with virtual assets, as they are abstract, and the threats to any given asset will continuously evolve as one bad actor after another comes up with a new way of attacking you. Moreover, the problem is made even more challenging because it is difficult to detect harm to an asset, since the asset is usually still there. For example, you can tell that the bank has been robbed because all of the money is missing. However, the equally vital bank records can be copied, in effect, stolen, without anyone being the wiser.

Hence, it is difficult to say with certainty that an assurance control is still safeguarding the virtual object it was set to protect. Therefore, the access control system is the essential mechanism for maintaining the assurance of the virtual asset base. That is because the complete set of tangible access controls is, in effect, the tangible representation of the security perimeter.

Consequently, if any of those controls are proven to be compromised or demonstrated not to ensure against unauthorized access, then it can be assumed that the protection objects within that security perimeter have all been compromised since access control is on the boundary, not within the actual secured space ... which, by the way, also argues that a proper solution must have multiple defense in depth perimeters.

Hence, defining the specific access control system is the critical next step in the process. As we have said, access control is defined and assured by the security perimeter. A security perimeter is the outer boundary of the particular instance of protected space. Defining a proper security perimeter is complicated by the feasibility factor, which refers to the likelihood that a task and purpose can be accomplished.

Feasibility is based on whether the solution fits within the available resources and capabilities of the organization. So, no matter how elegant the solution, it is useless if it is not feasible. For example, sophisticated biometric technologies can be used to ensure access control. Nonetheless, biometric solutions might not fit within the budget of the average college computer lab. Thus, a biometric solution for a minor application is questionable because it does not fit within the financial constraints. That would be the case even if the biometric control itself worked properly and fulfilled its purpose in every respect.

A circumstance that might change this would be if the college computer lab contained research data that was a highly sensitive element of national security. That change in conditions might justify the added cost and trouble of employing biometrics to protect it. However, if there were no apparent threats to the equipment or information, the price would probably not justify the means.

Hence, a central part of the design and implementation of a security perimeter is to assess and trade off the threats against the availability of financial and staff resources. Factors that might influence this thinking include considerations such as: what is the level of criticality for each of the information assets that may fall within the system's scope? And what is the degree of assurance required for each? In the worst case, a non-essential, low-risk resource might be left outside of the defensive perimeter.

A decision-maker uses this prioritization process to maximize resource utilization and optimize information assurance and security protection. As such, it is crucial to involve representatives from the organization, as well as relevant third parties, in the boundary definition process. This is particularly important when formulating a working security application, as real-world security boundaries are dynamic. Hence, the organization fine-tunes the deployment of security controls over time. In a holistic system, this must always be guided by the organization's business goals. Therefore, the planning process must incorporate a mechanism for obtaining ongoing feedback from stakeholders and operational units over time.

A formal feedback process is arguably the most critical element in formulating a practical security solution, as stakeholders are the ones in the trenches. Therefore, they are in the best position to identify a novel or potential operating threat and understand the harm that might ensue. Thus, they are in the best position to pass that information along to the centralized response function, which is a hallmark of the holistic process.

The individuals responsible for characterizing, e.g., analyzing, each reported threat will then assess and analyze the harm that might ensue from each reported incident and categorize the various options for response.

Operationally, the basis for the assessment is a comparison of a comprehensive set of standard best practice requirements against the current activities of the operation. The aim is to identify any divergence between what is recommended as proper and what is presently being done. The control must be modified when business circumstances change. Where no existing organizational activity meets the best practice requirements, the missing elements must be addressed through a new control procedure.

Once the risk exposures are identified, they are assessed to distinguish between active and latent threats, as a particular threat may not necessarily have a significant impact in a given situation. The control modification, or new control requirement, is carefully analyzed in relation to the business situation to determine its priority. If there are significant impacts, then the control is either modified or a new control is created. Other actions, such as risk acceptance or purchasing insurance, may be taken when the change is not justified by its business impact.

Step four: Asset valuation and tradeoff

The end product of this final phase is a concrete, real-world, holistic security strategy. The input that drives the development of that strategy is drawn from the outcomes of the prior three stages. The boundary-setting element in Phase Two is critical to the process since there is a direct relationship between the resources required to establish a specified security level and the extent of the territory that must be secured. Operational factors that enter into the development of this strategy include ... What is the level of criticality of each particular information asset that falls into the asset baseline? What is the specific degree of resource commitment required to assure it?

As a result, the most essential aspect of this might lie in the simple business valuation of the assets themselves. That is the case because, in the real world, there are never enough resources to secure every element of the information asset baseline absolutely. And since the baseline is overwhelmingly composed of abstract entities, the value of that asset base is also abstract, meaning it is unknown.

Therefore, each organization needs to adopt a uniform valuing system that will realistically and accurately prioritize its information assets. Consequently, it is our assumption that the critical success factors are defined at the business level, rather than by the system engineering process. That is because, as we've said, the tail doesn't wag the dog. The primary objective of the organization is to fulfill its business purpose, not to conduct security activities. Hence, any form of operational asset valuation must be rooted in and reflect the organization's vision, strategies, and purposes.

There are numerous ways to approach asset valuation. These range from the highly quantitative approaches, such as Economic Value Added (EVA), down to subjective instincts like "knowing the territory." Whatever approach is adopted, the aim is for the organization to document with certainty which of its business items require security assurance, which don't, and in what order.

Additionally, documentation of a formal process will demonstrate that due diligence was exercised in making the determination. This is crucial in protecting the organization from liability claims resulting from negligence. The best part of a quantitative valuation approach is that the organization can increase its valuation effectiveness and thus sharpen its control over its asset base as data is collected and refined over time.

The tradeoff process, a fundamental element in ensuring the proper utilization of resources, actually creates the holistic security scheme. Tradeoffs are the underlying activities used to implement the actual security solution.

It is a political rather than rational activity, which might seem like an odd statement given the methodological nature of the process to this point. However, the decisions about what to protect and what to leave out are driven by the organizational stakeholders' perceptions of importance, which is a subjective, qualitative judgment.

This is not a qualitative activity, although with precisely targeted information, decision-makers can move ahead with some assurance that they are basing their strategies on the realities of the situation. That decision-making is based on real-world knowledge of the financial, equipment, and personnel resources available to implement the desired level of security, as well as the pressing business concerns and the relative value of the asset. However, the goal is to maintain a straightforward approach to the asset base, which enables the deployment particulars to be planned with precision.

That should be both tangibly documented in the form of policy and procedure and also made visible to the entire organization. To ensure a daily basis for trust among participants, the organization should maintain long-term oversight of the ability of the formally documented and deployed control set to maintain alignment with the business purpose.

As we mentioned earlier, in order to continuously ensure the effectiveness of its security controls, the organization must establish an independent function at the top, specifically tasked with ensuring the alignment of business purpose with the security controls in the asset baseline. This top-level function is also responsible for maintaining the alignment of the actions of contractors and third-party service providers with the organization's business objectives. In order to do this properly, the organization should:

- Create a permanent top-level executive function to evaluate the effectiveness and performance of the security solution as it aligns with the business purpose.
- Continuously evaluate the effectiveness and performance of contractors and third-party service providers.
- Maintain assurance of compliance of control actions with all relevant laws, regulatory requirements, and contractual commitments.
- Evaluate and document the performance of the holistic security solution sufficient to assure its capable performance.
- Define policies and procedures sufficient to ensure proactive involvement of the audit function in the assurance of due diligence over time.

What is this final stipulation about? The organization must establish and maintain an audit capability to provide a formal basis for ensuring trust among participants. The aim is to provide a disinterested third-party guarantee of due diligence in the performance of the holistic security process. To continuously assure the effectiveness of the audit function, the organization should:

- Establish and charter a formal internal audit process
- Perform all audits using a standard and systematic process
- Establish controls sufficient to assure the independence of the audit function from any undue influence
- Specify explicit procedures for the performance of all audit work

Then, in order to continuously assure the effectiveness of the audit function, the organization should:

- Establish formal lines of communication for the timely and effective reporting of all audit findings to the appropriate parties
- Establish standards and enforce procedures sufficient to ensure the continuing competence of the audit function
- Conduct each audit project based on a formal plan.
- Ensure that the appropriate management entity, or responsible party, has authorized all audit plans
- Ensure that the audit function is utilized to assess the performance and effectiveness of all short- and long-range plans
- Establish and document a formal procedure to assure that follow-up activities recommended by the audit process have been carried out
- Establish an audit logging function
- Establish a definite period for retaining audit evidence
- Establish a process to ensure audit evidence is complete and correct

CHAPTER SUMMARY

Security solutions are multifaceted and multilayered, and all components must be present to establish a comprehensive response. The approach must be coherent because experience has shown that, if a flaw is found, it will be exploited. Therefore, all policies, procedures, and physical safeguards must be in place to ensure the security of the information asset. These are called security countermeasures. They must be established and seamlessly integrated into day-to-day operations to provide a trustworthy level of protection.

The critical first step is to develop a common understanding of the security requirements within the entire organization. This top-to-bottom understanding is difficult to maintain because it requires a continuous and strategically planned effort to ensure it. Additionally, the single point of failure in the formation of a security system is the complexity of the business process itself. Cybersecurity is an intangible condition, not a concrete objective. Thus, agreeing on the correct approach to ensuring it involves numerous conflicting points of view.

So, it is necessary to develop a standard agreement through a formal process. That process must allow all participants to examine and discuss the assurance situation. The outcome of this discussion is a design. Designs are important because they communicate the organization's understanding of how it will implement cybersecurity.

The design process should clearly articulate the fundamental policies and procedures. It should also enhance their acceptance among all participants. The design ensures that managers understand how to implement the operational relationships necessary to translate policies into day-to-day practices. An organization-wide awareness of security policies establishes an adequate level of understanding required to support proper and consistent practice. At a minimum, that design process involves the following activities:

- Identification and evaluation of the sensitivity of organizational systems and data
- Creation of plans to ensure security and control of every identified system
- Development and implementation of training programs to enable and enforce the understanding and the use of proper security measures

The competitive position of an organization relies on its ability to control its data and information assets. The plan and the planning process achieve those ends. The plan ensures that the necessary players and resources are in place to implement the policy effectively. The plan consolidates these elements into a single, coherent, and continuously evolving response. Every organization has strategic aims. Organizational policies for cybersecurity should naturally flow from these strategic imperatives. Because every organization is unique and implements security differently. The actual process will differ; however, all holistic security solutions address the practical requirements. That is, all information assets must be assured

- Correct.
- Confidential.
- Available.
- All relevant security needs must be represented in the solution.
- The responsibility for security must be explicitly assigned and understood.
- A system of accountability and enforcement must exist.
- Regular and systematic assessments must be performed.
- All participants must understand the importance of security.
- Continuity of operation must be ensured.
- Security functions must conform to legal requirements.
- Expense must be kept proportionate to the impact and likelihood of risk.
- The organization must ensure that information is used ethically.

In practice, organizations should follow the same systematic process to address these requirements. The outcome of the process is a concrete, organization-wide protection scheme that balances the aims of policy with real-world conditions and constraints.

The atomic-level components of the plan comprise a set of substantive actions that ensure the requisite level of security. They should be able to be traced directly back to the policies that defined them. The ongoing alignment of procedures to policies evolves the model and ensures its effectiveness in functional settings.

Therefore, the strategic planning process must establish a reliable security management scheme that can be verified. The tangible realization of that is a set of organizational behaviors, called controls, that are in place. Controls are designed to regulate a specific aspect of the organization's operations. Where they apply to security assurance, that control set is referred to as a holistic cybersecurity system. It substantiates policy by establishing tangible control over the information asset. A properly developed holistic security system ensures that a uniform control structure exists, extending from top to bottom within the organization.

Hence, defining the boundaries of the holistic security system is the critical first step in the process. This activity is based on the concept of security perimeters. A security perimeter is the outer boundary of the space that is to be secured. Defining a proper security perimeter is complicated by the feasibility factor. Feasibility is the likelihood that a task or purpose can be accomplished. It is based on whether the solution fits within the available resources and capabilities of the organization.

Thus, a central part of the deployment is to assess and trade off the threats against the availability of financial and staff resources. Factors that enter into this thinking include such considerations as: What is the level of criticality for each of the information assets that may fall within the system's scope? What is the degree of assurance required for each?

In the worst case, a non-essential, low-risk resource might be left outside of the defensive perimeter. Nevertheless, if that decision is based on precise knowledge of the capabilities of an established perimeter, this is informed risk. A decision-maker uses this prioritization process to maximize resource utilization and optimize cybersecurity and security protection. As such, it is crucial to involve representatives from the organization, as well as relevant third parties, in the boundary definition process.

This is particularly important when formulating a working security application, as real-world security boundaries are dynamic. With information assets, the system's boundaries are subject to ongoing refinement as threats and resources evolve. Over time, the organization fine-tunes the deployment of security controls. The proper modifications to the security controls can be accomplished based on feedback from the operational units over time. In that respect, the risk assessment activity is arguably the most essential element in formulating a proper security response, as it identifies potential threats, assesses the harm that might ensue from each, and analyzes and categorizes options for response.

Operationally, this process involves comparing the current operation's form to the comprehensive set of ideal best practice requirements specified in the framework model. This enables the organization to identify gaps in its security coverage. These gaps represent the vulnerabilities and weaknesses that new procedures must address.

Since a particular threat may not have a significant impact in a given situation, once the risk exposures are identified, they are assessed to distinguish those that would create specific and undesirable vulnerabilities. Next, these vulnerabilities are carefully analyzed in relation to the particular organizational situation to identify the specific weaknesses that the security system needs to target directly.

These weaknesses are prioritized so that those with the most critical impacts are addressed first. The product of this phase is a concrete security strategy whose input is derived from the outcomes of the risk analytic phase of the process. The perimeter setting element is vital to this consideration, as there is a direct relationship between the resources required to establish a specified security level and the extent of the territory that must be secured.

Operational factors that enter into the development of this strategy include ... What is the level of criticality of each particular information asset that falls into the asset baseline? What is the specific degree of resource commitment required to assure it? Thus, the deciding factor in shaping the security scheme is the simple valuation of the assets themselves.

That is the case because in the real world, there are never enough resources to secure every element of the information asset baseline absolutely. And since the baseline is overwhelmingly composed of abstract entities, the value of that asset base is also abstract, meaning it is unknown. Therefore, each organization needs to adopt a uniform methodology to systematically value and prioritize its information assets so that the most critical assets are targeted first.

Therefore, the critical success factors for a holistic solution are defined at the business level. Hence, any form of operational asset valuation must be rooted in and reflect the vision, strategies, and purposes of that part of the organization. The benefit of that approach is that the organization will know with certainty which item to secure and in what order. Additionally, following this process will document that due diligence was conducted in making that determination. The best part of this approach is that as data is collected and refined over time, the organization can increase its valuation effectiveness, thereby sharpening its control over its asset base.

The actual tradeoff process is a fundamental element of good strategic planning. Thus, it is a strategic, not a scientific, activity. However, with precisely targeted information, decision-makers can move ahead with some assurance that they are basing their strategies on the realities of the situation. The assumption is that the actual deployment of the security function will meet the requirements of the organization's security charter.

That decision-making is based on knowledge of the financial, equipment, and personnel resources available to implement the desired level of security, the pressing business concerns, and the relative value of the asset. The decisions produced by this process can then be used to implement the actual security solution. However, the point of this exercise is to have a straightforward fix on the asset base so that the particulars of the deployment can be planned with precision. This should be both tangibly documented in the form of policy and procedure and also made visible to the entire organization.

Chapter 5

Implementing the solution

Figure 5.1 Pencil drawing of a hand gently pressing a small seed into the soil, shown in close-up. In the softly shaded background, a lone tree stands at a distance, symbolizing patience, growth, and the quiet beginnings of future strength.

DOI: 10.1201/9781003603412-5

ACHIEVING HOLISTIC ASSURANCE

> *Plan for what is difficult while it is easy, do what is great while it is small.*
>
> **—Sun Tzu**

This chapter is devoted to the practical concerns associated with implementing an enterprise-wide, holistic solution. We aim to demonstrate how to establish operational assurance of the organizational threatspace ... as it evolves. As we said in the last chapter, implementation is the second formal stage in the process of developing a real-world, holistic control solution. It is, in effect, the practical, boots-on-the-ground phase that turns an organization's security design into a workable, everyday architecture of controls.

It goes without saying that the business must safeguard against all feasible threats to its valuable virtual assets. Thus, as business organizations grow and diversify ... more powerful security control solutions are required. In day-to-day application, this means that companies must consistently and systematically ensure that every critical business resource is adequately protected.

Achieving a verifiably proper state of assurance is a particularly challenging problem, given the layers of complexity present in any major organization. For instance, the threat environment of a multinational corporation contains an infinite number of vendors and operates across multicultural settings. And yet, the protection of all of that business's virtual assets must be fully ensured for the products of that business operation to be fully trusted.

As we have mentioned several times in this text, the coordination and control of complex work is based on a standard and coherent conceptual framework, or architecture, which enables all stakeholders in the organization to benchmark their security solution against best practices. The practical point of reference in this instance is the holistic security governance framework that was designed and discussed in the last chapter.

As such, this chapter will present and discuss the practical principles and methods that must be employed to develop a functioning, real-world, holistic governance architecture that will avoid the dreaded, gap-laden "piecemeal solution," which we discussed in Chapter 1. The goal of this process is to ensure a standard, fully documented, holistic security solution that incorporates all relevant security best practices. These practices are then implemented through a tangible and comprehensive infrastructure of well-defined management actions, specifically designed to optimize the effectiveness of the security solution.

But first, we need to spend some time explaining what that enterprise-wide holistic architecture ought to look like and how it will function in an applied setting. Holistic architecture is composed of a rational set of commonly understood and accepted components arranged within a logical array of inter-organizational relationships. These are then used to ensure and control the organization's information asset base. The effectiveness of that approach then depends on the practical implementation of a comprehensive organization-wide assurance system and culture, rather than the development of ad-hoc security solutions for each identified threat.

Essentially, the business defines and documents a coherent framework of actions that encompasses all the requisite management roles, organizational behaviors, and strategic policies necessary to ensure a fully secure organization. This solution is made tangible and practically overseen by a regularly executed and rational assessment process that allows the organization to maintain an effective set of security controls.

Assessment is a primary player in the long-term implementation and operation of any security architecture. The assessment process typically involves comparing current organizational practices against a commonly accepted, best-practice-based reference model or standard, such as ISO 27000. Depending on the outcome of the assessment, a prolonged period of trade-offs and refinement of the control architecture may be required before an eventual resolution can be reached.

Nevertheless, the final documented solution must always address the vulnerabilities and threats that were identified during the design process. Thus, accordingly, the end product will always describe a concrete and coherent set of recommendations that meet all of the necessary security requirements for that particular setting. The specific security control requirements are elicited once the problem space has been sufficiently understood. These might amount to nothing more than a simple natural language statement of what has to be done, or they could be expressed using any one of several formal description methodologies. The documentation outcome is most typically a set of detailed specifications of the real-world form of the security design architecture. As we have stated, architecture must directly address every issue identified in the risk assessment and satisfy all known constraints. All design architectures exhibit these common characteristics:

- They are complete in the sense that they encompass the entire solution.
- They are correct in that all elements of the solution that logically should be present are.
- They are understandable in how they communicate the form of the solution.
- And all of the elements in the architecture are traceable to a particular business purpose.

The formally documented design architecture also establishes the quantitative basis for the continuous assessment function. Assessment is the tool that the organization utilizes to evaluate and judge the success of the real-world system itself. Hence, the documentation must ensure that stakeholders can trace the discrete technical and behavioral controls that represent the solution to their specific business purpose. That means that, from a resource management standpoint, all of the necessary operational business issues are characterized and resolved in the architectural representation.

Hence, it is the documentation that actively and intentionally aligns the form of the security solution with the organization's explicit business needs. This outcome might be just as appropriately termed "realization" or "implementation" of the security design, because its product is the actual, substantive set of controls that ensures the processing and storage of organizational business assets embody the proper set of best practices.

Consequently, assessment is the fundamental element of practical organizational control. And accordingly, a formal and consistently applied practical measurement process is always required to confirm that appropriate controls are in place and functioning correctly. This is accomplished by conducting regular reviews of operational elements at pre-planned and mutually agreed-upon intervals. The organization can engineer or at least think through the operation of its security solution by evaluating performance at formally designated points in the process.

Measurement programs are typically founded on a range of standardized metrics. When correctly set up and maintained, the measurement program will monitor the security function and bring any deviations to management's attention. However, there are no universally recognized standard metrics for doing this. Instead, individual organizations choose the measures that they feel best fit their particular situation.

The rule for this is straightforward: the evaluation activities must be uniformly and consistently applied. In particular, since security operations are focused on preventing breaches, there is a need for a uniform definition of what constitutes a security violation. The result of executing this process is a comprehensive, coherent, and fully managed security architecture that is precisely aligned with the business purpose requirements of the circumstances. The mechanism for conceptualizing and then operating an effective measurement program will be discussed in much greater depth in the next chapter of this book (Chapter 6).

Formulating a best practice solution

The recommendations that are embodied in a best practice standard serve as the basis for characterizing and implementing a wide range of real-world security functions. In concept, the recommendations of a best practice standard are not standalone elements. They are meant to substantiate an integrated set of requirements that the security function must satisfy. These best practices, when taken together, constitute the industry's understanding of cybersecurity.

Accordingly, the recommendations of a commonly accepted standard of best practice comprise a complete and rational solution, which, when tailored adequately within a given situation, will produce a fully secure operational solution. In essence, best practice standards such as ISO 27000 are formal mechanisms that enable an organization to specify its particular rules for control, as well as the method for ensuring the ongoing status of those controls.

Nine commonly recognized factors are considered indicative of a properly organized and implemented security solution. These are:

1. The existence of a formally documented security policy
2. Implementation model that fits with organizational culture
3. Visible support and commitment from management
4. Organization-wide understanding of security requirements
5. Formal risk assessment and risk management procedures
6. Effective marketing of security to all managers and employees
7. Appropriate training and education
8. A comprehensive system of measurement
9. The provision for feedback and suggestions for improvement

These factors are all realized in a standardized method of operation that falls under the general rubric of the "security of operations" function, which we will discuss in the next section.

SECURITY OF OPERATIONS: ENSURING REAL-WORLD ASSURANCE

Even the finest sword plunged into salt water will eventually rust.

—Sun Tzu

The security of operations function is orthogonal to everything we have discussed so far, in that its primary role is the continuous, every day assurance of the integrity and appropriate performance of the control factors that we just listed. In essence, security of operations ensures that all specified security criteria are satisfied and that the business function operates as intended in the day-to-day performance of its activities. To ensure proper performance, the security of operations function monitors and evaluates the day-to-day operation of all controls within the assurance architecture. It achieves this by verifying that all behavioral and technical countermeasures are in place and operating correctly.

Ultimately, when threats are detected, security of operations is also responsible for coordinating the corrective action response. Hence, the organization would not be able to guarantee the long-term viability of its information asset base without ensuring the security of its operations. The security of operations function entails such critical actions as:

- Ensuring that current operating controls are correctly aligned with the business purpose as specified in the strategic plan.
- Monitoring the everyday performance of the security architecture to confirm that controls are functioning correctly and continue to align with the business purpose.
- Performing standard operational assurance actions to validate the correctness, proper functioning, and alignment of all of the controls in the security solution.

As the name implies, security of operations is less involved with strategy and development, which were the topics discussed in the prior chapters, than it is with ensuring the reliable day-to-day execution of the security solution. The security operations function accomplishes this task by ensuring that security best practices always align with business stakeholder requirements.

Every business has a given set of security objectives. Logically, those objectives must be satisfied for the organization to consider itself secure. Nevertheless, the overall operating environment is constantly changing, and therefore, to ensure proper alignment, the objectives must also change. Factors that can affect change include:

- The people who use the system, or their motivations.
- Any system that is interconnected with the organization's systems.
- The type, or sensitivity of data flowing to, through, or from the organization's system.
- The way the organization does business, or the type of business that is conducted.
- The rigor, application, or extent of the security objectives.

Obviously, suppose a particular practice is demonstrated to be no longer effective or is shown to be out of alignment with the business purpose. In that case, the organization must undertake an evaluation process to determine and specify corrective action. Typical corrective action changes might include

- Simple administrative actions like reclassification of the asset to a different sensitivity level.
- Altering the practice to conform to the new purpose.
- Eliminating or replacing the practice entirely.

Factors that may need to be evaluated before a decision is made include common concerns such as feasibility and resource availability, as well as the existence of practical alternatives. In every case, however, the only acceptable outcome is that the new solution must align with best security practices and the business purpose.

Security of operations and business alignment

The role of security of operations is to maintain accurate alignment between the organization's business goals and its security practices. Security of operations is responsible for monitoring the execution of each business process and the associated set of controls that have been implemented to ensure security. The aim is to underwrite continuous alignment between business purpose and the security solution.

The real-world monitoring activities focus on detecting meaningful deviations from either business purpose or proper practice. Typically, this is accomplished by identifying and recording problems as they occur, analyzing each situation to determine how it can be mitigated, and taking the appropriate corrective, adaptive, perfective, or preventive action to ensure proper realignment with the business purpose and the nature of the threat.

Furthermore, because the security environment and the organization itself are constantly evolving, confidence in the integrity of the security response must be continuously renewed. As a result, security of operations must also periodically verify and certify the effectiveness of the currently instituted security solution. Hence, the security of operations function routinely reviews, inspects, tests, and audits the performance of the elements and interrelationships that comprise the security architecture. Where problems are encountered, the security of operations is responsible for initiating and coordinating the resolution of these problems.

Therefore, in essence, the direct accountability for response makes the intrusion detection function an applied subset of the overall security of operations purpose ... which is to ensure that every conceivable threat is identified and appropriately responded to.

Managing and maintaining an effective security of operations function

The overall holistic architectural framework must be planned, designed, administered, and maintained to ensure a secure organization. As we said in Chapter 4, planning and design are the first steps in implementing a comprehensive, holistic security infrastructure. The administration and maintenance of that infrastructure is the province of the security of operations function. Thus, the purpose of the security of the operations management function is to ensure that leadership vision and expertise are consistently applied throughout the ongoing operational assurance process.

As we mentioned earlier, an infrastructure is required to ensure a proper and timely response to all potentially significant threats. The role of the security of operations management function is to oversee and maintain appropriate alignment of that architecture. The overall purpose is to maintain correct alignment between the business purpose and the tangible security response. This involves the development and continuous maintenance of the most appropriate and capable countermeasures, along with their placement in a rational set of interacting mitigations.

Holistic assurance is founded on a comprehensive, unitary organization-wide, policy-based architecture of operational controls and countermeasures. The role of security of operations is to maintain the relevance and effectiveness of those controls. The primary aim of the overall process is to ensure the most effective response to current and emerging threats in the evolving threat environment. It is a given that this activity all takes place within the context of a dynamically changing situation.

In its most basic terms, effectiveness can be characterized as the assurance of timeliness in the threat response, as well as detection and reaction to external or internal intrusions or security violations. That includes ensuring that both proactive and reactive problem responses are supported by continuous and ongoing threat sensing, analysis, and response operations. The sensing function encompasses all monitoring, testing, and assessment activities necessary to accomplish that purpose. Sensing's purpose is to identify all meaningful intrusions (e.g., a break-in), violations (e.g., an inappropriate access), or vulnerabilities (an identified weakness that a threat can exploit).

The analysis function then facilitates an understanding of the risk involved. This is a simple risk analysis in the operational space. It assesses the frequency of occurrence and impact and considers and evaluates all risk avoidance, risk mitigation, and risk transfer options. The organization then selects and authorizes the remediation option. Once that is done, the organization monitors and ensures that any required changes are implemented and that the correct reintegration of new security policies, procedures, or countermeasures into the operation is achieved. This is always under the oversight and authorization of the relevant decision-maker. This will be detailed at much greater length in the next chapter.

The actual remediation actions fall into three categories: preventive, reactive, and *emergency* action. Preventive action involves identifying and immediately removing vulnerabilities, as well as correcting errors, before they can be exploited. Adaptive action adjusts the security response to new or changed conditions. Hence, preventive action involves identifying and detecting latent vulnerabilities (e.g., the system is found to be vulnerable to a particular class of intrusion).

With *proactive* assurance, decision makers have time to consider and authorize either a preventive, perfective, or adaptive response. Perfective action also involves improving the performance, dependability, and maintainability of the existing solution.

Reactive action is the second general category of response. Unlike preventive assurance, decision-makers rarely have the time to conduct extensive analysis with reactive assurance. But they DO have the option of authorizing the corrective or emergency response based on a previously defined response strategy. Hence, much of reactive assurance is supported by proactive contingency plans. The security principle is that the general response should be thoroughly thought through in advance.

Finally, *emergency* action is a corrective action that is carried out on a 'do-it-now' (DIN) basis. Hence, emergency action refers to an unscheduled corrective response (e.g., an intrusion or violation has occurred, requiring an immediate response). Because emergency actions are rarely planned or systematic and have the potential for extensive damage, they are authorized only where preliminary analysis indicates a high probability of harm if the threat is not addressed immediately.

The role of continuity planning in everyday assurance

The duty of the operational response process is to be always ready to resolve problems as they arise. The organization's continuity planning process establishes the overall approach to ensuring operational continuity. However, it is the responsibility of the security operations function to ensure that all pre-planned responses remain appropriate and that the organization can identify, report, and respond to incidents in a timely and effective manner using those responses.

Therefore, a crucial aspect of operational security is to ensure that the organization always has an effective operational response available. That operational response is established and maintained through a plan that integrates the principles of sensing, analyzing, and responding into substantive procedures that meet the organization's security needs.

These principles apply regardless of whether the event was foreseen or unforeseen. The only difference is that, if the event was anticipated, the response is determined in advance. For example, there is always a set of operational contingencies in place to respond appropriately to a fire, and most organizations conduct regular drills to ensure that the response is understood and reliably executed. The presence of that predefined response ensures that an optimal solution is provided in as timely a manner as possible.

However, many events are unforeseen and can often be the most hazardous. If the incident is unpredictable, the security of operations process aims to ensure a coordinated and appropriate response. The difference is that, due to the incident being unforeseen, there is a much greater emphasis on timely analysis, leading to a rapid and intelligent response. That timeliness is underwritten by effective incident reporting; in essence, incident reporting triggers the operational response process.

Incident reporting ensures that every significant event that could compromise the organization's information is identified and reported. These incidents are not limited to events that make the six o'clock news, such as the occasional Internet-wide denial-of-service attack. They include everything from significant, time-sensitive attacks all the way down to routine reports of potential vulnerabilities identified by the staff.

Therefore, a successful reporting function is founded on a range of sensing measures. These measures are placed around the organization, both on the perimeter and embedded within operational practice. The goal is to identify security violations, attempts to exploit security vulnerabilities, or inadvertent breakdowns in security functioning as quickly as possible. Sensing measures can be as varied as:

- Automated intrusion detection (IDS)/intrusion prevention (IPS) systems.
- Software-driven scans, such as malware and virus checkers.
- Tips or direct reports from guards, law enforcement officials, or other outside sources.

Proper security practice dictates that incident reports go to a single central coordinator for confirmation, analysis, and subsequent action. Central coordination is necessary because attacks and compromises rarely present themselves in a single, neat package. Instead, a series of suspicious happenings begins to form the signature of an impending attack. As a result, there has to be a single coordinating entity to collect and analyze the information.

Once an incident can be confirmed, its impacts must be at least minimally understood to initiate the proper response. The role of the staff at the central coordinating agency is to connect the dots. Potential incidents include pre-attack probes, unauthorized access attempts, denial-of-service attacks, or infrastructure vulnerabilities identified by the staff. Another possible source could be a notification from an outside entity, such as Microsoft or the Computer Emergency Response Team Coordination Center (CERT/CC). Reports of potential incidents are typically generic and often result from routine data gathering and analysis.

The various system-based monitoring devices typically generate incident reports. One of the most common methods is called operational event logging. Automated event logging is routinely executed as a subsystem within the operating system. It is necessary for the security of operations because it monitors events that occur within the system itself.

Instituting the process: The holistic plan

Security of operations is embodied through a standard organizational planning process. The plan operationalizes and coordinates most of the elements of the security of operations process, guiding the allocation of resources for its overall conduct. Therefore, the first step in establishing a security of operations function is to develop a comprehensive, cross-functional, and cross-organizational plan. The purpose of that plan is to ensure that the security of operations function is fully and correctly deployed and embedded in the day-to-day operational fabric of the organization. The outcome of this planning process is a practical long-term specification of the methodology for performing the security of operations function.

That methodology will encompass all organizationally approved processes and practices that the business intends to adopt and follow to maintain the ongoing effectiveness of the security operation function. Since operational assessment is a critical aspect of maintaining the practical security of operational functionality, the specific procedure and metrics that will be utilized to track performance must also be specified.

A formally sanctioned security operations plan is a crucial baseline document. It serves as a practical point of reference in the evolution and day-to-day management of the security of operations function. The plan delineates the operational requirements necessary to ensure a robust and persistent state of holistic assurance. It explicitly specifies the standard practices and the schedule, or timetable, that will be followed.

Ensuring effective understanding: Operational information exchange

The definition and design of that information exchange process are an integral part of the operational planning process and must be revised and updated as the security situation changes. To enforce proper control, all of the organization's significant stakeholders must be tied together through coordinated information. The definition and design of that information exchange process are an integral part of the operational planning process, and they must be revised and updated as the security situation changes.

Every significant organizational process has to be monitored and controlled. To ensure this, the relevant information must be collected and distributed to the appropriate decision-makers. That distribution list should include top and mid-level managers responsible for overseeing the process, as well as the technical participants involved in that process. Communication is a critical part of the tracking function. It is also essential in ensuring that the process is properly controlled. To enforce proper control, all of the organization's significant stakeholders must be tied together through coordinated information.

Like the strategic plan, the operational security plan should be easily understood by all participants. It should leave all staff members knowing precisely what activities are required and the timing for performing them. The operational plan then organizes and focuses the deployment of those activities in a way that allows them to function most effectively. In essence, it enables decision-makers to align their safeguards with available resources.

The operational plan is a crucial source of support for the organizational budgeting process, as it embodies and makes explicit the organization's security objectives. These objectives serve as the foundation for deploying the overall security function and provide an excellent means to gauge ongoing performance.

More importantly, the operational plan organizes the technical and procedural response in a way that ensures the proper countermeasures are in place to address the relevant security requirements. Finally, because the plan details the criteria for performance, it also serves as an effective mechanism for assessing whether the organization's contractual and regulatory obligations are being met.

Timing-wise, operational planning is done on an annual basis. However, it can be done as often as required if the situation warrants. For instance, if the circumstances are remarkably fluid, this type of planning might be necessary on a quarterly, monthly, or even weekly basis.

Status assessment: Mapping the solution

The first step in the operational planning process is an assessment of the organization's current status. This assessment characterizes the near-term threat environment and specifies the resultant security requirements. That baseline process documents the current security situation and defines the ensuing set of security requirements. The concrete outcome is a baseline, or benchmark set off by findings that describe the current status of the security situation.

After the current status has been established and documented, required changes to the current operation are defined. These could be internally focused and only apply to a particular unit. Or they might be global recommendations about policy. The purpose of the global recommendations is to offer a roadmap for explicitly aligning the security of operations function with the business purpose. This roadmap documents each relevant issue and the priorities that will shape the operational security function's conduct throughout the specific planning period.

That roadmap must also specify a management framework for the technical and procedural countermeasures that will be adopted. To accurately determine the feasibility of these approaches and the resources required, decisions should be based on a thorough analysis and understanding of the risks and filtered through the threat prioritization process.

That roadmap is then used to develop the security architecture. Once the direction is decided on, planners document an appropriate infrastructure of operational procedures. The aim is to create a secure and stable day-to-day operational security function. The outcome of this stage is a set of defined practices and work instructions that dictate operational security practice. The aim is to ensure a thorough understanding of the procedures required to support every aspect of day-to-day security operations. This is typically communicated through a policy and procedure manual.

Documenting and publicizing best practice: The procedure manual

Every business must compile, distribute, and update a procedure manual that contains the recommended best practices for that particular organization. The purpose of this manual is to outline all necessary procedures that will be carried out to ensure the continuous security of operations. Finally, there should be a clear statement of the interrelationship between related procedures.

The manual must prevent the organization's workforce from omitting something meaningful in their day-to-day security practice. Therefore, at a minimum, there should be a simple checklist that provides clear instructions on how to perform routine cyber-hygiene activities.

Procedure manuals also specify the standard, commonly accepted remediation options. For example, if there were frequent instances of equipment failures, a proper recovery procedure might be defined as a corrective action. At a minimum, every documented procedure should ensure that the required steps are specified, the expected results are clearly stated, and the criteria used to determine whether the goals of the procedure manual have been met are specified.

Logically, the security of operations manual must contain a detailed specification of the technologies and products that will be used during the planning period. Technology alone will not secure the organization. But it is obviously a critical aspect of the process. Therefore, the operational security plan should directly specify all security-related products and their specific applications. Once the supporting technology has been identified and the system implemented, there is an obligation to do ongoing status assessment and monitoring.

Because the procedure manual publicizes the security of operations to the organization at large, it must be kept up to date and current. Once tangible security procedures and technical countermeasures have been fully characterized and publicized in the policy and procedure manual, the organization uses that manual to build awareness. That typically involves focused employee education and training programs. The commonsense goal of operational security is to anticipate all likely security events and have a predefined response in place. This leads to the final aspect of the security of operations function, ensuring a timely response.

Addressing all eventualities

Finally, it is clearly insufficient to create a set of procedures without fully informing the user community of their personal responsibilities regarding any defined practice that involves them. Therefore, proper education and awareness are one of the cornerstones of the implementation process. The educational program is deployed and administered as part of overall operations planning. This is a continuous responsibility. The specific education, training, and awareness activities are constantly referenced in these procedures and are developed for a particular period.

ELEMENTS OF OPERATIONAL SECURITY

> *To secure ourselves against defeat lies in our own hands.*
>
> —Sun Tzu

As we mentioned earlier, the operational security process consists of four primary functions. These functions represent the four principal elements of the operational security process: sensing, analysis, response, and management. It is now time to explore the implementation and operation of these functions in detail.

Operational sensing, analyzing, and responding to the threat

Operational sensing is the cutting edge of holistic security. That's because it continuously monitors the three legitimate attack surfaces – electronic, human, and physical – seeking to maintain a secure state as well as respond to new threats. In essence, it serves as the eyes and ears of the organization when it comes to threats. Besides identifying and responding to changes in the threat environment, the sensing process also effectively monitors and evaluates the organization's control infrastructure to detect potential vulnerabilities and address security violations as they arise.

The operational sensing function is implemented and executed based on a defined set of policies, procedures, tools, and standards that the organization specifies as part of the overall strategic plan. Operational sensing is primarily a proactive activity. Therefore, it is continuously executed. It identifies and resolves operational anomalies as they arise. Since those anomalies can be associated with almost any kind of hostile activity, sensing is not limited to electronic oversight. Instead, it extends as far as feasible into the organization's operating environment, including all human and societal attacks, such as phishing, as well as functional considerations like noncompliance with regulations.

Operationally, threat sensing monitors (e.g., sensors) detect the general threat context across all three common attack surfaces of the organization. The process must be continuous because threats can arise at any point in time and can represent a range of unanticipated harms. Accordingly, monitoring of the operational threat space must be performed on a disciplined and regularly scheduled basis. It is also necessary to report all potentially adverse outcomes through a standard and disciplined process.

Threats are generated in the everyday operation of the organization, within the context of its business purpose. Therefore, it is a best practice to continuously analyze the outcomes of the sensing process to identify and determine the best response to each potential security threat, exposure, vulnerability, security violation, or unauthorized deviation from the organizational purpose.

The sensing and analysis function aims to respond as quickly and effectively as possible to emerging threats, malfunctions in the operation, or incidents. That is a typical operational requirement of any security process, which is why ensuring the success of the security operations process requires that sensing and analysis be performed on a standard, fully documented, and continuously coordinated basis.

Thus, an operational security infrastructure must exist to guarantee that the sensing process is executed as effectively and efficiently as possible. It must also be performed to ensure that the status of the threatscape is continuously known and evaluated. That includes ensuring that the policies, procedures, tools, and standards utilized to carry out that process provably achieve the business purpose they are deployed to address.

Management and end-user behavior are qualitative, subjective conditions. Therefore, they are assessed through verifications, such as reviews. Verifications are periodic activities that are scheduled, as appropriate, to evaluate the effectiveness of everything from personnel security to technical configurations. Verifications underwrite qualitative judgements. They can be both managerial and technical.. Those types of reviews comprise walkthroughs, inspections, or audits.

The activity that typically supports technical assurance practices is the classic testing function. Besides conventional testing practices, testing can also include intrusion detection, penetration testing, and assessment of procedural violations. Threats, vulnerabilities, and violations that are discovered through either the testing or review process are recorded and reported using a defined anomaly reporting and problem resolution process.

To produce rationally derived changes, the threat analysis process must be structured to allow decision-makers to authorize corrective action based on an objective understanding of the threat and risk. Ideally, tests and reviews should be conducted against an established benchmark. This benchmark typically represents the point in time when the organization was last known to be in a secure state. At a minimum, the evidence of a safe state requires documentary evidence of:

- A feasible security perimeter
- An overall concept of standard operating procedure
- A generic operational testing and review plan
- Policies to ensure appropriate response to unexpected incidents
- A secure site plan
- A Business Continuity Plan (BCP/DRP) with Recovery Time Objectives (RTO), Network Recovery Objectives (NRO), and Recovery Point Objectives (RPO) fully established

Analyzing: Underwriting smart decisions

To make effective decisions about an identified threat, it is essential to understand all its consequences and potential impacts. Everything involved with the threat must be included in that analysis, not just the effects on the technology. For instance, it is not sufficient to understand the security implications of a change to the password system. It is also necessary to understand specifically what that means in terms of potential impacts on overall worker productivity as well as how it will change worker behavior.

An appropriate understanding of the consequences of a threat will ensure a coordinated response. A proper understanding requires identifying the elements within the organization that are affected. Those elements need to be adequately understood to precisely define the impacts of the threat and any prospective changes on them. Hence, the effects on an element's existing policies, procedures, and countermeasures must be characterized along with any cascading or ripple effects that might occur within the organization. This could also involve understanding what overall security policies, legal, regulatory, and forensic requirements are affected, beyond the obvious technical or procedural implications involved.

To implement the correct response, it is necessary to evaluate all feasible alternatives. That requires the organization to conduct a comprehensive and detailed impact analysis, which should be based on a structured approach. The methodology should ensure a thorough and unambiguous understanding of all of the operational implications of a given response strategy, its resource requirements, and the associated changes required.

Logically, to understand all the strategic implications, it is necessary to classify the threat by type, criticality, scope, particularly as it impacts resources, and finally, to identify the feasible options that fit within all the given constraints. Once these have been fully understood, the results and recommendations are communicated to the proper decision-maker for official authorization.

To provide intelligent authorization, the decision maker must understand the type and extent of the impacts and risks associated with each option, as well as the likelihood and feasibility of each risk. It should be possible to estimate the security and resource implications that would be required to respond to the threat, as well as those of not responding, from this analysis process. That includes an intelligent estimate of the impact of:

- Policy and procedure on creation and maintenance of a secure operational state.
- Business continuity/disaster recovery strategies on long-term organizational viability.
- Return on investment of the security scheme (note: the return on investment should include a feasibility estimate along with resource estimations).

The results of the analysis phase must support explicit decision-making about any potential operational change. To support intelligent decision-making regarding the given response, it is necessary to provide a comprehensive and detailed analysis and description of the implementation requirements for each feasible direction. Hence, the analysis report must clearly outline both the estimated impacts and be plainly and explicitly traceable to the business case.

Responding: Making informed changes in the structure of the operation

Change is inevitable in any organization, especially in response to the constantly changing threat environment. The organization implements any corrective action that may be authorized as a result of the decision analysis process. In some cases, there might be a reasonable operational justification for not responding to a threat, or for not responding to it as immediately as possible, such as resource constraints or the current infeasibility of the recommended response. Therefore, this is a considered decision-making process, not a standard operating procedure.

Nevertheless, whether a decision to respond is authorized or not, it is essential for the security of operations to continuously monitor all known threats and react appropriately when a response is required. The agent responsible for actually modifying the protection scheme must understand all of the requirements and restrictions involved in making a specified alteration to the current operational form of the solution. That applies whether it is a technical fix or a change in policy,

Consequently, a process must exist to specify and convey to the agent that will implement the change, all of the technical and behavioral requirements of any authorized alteration to the security operation. Additionally, a standardized and disciplined process must be in place to ensure that any action taken with respect to the security solution is performed in a consistent and controlled manner. A comprehensive testing, review, and audit program typically supports this. In essence, operations staff should continue to monitor and analyze the security solution to verify that the intended results have been achieved.

That assessment process certifies that the threat has been successfully addressed and a reliable degree of protection has been re-established. The actions that must occur and the criteria that must be met to ensure compliance are specified. These are specified as part of the decision to alter the security scheme. Additionally, to provide confidence, particularly in highly secure settings, it may be necessary to perform a third-party assessment or audit to certify the suitability and correctness of the response.

Managing: Enforcing accountability

Enforcement is a critical success factor. Therefore, to ensure security, explicit enforcement requirements and consequences for non-compliance must be designated for every role in the security process, from the CISO down to the most junior worker. Therefore, once the security plan has been itemized, documented, and publicized, the appropriate measures have to be defined to enforce secure behavior. In this respect, the consequences of non-compliance must be explicitly understood and personally agreed upon by every member of the organization. This is necessary to ensure that employees will faithfully perform their assigned security duties. Moreover, enforcement must be administered from the top of the organization and practiced continuously as a commitment throughout the organization.

THE PEOPLE FACTOR IN OPERATIONAL ASSURANCE

Opportunities multiply as they are seized.

—Sun Tzu

Threats to corporate assets can appear in many forms. Those range from penetrations of the network by technically sophisticated "hackers, all the way down to petty thefts perpetrated by people who knowingly, or even unknowingly, take something of value. All the same, each of these is a violation. Therefore, to ensure total security, each viable threat must be countered by a substantive response.

This means that a valid and appropriate array of procedures must be developed and consistently applied throughout the lifecycle of the security system to counter both behavioral and electronic threats. As we have said, technology is a critical factor in any protection scheme. However, that factor alone cannot assure reliable security performance. To ensure a consistent state of security, it is necessary for the people the system serves to adopt and follow highly disciplined security practices.

Therefore, human factors themselves are also essential and substantive contributors to the success of the holistic security process. It is easy for people on the technical side of the security operation to trivialize the importance of human behavior in the success of a security system. That is, because the assets are virtual – e.g., electronic and harmful actions of people against system resources are hard to classify. Even more problematic, they are almost impossible to predict.

Nonetheless, a dependable day-to-day security system implicitly relies on people to operate and use the technology properly. For instance, no matter how robust the access control and how stringent the policies, it is the workers who are susceptible to every conceivable form of social engineering. Therefore, they are the logical point of attack if an adversary seeks to compromise system security. For instance, among other things … the people in any organization will:

- Willingly share their password with others.
- Never refresh expired ones.
- Write critical access information on the front of their terminal so they won't forget it.
- Leave their workstations unattended.
- Click on links without considering the security implications.

As a consequence, humans are the weakest link in the system, and because of this, their behavior cannot be left to chance when it comes to security operations. Human behavior must be addressed by a tangible set of practical countermeasures, designed to eliminate uncontrolled human behavior as the primary vulnerability.

As we mentioned in Chapter 2, consistently ensuring the adequate performance of the security system is almost impossible where people are involved, and there are countless mundane ways that people can completely compromise even the most secure situation.

The root cause lies in the fact that information is highly abstract, making it difficult for designers to consider every way it can be compromised by human behavior. As a result, it isn't easy to trust that the people involved in the day-to-day process of handling information will consider everything necessary to protect the organization. That is the reason for best practice. However, best practice procedures must be known and consistently followed to be effective. Therefore, the human security process is built on softer elements, such as training and awareness, rather than complex, technological methods.

Human factors influence security performance because every worker has an individual understanding of how rigorously rules should be followed and how consistently prescribed action requirements are adhered to. As a result, the human aspect of assurance must be addressed through a substantive set of control procedures, and accountability must be built into the process. Moreover, it is necessary to tailor those controls to each role, since no single individual is responsible for maintaining security end-to-end throughout the operation.

Most failures in security stem from the execution of the process rather than the plans that establish it. That is because security work depends on all participants having an adequate understanding of what is required of them, and that is rarely the case where typical business operations are concerned. Nevertheless, adequate assurance is only possible if all individuals in the organization understand their precise responsibilities within the security process.

Therefore, one of the key elements of holistic security is the simple requirement for the organization to ensure predictable and trustworthy behavior among all stakeholders. Accordingly, it is the organization's duty to provide a satisfactory level of understanding of all relevant best practice requirements to every member of the organization, whether formally acknowledged or not.

This last condition means that everyone who works in or is a stakeholder in the organization must precisely understand what is expected of them, as well as the consequences of non-compliance. That level of knowledge can only be ensured through a formal organizational process that aims to ensure everyone has mastered their security responsibilities. Hence, it is the organization's duty to establish a formal awareness and training program as part of the overall security of operations process.

The point of a formally designed and operated training and awareness process is to establish security discipline organization-wide. The term discipline denotes nothing more than the reliable performance of the best practices required of them. Holistic security systems require disciplined execution because all participants must uniformly perform the formally specified security procedures at all times to ensure consistent and complete protection. That is because inconsistent performance can lead to security breakdowns and harm to the resource.

Implementing and maintaining a disciplined system of rules of behavior for all participants ensures that protection will be reliable. Hence, one of the first conditions for instituting systematic information assurance is the establishment of a formally documented description of disciplined practice as interpreted by that particular organization. Nevertheless, because the required security practices tend to impose additional worker requirements, people often do not adopt highly rigorous secure behaviors. They must be motivated to do that.

Hence, motivation is the other important human factor in the information assurance process. Motivation is the aspect of human behavior that initiates, directs, and sustains all forms of interaction among people. It is the driver that maintains a person's willingness to carry out a given task or achieve a goal. It determines the degree, direction, and persistence of an effort over a set period of time.

Motivation is only possible if there are sufficient incentives in place. These are enforced through an accountability system that rewards correct actions and discourages improper ones. It is impossible to establish accountability if the explicit rules of behavior are not formally written and understood. Therefore, the organization must also ensure that all employees understand the consequences of violating these rules. For that reason, the second critical role of the human security process is to ensure that every member of the organization understands all accountabilities.

Unfortunately, however, the technological areas in cybersecurity are much better documented and accepted than the behavioral ones. Technology has an established body of knowledge, and the elements of the domain are relatively well understood and agreed on within the profession. However, the body of knowledge associated with assuring a proper level of security competency among the human elements is only just beginning to emerge.

Nevertheless, human behavior must be controlled to ensure a long-term, holistic security process. It is also evident that establishing that control requires fitting different levels of knowledge and capability requirements to each job type. For instance, a secretary will require a different level of security capability than a system manager. But they will both need to exercise those differing capabilities on a disciplined basis. That is because each of these different business responsibilities requires a different type of security knowledge.

Thus, the specific security needs and abilities of individual roles will vary across the organization as a whole. Hence, each organization needs to formulate and document a formal model of the basic security behaviors required for each role. The documentation would itemize the general types of behavior that must be practiced within each generic role. It would then serve as a point of reference for establishing the desired level of assurance within the organization.

A properly functioning statement of security behaviors would enable an organization or individual practitioner to build their overall security capability. It would do this by itemizing the required security best practices for a set of generic roles within the overall business structure. There are five states of security behavior. These are: running from least desirable to most desirable:

Recognition – the individual recognizes the need for cybersecurity but is unsure of how to address it.

Awareness – the individual performs informal security practices on an undisciplined basis.

Application – the individual performs best practice security practices on a disciplined basis.

Control – the individual makes choices about security based on analysis and best practices.

Adaptation – the individual is adaptive and creative in responding to unanticipated threats.

Societal security factors

A set of societal factors must be considered when establishing a functioning, day-to-day security response. Those are the general societal-centered qualities that cybersecurity must ensure, including individual privacy rights, legal and regulatory compliance, and the prevention of criminal behavior in virtual space. In many respects ... because this is such a broad and catch-all category, these cybercrime factors account for a majority of the exploits and actual losses recorded every year. Hence, the considerations that are rooted in our larger society and that generate real consequences are genuine concerns that must be substantively addressed when implementing a holistic response.

Societal security involves a concrete set of collective duties that generally dictate how organizations and individuals should behave in a given circumstance. That advice is necessary for every profession, as it enables practitioners to distinguish right from wrong and thereby make informed choices. The practical value of a formal set of duties is that it formalizes the principles of acceptable behavior for the group. That foundation provides the group's decision-makers with an effective yardstick to evaluate the conduct of employees and peers.

Although they are intangible concepts, considering societal factors such as privacy and compliance is a practical aspect of the cybersecurity process, as these factors have real-world consequences in both litigation and organizational reputation. Thus, they are a critical part of the operational security process. Practically, there must be a shared understanding of what factors, such as compliance and privacy, represent to the organization.

Having a clear statement of the organization's societal values is essential, since the policies that shape holistic assurance are formulated in the light of an understanding of what those values mean to the specific organization. Or, in practical terms, the societal perspective guides an organization's approach to its overall commitment to operating in a trustworthy manner. Hence, that point of view must be both clearly expressed and unmistakably understood across the organization.

The goal of a formally documented statement of organizational principles is to enable individuals within the organization to make informed, day-to-day decisions. These choices must balance what is suitable for the individual or the group against the greater good of society. That balancing act is dynamic, in that there is absolutely no correct answer. Consequently, such a system centers on the description of a commonly accepted set of societal norms and principles, as well as practical guidelines for applying them.

Those principles embody the group's value system and must be formally defined and endorsed by the organization as a whole. The interpretation of how these principles should be applied is up to the individual and relies on an appropriate understanding of the behavior that is required. In the practical universe, this means that the group value system directs the routine behavior of individual members.

The principles serve as a stable and reliable navigation beacon, ensuring that every individual decision aligns with the organization's shared ethical values. Therefore, they must also ensure that unacceptable behavior is recognized and evokes an appropriate response. The documentation of a business enterprise's values is referred to as its ethical code of conduct.

An ethical code of conduct is the organization's standard for proper behavior in a given instance. It defines the accepted values and principles of its particular domain. It dictates the duties and obligations of individual workers in reference to the group norms. Accordingly, it offers the ability to manage the ethical behavior of that specific group. These rules are either normative – they establish general right and wrong – or descriptive – they define what the group believes and how people should act in reference to that belief.

Ethical codes delineate the correct choices for individuals in relation to the overall norms of the group. In a practical sense, a defined moral code enables an organization to determine when an individual is not behaving correctly. Proper behavior is demonstrated by the individual's capacity to make consistently correct decisions in the light of the values of the organization. Consequently, a properly designed ethical system will always provide a concrete point of reference for proper behavior and an explanation of the consequences of deviating from group norms. Thus, in practical application, an explicit enforcement mechanism is an absolute necessity for a properly functioning code of conduct.

However, since codes of conduct define group norms and all groups are different, there is no universally valid set of rules of behavior. For instance, the code of conduct for the hacker community differs from that of the Business Software Alliance. Although the legitimacy of the former group's ethics may be questioned, their code represents their customary group behavior. Accordingly, the underlying basis and intent of every ethical system have to be fully understood when judging what the code of conduct means.

Professional codes of conduct outline the specific duties and obligations that members of the profession owe to each other and their clients. Professional codes of conduct outline the proper way for members of a practitioner group to interact with one another. Finally, and most importantly, they define how the overall profession proposes to interrelate with society as a whole. Thus, professional codes of conduct are the formal ethical models that embody and communicate the accepted norms that a specific group has adopted.

They are based on each organization's understanding of correct professional behavior. In the case of assurance, the code must describe the organization's position regarding security, as well as its policies for the appropriate use of resources. Thus, professional codes of conduct are essential in guiding the field of cybersecurity. That is because they speak to a broad range of concerns raised by the increasing use of technology. They provide ethical guidance with respect to such significant issues as:

- The rights of individuals
- The effect of the global information grid on intellectual property
- The degree of commitment required
- Professional competency

Defining capability

A common understanding of proper, professional behavior is an essential building block in guiding real-world operational solutions. But a commonly understood and accepted definition of individual capability and expectations for cybersecurity workers might be an even more critical aspect of the profession. That is because cybersecurity workers operate under the assumption that practitioners have an elevated level of knowledge.

That presumption is a crucial factor in other professions where public trust must be ensured. For instance, in the case of a doctor, the minimum standard level would be the probability that a medical condition would receive the proper diagnosis and treatment. Doctors are held to a high standard of expectation in this respect because of their advanced skills, training, and knowledge. Their medical license attests to that. Similarly, lawyers are held to a higher professional standard in matters related to the law because they have to pass a State Bar exam. Both ensure confidence in the profession.

The problem is that a standard proof of capability isn't enforced for cybersecurity professionals. Or in simple terms, at present, the people working in the area generically termed "cybersecurity" are not subject to any formal requirements regarding proof of capability. There are general expectations regarding the background and education they require. However, there is no explicit mechanism to ensure professional capability. That implies concrete consequences for organizations, as employee incapability has profound negative implications for the group's interest.

There is no formal definition of the knowledge or competencies required to ensure the successful performance of professional work, particularly in holistic security, nor is there a specified minimum level of education and training that a competent cybersecurity professional must possess. Hence, although there are several representative common bodies of knowledge, the field lacks a single system to guarantee the professional competence of practitioners. Accordingly, there is extreme variability in skills and competencies within the profession, which only serves to reinforce the stovepipe nature of the field.

As we have frequently stated, stovepipes can have a potentially profound impact on the type and degree of protection that can be expected for a given solution, as they create and encourage gaps. Moreover, the potential for misunderstanding and miscommunication is obvious. As a result, ordinary people who have faith in the ability of a security professional have no guarantee that their confidence may not be misplaced. Therefore, the assurance of overall trust is obviously a societal factor that must be considered in any cybersecurity solution, whether holistic or otherwise.

CHAPTER SUMMARY

Implementation is the second formal stage in the process of developing a practical, holistic control system. The coordination and control of complex work requires a common and coherent conceptual framework, or architecture. This allows all stakeholders in the organization to benchmark their performance against best practices.

As such, in this chapter, we present the principles and methods that must be employed to create a functioning, real-world, holistic governance architecture. The goal is to formulate a standard, fully documented, holistic security solution that embodies all appropriate security best practices, as documented by a tangible and comprehensive infrastructure of well-defined management practices.

In this respect, the business defines and then documents a coherent framework of actions that encompasses all the requisite management roles, organizational behaviors, and strategic policies necessary to ensure a fully secure organization. This is made tangible and overseen by a regularly performed and rational assessment process that allows the organization to implement an effective set of security requirements. Accordingly, the end product consistently embodies a concrete and coherent set of recommendations. The particular system requirements are elicited once the problem space has been sufficiently understood. All architectures exhibit common characteristics:

- They are complete in the sense that they encompass the entire solution.
- They are correct in that all elements of the solution that logically should be present are.

- They are understandable in how they communicate the form of the solution.
- And all of the elements in the architecture are traceable to a particular business purpose.

The real-world system actively and intentionally aligns the form of the security solution with the organization's explicit business needs. A properly set-up and maintained solution will monitor the security function and bring any deviations to management's attention. The result of executing this process is a comprehensive, coherent, and fully managed security architecture that is precisely aligned with the business purpose requirements of the circumstances. Nine commonly recognized factors are considered indicative of a properly organized and implemented security solution. These are:

1. The existence of a formally documented security policy
2. Implementation model that fits with organizational culture
3. Visible support and commitment from management
4. Organization-wide understanding of security requirements
5. Formal risk assessment and risk management procedures
6. Effective marketing of security to all managers and employees
7. Appropriate training and education
8. A comprehensive system of measurement
9. The provision for feedback and suggestions for improvement

These factors are all realized in a standard method of operation that falls under the general rubric of "security of operations." The security of operations functions orthogonally to the initial development and design functions. Its primary role is to ensure the integrity and proper performance of the holistic security system, as conceptualized and operationalized in the design. In essence, operational security ensures that all necessary day-to-day security requirements are functioning as intended in the business's day-to-day operations.

To ensure security, operations security monitors and evaluates the day-to-day execution of all controls within the assurance architecture by verifying that all behavioral and technical countermeasures are in place and operating correctly. Ultimately, when threats are detected, security of operations is responsible for coordinating the corrective action response.

As the name implies, security of operations is less involved with strategy and development than it is with underwriting dependable day-to-day performance of the security solution. The security operations function accomplishes this by ensuring that security best practices always align with business stakeholder requirements. Every business has a given set of security objectives. Logically, those objectives must be satisfied for the organization to be considered secure. Nevertheless, the overall operating environment is constantly changing, and therefore, the objectives must adjust accordingly to ensure proper alignment. Factors that can affect that include changes in:

- The people who use the system, or their motivations.
- Any system that is interconnected with the organization's systems.
- The type, or sensitivity of data flowing to, through, or from the organization's system.
- The way the organization does business, or the type of business that is conducted.
- The rigor, application, or extent of the security objectives.

Security of operations and alignment

The role of security of operations is to maintain proper alignment between the organization's business goals and its security practices. Security of operations is responsible for monitoring the execution of each business process and the set of controls implemented to ensure security. The aim is to provide continuous alignment between business purpose and the security solution.

That monitoring activity focuses on detecting meaningful deviations from either business purpose or proper practice. Typically, this is accomplished by identifying and recording problems as they occur. Analyzing each situation to determine how it can be mitigated and taking the appropriate corrective, adaptive, perfective, or preventive action to ensure proper realignment with the business purpose and the nature of the threat.

Furthermore, because the security environment and the organization itself are constantly evolving, confidence in the integrity of the security response must be continually renewed. As a result, the security of operations must also be periodically verified and certified for the effectiveness of the currently instituted security solution. Hence, the security of operations function routinely reviews, inspects, tests, and audits the performance of the elements and interrelationships that comprise the security architecture. Where problems are encountered, the security of operations is responsible for initiating and coordinating the resolution of these problems.

The purpose of the security operations process is to maintain the most effective possible response to threats and the evolving threat environment, within the context of a dynamically changing situation. Holistic assurance is founded on a comprehensive, unitary organization-wide, policy-based architecture of operational controls and countermeasures. The role of security of operations is to maintain the relevance and effectiveness of that system.

Instituting the holistic process: The plan

Security of operations is embodied through a standard organizational planning process. The plan operationalizes and coordinates most of the elements of the security of operations process, guiding the allocation of resources for its overall conduct. Therefore, the first step in establishing a security operations function is to develop a comprehensive, cross-functional, and cross-organizational plan.

The purpose of that plan is to ensure that the security of operations function is fully and correctly deployed and embedded in the day-to-day operational fabric of the organization. The outcome of this planning process is a practical long-term specification of the methodology for performing the security of operations function.

A formally sanctioned security operations plan is a crucial baseline document. It serves as a practical point of reference in the evolution and day-to-day management of the security of operations function. The plan delineates the operational requirements necessary to ensure a robust and persistent state of holistic assurance. It explicitly specifies the standard practices and the schedule, or timetable, that will be followed.

The operational plan is an instrumental support to the organizational budgeting process because it embodies and makes explicit the organization's security objectives. These objectives serve as the foundation for deploying the overall security function and provide an excellent means to gauge ongoing performance.

Like the strategic plan, the operational security plan should be easily understood by all participants. It should leave all staff members knowing precisely what activities are required and the timing for performing them. The operational plan then organizes and focuses the deployment of those activities in a way that allows them to function most effectively. In essence, it enables decision-makers to align their safeguards with available resources.

The operational plan organizes the technical and procedural response in a way that ensures the proper countermeasures are in place to address the relevant security requirements. Finally, because the plan details the criteria for performance, it also serves as an effective mechanism for assessing whether the organization's contractual and regulatory obligations are being met.

Human security factors

Threats to corporate assets can appear in many forms. Those range from penetrations of the network by technically sophisticated "hackers, all the way down to petty thefts perpetrated by people who knowingly, or even unknowingly, take something of value. All the same, to ensure total security, each of these threats must be countered by a substantive response. This means that a valid and appropriate array of procedures must be developed and consistently applied throughout the lifecycle of the security system.

As we have said, technology is a critical factor in any protection scheme. However, that factor alone cannot assure reliable security performance. To ensure a consistent state of security, it is necessary for the people the system serves to adopt and follow highly disciplined security practices. Consequently, human factors themselves are also essential and substantive contributors to the success of the holistic security process. For instance, no matter how robust the access control and how stringent the policies, it is the workers who are susceptible to every conceivable form of social engineering. For instance, people:

- Willingly share their password with others.
- Never refresh expired ones.
- Write critical access information on the front of their terminal so they won't forget it.
- Leave their workstations unattended.
- Click on links without considering the security implications.

As a consequence, humans are the weakest link in the system, and because of this, their behavior cannot be left to chance. Human behavior must be addressed by a tangible set of practical countermeasures, designed to eliminate the human factor as the primary vulnerability.

This can only be ensured through a formal organizational process that ensures that everybody has mastery of their responsibilities. Hence, it is the organization's duty to establish a formal awareness and training program as part of the overall security of operations process.

The point of a formal process is to establish security discipline organization-wide. The term discipline denotes nothing more than the reliable performance of a method of best practice. Holistic security systems require disciplined execution because all participants must uniformly perform procedures at all times to ensure protection is consistent and complete. Inconsistent performance can lead to security breakdowns and harm to the resource.

Societal security factors

A larger set of social factors must be considered in establishing a functioning, day-to-day security response. Those are the societal-centered qualities that cybersecurity must ensure, including individual privacy rights, legal and regulatory compliance, and the prevention of criminal behavior in virtual space. In many respects, the cybercrime factor accounts for a vast majority of the exploits and actual losses recorded every year. Thus, the considerations that are rooted in our larger society and that generate real consequences are genuine concerns that must be kept in mind when implementing a holistic response.

Although they are intangible concepts, considering societal factors such as privacy and compliance is a practical aspect of the cybersecurity process, as these factors have real-world consequences in both litigation and organizational reputation. Thus, they are a critical part of the operational security process. Practically, there must be a shared understanding of what factors, such as compliance and privacy, represent to the organization.

The complete set of these principles embodies the group's value system and must be formally defined and endorsed by the organization as a whole. The interpretation of how these principles should be applied is up to the individual and relies on a proper understanding of the behavior required. In the practical universe, this means that the group value system directs the routine behavior of individual members.

The principles serve as a stable and reliable navigation beacon, ensuring that every individual decision reflects the organization's common ethical principles. Therefore, they must also ensure that unacceptable behavior is recognized and evokes an appropriate response. The documentation of a business enterprise's values is referred to as its ethical code of conduct.

Chapter 6

Managing the solution

Figure 6.1 Pencil drawing of two contrasting figures: on the left, a calm, bearded man studies a map at a table, marking it thoughtfully with a stylus; on the right, a fierce warrior shouts while raising a sword overhead. The scene contrasts quiet strategic planning with impulsive aggression and direct combat.

DOI: 10.1201/9781003603412-6

ENSURING HOLISTIC CONTROL

It is more important to outthink your enemy, rather than outfight him.
—Sun Tzu

This chapter is devoted to all of the practical concerns associated with creating and managing a fully implemented, enterprise-wide, holistic security solution. We discuss the purpose and functioning of all eight generic elements of a holistic solution, considered as a unified entity. Our primary aim here is to demonstrate where and how the merger of the traditional electronic aspects of the cybersecurity process with the necessary behavioral elements will create a single, fully converged strategic process that aligns business purpose with practical protection.

As we mentioned in Chapter 2, the electronic countermeasure areas are what people typically think of when they hear the term cybersecurity. That's because those control actions, or at least their outcomes, are both observable to the stakeholder community and can be expressed in easy-to-relate-to, quantitative terms, such as permitted and/or blocked access attempts.

Nevertheless, other adverse events are difficult to characterize, such as phishing attempts, lost or stolen equipment, or unauthorized access to secure spaces by unvetted individuals in the course of their daily tasks, for instance, security guards or the janitorial staff. Each of these eventualities is a potential source of loss or harm to the organization. Therefore, they must be included in the consideration of the shape and content of the protection scheme.

There are four generic classes of considerations that guide the consideration: attack surface, threat agent, threat source, threat community, and threat consequence.

Attack surfaces

The attack surface is the sum of diverse points, e.g., attack vectors, where an unauthorized user – e.g., the "attacker" – can attempt to enter or extract data from a target object. For example, in the case of electronic attacks, the attack vector refers to the method that the adversary uses to compromise a given system, such as buffer overflows, command injections, and networking protocol exploits. Thus, the general strategy for securing the electronic security function is to reduce the size of the overall electronic attack surface, e.g., restrict the possible points of access. The basic methods for attack surface reduction are to:

- Reduce entry points available to untrusted users
- Eliminate services requested by relatively few users
- Reduce the amount of running code

Threat agents

The term 'threat agent' categorizes an individual or group that can pose a threat. A threat agent exploits a weakness/vulnerability of the system and the related controls through an *attack vector*. Thus, when considering this, it is essential to identify who would want to exploit a given business asset and how they might use it against the company. Threats can be classified according to their type, origin, and the damage they cause. Electronic damages include:

- compromise of information
- eavesdropping
- theft of media
- retrieval of discarded materials
- technical failures
- equipment damage
- software failures
- capacity saturation
- compromise of functions
- error in use
- abuse of rights
- denial of service, or actions

Practically anyone and anything can be a threat agent under the right circumstances. That includes such diverse constituencies as the well-intentioned, but inept, computer operator who trashes a security scan by typing the wrong command, the regulator performing an incorrect audit, or the squirrel that chews through a data cable. Threat agents can take one or more of the following actions against an asset:

- Access – simple unauthorized access
- Misuse – unauthorized use of assets (e.g., identity theft, etc.)
- Disclose – the threat agent illicitly discloses sensitive information
- Modification – unauthorized changes to an asset
- Denial of access – includes destruction, theft of a non-data asset, etc.

It's essential to recognize that each of these actions affects different assets differently, which in effect determines the degree and nature of loss. These individuals and groups can be classified as follows:

- Non-Target Specific – Threat Agents are viruses, worms, Trojans, and logic bombs.
- Employees – staff, contractors, operational/maintenance personnel, or security guards.

- Organized Crime and Criminals – target information that can be converted into money.
- Corporations: competitive intelligence. Partners and competitors fall into this category.

Threat sources

Threat sources describe the actual individuals or organizations that benefit from a compromise. This is often separate from the actual perpetrator, as it is typical for entities like nation-states to employ a wide range of threat agents to accomplish their nefarious purposes. Hence, threat source is a term used to distinguish the beneficiary from the threat agents/actors who actually carry out the attack and who may be commissioned or persuaded by the threat actor to knowingly or unknowingly act. This is a crucial distinction when evaluating potential risks.

Threat communities

Threat communities are subsets of the overall threat agent population. They share key characteristics that are essential clues when considering the type of threat. For instance, the Cyberpunk we discussed in Chapter 1 is a perfect example of an individual motivated by a distinctive purpose. Those reasons, for instance, counterculture actions, must be considered when devising a defense and/or investigating a breach.

The concept of threat communities is a powerful tool for understanding who and what we're up against as we try to manage risk. For example, the probability that an organization would be subject to an attack from the terrorist threat community would depend in large part on the characteristics of your organization relative to the motives, intents, and capabilities of the terrorists. Questions to answer would be:

- Is the organization closely affiliated with an ideology that conflicts with known attackers?
- Does the organization represent a high-profile, high-impact target?
- Is the organization a soft target?
- How does the organization compare with other potential targets?
- What components of the organization would be likely targets?

Threat consequence

Threat consequence is the outcome of a specific threat action. That includes such generic harms as disclosure, deception, disruption, and usurpation. Examples of this include ... The intentional release of sensitive data to an unauthorized entity or searching through data residue to gain unauthorized knowledge of sensitive data is referred to as OPSEC.

Of course, there is always human error, where a human action or inaction unintentionally results in an entity gaining unauthorized knowledge of sensitive data. Finally, there is a hardware/software error, which is a system failure that results in an entity gaining unauthorized knowledge of sensitive data. These all have different motivations and are subject to distinct sets of countermeasures. Therefore, each eventuality must be identified and factored into the planning for the holistic system. These include:

- Theft- gaining access to sensitive data by stealing it.
- Wiretapping (passive) monitoring and recording data flowing between two points.
- Emanations analysis – gaining direct knowledge by monitoring system signaling.
- Inference – reasoning from characteristics or byproducts, aka OPSEC.
- Traffic analysis – gaining knowledge of data by observing characteristics of communications.
- Signals analysis – gaining indirect knowledge by analyzing a signal.
- Intrusion – unauthorized access by circumventing a system's protections. This includes:
  - Trespass – gaining unauthorized physical access.
  - Penetration – gaining unauthorized logical access to sensitive data.
  - Reverse engineering – disassembling and analyzing the design of a system component.
  - Cryptanalysis – transforming encrypted data without having prior knowledge of encryption parameters or processes.

CREATING SUBSTANTIVE COUNTERMEASURES

Countermeasures are deliberately designed security controls. When these are applied to protect the system itself, they are referred to as security services. The goal of holistic security is to ensure that the appropriate set of countermeasures is deployed to safeguard against every potential harmful eventuality. As such, those controls must be mutually interoperating. For instance, an electronic log can be used to record physical access, or an accumulated blacklist of dangerous sites can thwart access to a known phishing site. However, these actions must be carefully planned and coordinated.

In that respect, then, holistic security is built around the twin concepts of planned *convergence* and deliberate *integration*, where the only acceptable outcome is a fully harmonized set of control actions that will directly mitigate every priority threat within the overall context of the business purpose. Thus, the primary goal of holistic security is to define and combine every single logically required electronic, human, and physical control into a unified, comprehensive, and correctly interacting real-time solution.

As we have stated, this aim is achieved through a deliberate design activity and managed through a formally coordinated assurance process. However, the question remains: how do these eight common protection areas work together to ensure comprehensive cybersecurity assurance? That is what we will talk about here. Accordingly, this chapter will explain the purpose and intent of each area's standard controls and discuss how to converge those controls into a single integrated solution.

It is given that you must reliably secure three different attack surfaces for the cybersecurity solution to be effective, and that any control on any attack surface is likely to be interdependent with controls from other attack surfaces. For instance, electronic access controls rely on identity management, which is closely tied to HR. Accordingly, a proper protection scheme comprises a complete array of intelligently designed and fully integrated best practices that are typically derived from a commonly accepted, industry-sanctioned standard.

Those best practices are then suitably tailored to address all identified risks, and from there, they are properly interrelated to serve a specified business purpose. Afterward, the operational solution is continuously monitored for effectiveness, both in terms of the desired performance outcomes and their interactions with other interdependent controls.

ENSURING EVERYDAY HOLISTIC PROTECTION

> *Knowing the enemy enables you to take the offensive; knowing yourself allows you to stand on the defensive, as Sun Tzu advises.*

Cybersecurity doesn't just happen. It must be intentionally designed and embedded into the organization as an ongoing operational process. Thus, the term architecture describes the discrete, usually formal procedure that assures the development of a coherent and practical framework of controls. All required functions must be substantively verifiable as embedded into that structure. The responsibility for developing the generic framework for this activity lies within the general domain of the security architecture function.

As we mentioned, the term "security architecture" refers to the tangible representation of the security requirements for a particular setting. Architecture serves two fundamental purposes. First, it requires a detailed examination of the functions that must be addressed to ensure the necessary level of security. Second, it describes the precise actions that will be taken in each category to bake that solution directly into the security function. As such, holistic security operations embody the necessary practices to safeguard the organization against the likely challenges of operational failure.

The holistic security function ensures that the appropriate set of security principles and best practices is implemented and adhered to. It monitors and evaluates daily electronic and behavioral security practices to ensure that they are being performed in a disciplined and continuous manner. It assures the overall integrity of the security solution by performing the necessary monitoring, testing, and housekeeping tasks that the organization considers essential to security. As we said, that includes such things as making certain that the most relevant security principles and practices are correctly aligned with the organization's threat situation,

Every holistic system design is based on a coherent set of assumptions about the threat environment; therefore, any belief that is not identified and documented is a potential security vulnerability. The design of a holistic security strategy and the necessary security policies can only be guided by a proper understanding of the specific situation's requirements.

That requires the organization to make a precise set of estimates about its business needs and purposes, the types of protection required, and the kind of intruders it will face. In essence, the designer must consider who might attempt to breach the current security measures and why they might want to do so. Doing so is always a guess, the success of which requires continuous refinement of the understanding of the threat environment.

As we mentioned in Chapter 1, much of this relies on identifying the various types of malicious agents and their motivations. No security measure can ever be expected to protect the target asset from a directed attack absolutely. They can only delay the inevitable long enough for the proper response to be formulated. Consequently, the goal of the countermeasure deployment process is to identify and then establish the appropriate set of responses to mitigate the danger. As we also pointed out in Chapter 1, the response is based on the likely motivations and capabilities of all known attackers.

Finally, deployment of an effective response is as much a people problem as it is a technical design issue. That is because most security measures impact ease of use. Accordingly, the design and deployment of the holistic security scheme have to be done to justify the likely costs and benefits. Thus, the first primary requirement of holistic security is a set of policies outlining the organization's desired level of security protection. That list can be lengthy and may vary depending on the unique situations within an organization. The typical set of policies will include:

- Scope and purpose of the holistic security system
- The business and assurance case for the protected space
- Management accountability and acceptable use
- System solution configuration management and change policy

- Access control policy
- Remote access policy
- Telework security policy

The role of the holistic security scheme is to ensure the integrity of the business's overall information processing, transmission, and storage activities, thereby safeguarding virtual data from all theft, fraud, repudiation, and dispute hazards. Since virtual data is an essential part of modern business, that responsibility alone would justify robust, holistic security funding. However, the actual support for holistic security operations is a matter of each corporation's risk appetite, which is often influenced by business factors that are not necessarily geared towards adequacy of protection.

We already know that the various components of a modern business operation and the risks associated with each element must be identified and related to one another in a coherent and systematic manner. Then, the right policies, practices, and technologies must be selected, and their use must be monitored. That is a duty of strategic managers, not the organization's information technology function, since that is a generally electronic operation.

Accordingly, the responsibility for interfacing between the user community and the wide range of electronic devices lies at a higher level within the organization than the network or application assurance functions. That is also why cybersecurity cannot be considered a purely electronic problem.

Ultimately, in the broadest sense, the holistic security function ensures the integrity of confidential and publicly available information. In effect, a well-organized, holistic cybersecurity operation serves as the logical management control point to ensure that information intended for public release is properly authorized before publication and that all authorizations are subsequently adhered to. This may seem like a minor concern unless one considers the value of proprietary information to an organization.

Creating and maintaining capable countermeasures

A proven, capable array of countermeasures is the conceptual ideal state for cybersecurity. That state of assurance is achieved through the realization of three generic conditions: adequate threat detection, effective threat prevention, and immediate threat response. That is all based around a set of deliberately designed and implemented countermeasures.

In cybersecurity, a countermeasure is an action, device, procedure, or technique that mitigates a threat, vulnerability, or attack. It does this by eliminating or preventing it, or by minimizing the harm it can cause. Countermeasures identify and report potentially harmful events, allowing for corrective action to be taken.

Modern cybersecurity countermeasures tend to be "preventive" in nature. Electronic measures, such as access control mechanisms, firewalls, or intrusion detection systems, are examples of this. The whole point of a countermeasure is to mitigate attacks before they can do much damage. In practical terms, this means that existing vulnerabilities must be identified and either patched or eliminated as they are discovered. Operationally, this approach relies on the formal segmentation of the organization's information processing and data communications functions, which is typically referred to as defense-in-depth.

The goal of a defense-in-depth architecture is to prevent intruders from exploiting other areas of the system if one element is breached. The strategy focuses on controlling access through multiple perimeters. This arrangement has been termed a "defense-in-depth." For example, the tangible components in a segmented network topology are the routers and firewalls that secure the perimeter of each layer.

A risk analysis is always necessary to identify the specific risks to a particular given segment of a system or network, its equipment, resources, and its data. That activity involves identifying and labeling the organizational assets in that layer, or segment, and arraying them into an asset baseline. Then, each baseline is assessed and prioritized to determine the appropriate level of protection to be applied to it. Detailed actions are then documented, which will be used to secure each layer, including the baseline sensitivity level, the degree of assessed risk, and the specific mitigation scheme.

Once a set of mitigations is determined for each layer or segment, the next step is to identify the various types of users and their privileges within that space. The degree of potential compromise will depend significantly on the types and levels of privilege assigned to individual users. Their access requirements will determine the placement of that layer, or segment, within the overall defense-in-depth scheme. For instance, users with a high level of privilege will require more powerful countermeasures than users with lesser privileges. The five most common types of users (in descending order of priority) are:

1. Administrators are responsible for the management of network resources.
2. Privileged internal users with a need for an elevated level of access.
3. Internal users with general access.
4. Trusted external users with a need to access some resources.
5. Other untrusted external users or customers.

Perhaps the easiest way to illustrate this is from a physical network topology standpoint. The outermost layer, or segment of a network, constitutes the dividing point between the assets that the organization wishes to control and the ones that it does not protect. Within that perimeter, each succeeding layer, or segment, would imply increasing levels of investment in countermeasures.

In electronic data interchange terms, boundaries are established at the point that separates a more trusted network from a less trusted one and, so, the outermost perimeter of the organization's network is by definition the most insecure part. That is because it is the area that is the easiest to gain access to and thus it is the point that is most frequently attacked. For that common sense reason, then, sensitive organizational information should never be placed close to the boundaries of the system. Instead, sensitive information should always sit behind the maximum practical number of firewalls and behavioral filters.

Because it involves the use of technology, the cybersecurity operation must have the ability to monitor, control, and rationally evaluate and evolve the configuration of its software and hardware components over time. Likewise, proper protection procedures must be maintained in light of developing best practices. Naturally, there are several elements encompassed by this process, but the primary issues are those of trust, boundaries, assumptions, and human factors.

ENSURING TRUST

Given the purpose of the overall cybersecurity assurance process, the first issue that must be addressed is how to deal with trusted, untrusted, and unknown entities. This is the essential decision factor in maintaining any security operation, as the primary purpose of a formal protection process is to ensure the organization's assets are protected against access by untrusted entities. The ideal is to maintain an accurate understanding of the entities that can be trusted.

Trusted entities are the ones that have been adequately vetted and assigned access privileges. In practical terms, this means that these are the elements that have access rights within the organization's own security scheme. Therefore, by definition, a trusted entity can be allowed to cross the defined security perimeter of a layer or segment.

Untrusted entities are any person or process that has not been vetted and assigned access rights, and are untrusted because their trustworthiness is questionable, by definition. Moreover, although an organization might still communicate with an untrusted entity, it needs to be specifically protected from possible harm that might originate from that untrusted source. That is why firewalls are set on the perimeter of a trusted layer, or segment. The purpose of these utilities is to filter incoming access requests or information from untrusted sources and take a specified action. For instance, if a request has been blacklisted, it is automatically denied.

Unknown entities are neither trusted nor untrusted; therefore, a decision must be made about their status and rights. Because they are unknown, it is not possible to automatically respond to the request. In most cases, the proper approach is to handle unknown requests in the same manner as untrusted ones.

However, there are built-in responses to most eventualities in the case of access attempts from untrusted entities, because the likely threat is known and specific actions to mitigate it have already been defined. That is not the case with unknown entities, so their access requests are always treated with the most significant degree of restriction.

THE EIGHT GENERIC ELEMENTS OF CONTROL

A threat is a potential danger that could exploit a vulnerability to compromise security. A threat can be either intentional, e.g., an individual cracker or a criminal organization, or accidental, encompassing the possibility of a computer malfunction, a natural disaster, or an unanticipated circumstance, capability, action, or event. ISO 27005 defines threat as a potential cause of an incident that may result in harm to systems and the organization. FIPS 200 describes it as any circumstance or event that has the potential to adversely impact an organization's operations, including its mission, functions, image, or reputation.

The potential for theft or damage of critical data always exists if there isn't a rigorous and practical control process in place to mitigate the circumstance. Thus, the holistic security operations function ensures and maintains assurance that no sensitive information is released without authorization and that any released information has been adequately validated for correctness and accuracy.

The complete set of best practice controls can be factored into eight generic countermeasure areas, which can subsequently be organized into two subdomains. The first sub-domain encompasses all of the traditional technical control areas. These are deliberately focused on securing the electronic attack surface and are generally wholly electronic. As we mentioned, they tend to be viewed as part of the entire cybersecurity operation because they are visible to end users and have a strictly digital focus. These are:

1. Network and communication security countermeasures
2. Application and system software security countermeasures
3. Encryption measures

The second sub-domain is less conventional, but it is nonetheless essential. These are the environmental, contextual, and behavioral countermeasures that the organization establishes to address non-electronic attacks on both human and physical attack surfaces, such as phishing or physical theft. Those fall into five generic categories:

1. Business continuity and disaster recovery planning
2. Legal and regulatory compliance
3. Secure software assurance

4. Personnel security assurance
5. Physical security assurance

Just as electronic controls must be explicitly specified, designed, and substantively implemented, the behavioral controls in these two subdomains also need to be documented to achieve their specified purpose. All these control areas aim to ensure rational and interoperable assurance of the organization as a whole.

DOMAIN ONE – ELECTRONIC SECURITY: ENSURING THE USUAL LIST OF SUSPECTS

Correct your mistake as soon as you have found it.

—Sun Tzu

Electronic security relies on concepts that implement trustworthy systems. These concepts are generally based on science developed in the 19th century, which have been used since that period to define the basic shape of operating systems and application protection. In that regard, secure operating systems embed functionality in the system kernel that enforces security policies in conventional use.

Electronic security is enabled by rigorous control over the enterprise's software assets and the cross-referencing of what each electronic function will do to ensure the business purpose. This leads to the conceptualization and documentation of a functional security profile for each piece of software running in the system, including the software that supports external data communication. Those profiles characterize every adverse event, and an explicit set of electronic controls must be prescribed to counter each relevant threat to the business purpose.

Both physical and logical resources can contain one or more vulnerabilities that a threat agent could exploit. Due to intentional or unintentional dependencies, those agents can potentially compromise the confidentiality, integrity, or availability of resources other than the resource that is vulnerable to attack. A threat is active when it attempts to alter system resources or affect their operation. A "passive threat" attempts to learn or make use of information from the system without affecting system resources, thereby compromising confidentiality.

Since passwords are the most widely used countermeasure for ensuring confidentiality, password cracking is perhaps the most common method of exploitation. Password cracking, also known as "guessing," is the process of recovering passwords from a system as a means of gaining unauthorized access. The brute-force attack is the most common example of a cracking exploit. Brute force attacks attempt every conceivable iteration of a password – such as AAAA, AAAB, etc. – until the right combination is found. Obviously, this approach requires computer support for the entry process.

Another popular example is MAC spoofing. The process of masking a MAC address is known as MAC spoofing. Essentially, MAC spoofing involves altering a computer's MAC address for nefarious purposes. MAC spoofing changes the factory-assigned Media Access Control (MAC) address of a network interface controller (NIC) to fool an operating system into believing that the attacker's network interface has the target's MAC address. This obviously requires tools and sometimes direct access to the machine.

A zero-day (also known as zero hour or 0-day) vulnerability is an undisclosed and uncorrected computer application vulnerability that could be used to exploit the computer's programs, data, or additional computers on a network. It is known as a "zero-day" vulnerability because once a flaw becomes publicly known, the programmer or developer has zero days to fix it before disclosure. Zero-day attacks can occur because a vulnerability window exists between the time a threat is released and the time security vendors release patches to address it. Thus, zero-day attacks are a severe threat.

Additionally, there are internet bots, also known as bots. These are software applications that run automated tasks over the Internet. Typically, bots perform tasks that are both simple and structurally repetitive, at a much higher rate than would be possible for a human alone. Bots are used for the coordination and operation of automated attacks on networked computers, such as denial-of-service attacks by botnets. Victims acquire a bot by clicking on a link that appears harmless but is actually designed to install the attack software surreptitiously.

Often, the only way an organization will know it is under attack is from suspicious behavior in the system's operation. The following are examples of warning indicators: Suspicious e-mail – may include bad grammar, misspellings, and/or generic greetings. These are designed to appear as if they come from a position of authority or a legitimate company. However, they contain maliciously crafted attachments with varying file extensions or links to a malicious website. The suspicious message will ask the user to update or validate information, or click on a link, and it threatens dire consequences or promises a reward. The effects of any of these attacks include, but are not limited to:

- Corrupt files and destroyed or modified information
- Compromise and loss of information
- Hacker access and sabotaged systems
- Being placed in a Bot

Microsoft has proposed a general classification structure for cyber threats. The model is called STRIDE, derived from the initials of the threat categories: Spoofing, Tampering, Repudiation, Information Disclosure, Denial of Service, and Elevation of Privilege. In conjunction with this, Microsoft proposed a risk rating called DREAD. The DREAD name comes from the initials of the five categories listed.

- Damage – how bad would an attack be?
- Reproducibility – how easy is it to reproduce the attack?
- Exploitability – how much work is it to launch the attack?
- Affected users – how many people will be impacted?
- Discoverability – how easy is it to discover the threat?

When a given threat is assessed using DREAD, each category is given a rating – for example, 3 for high, 2 for medium, 1 for low, and 0 for none. The sum of all ratings for a given exploit can be used to prioritize among different exploits.

Artificial intelligence (AI) applications are the most recent solutions for managing the constant electronic threats to a network. That is because AI enables advanced situational awareness by providing early identification of anomalous behavior and data-driven support for accurate decision-making, leading to timely deployment of threat-mitigating actions. AI applications offer automated intelligence gathering and comprehensive methodologies for real-time monitoring, including advanced techniques such as behavioral modeling and threat analytics. Adverse actions against a computer or network system can typically be classified into one of the categories below:

Backdoors in a computer system, a cryptosystem, or an algorithm are any secret method of bypassing standard authentication or security controls. They may exist for several reasons, including original design or poor configuration.

Spoofing of user identity describes a situation in which one person or program successfully masquerades as another by falsifying data.

Tampering refers to the malicious modification of products. So-called "Evil Maid" attacks and security services' planting of surveillance capability into routers are examples.

Privilege escalation refers to a situation where an attacker with limited access can, without authorization, elevate their privileges or access level. For example, a standard computer user may be able to fool the system into granting them access to restricted areas, thereby reducing vulnerabilities.

Social engineering and direct computer access (physical) attacks can only be prevented by non-computer means, which can be difficult to enforce, relative to the sensitivity of the information.

Even in highly disciplined environments, such as military organizations, social engineering attacks can still be challenging to foresee and prevent. It is possible to reduce an attacker's chances by keeping systems up to date with security patches and updates, using a security scanner, and/or hiring competent personnel responsible for security.

Characterizing the threat environment

Generally, the profession refers to the process of considering the impact of the threat environment on a given situation as "threat modeling." Threat modeling is a methodology that allows organizations to optimize the electronic cybersecurity by identifying and associating vulnerabilities with business objectives. That lets the organization visualize and deploy the appropriate countermeasures for each relevant threat.

Within the context of a threat model, a threat is any potential or actual adverse event that can compromise an enterprise's assets, including both malicious events and unplanned occurrences. The key to threat modeling is determining where the most effort should be applied to sustain a secure response. This is a variable outcome that changes as new factors develop and become known, applications are added, removed, or upgraded, and user requirements evolve. Thus, threat modeling is a continuously iterative process that consists of:

- The explicit definition of business assets
- The cross-referencing of what each application does to each asset
- The creation of an explicit profile of security functions for each application
- The identification of potential threats
- The prioritization of potential threats
- Documenting adverse events and the actions that each controls to mitigate them

The most significant challenge in real-world cybersecurity operations is the constantly evolving nature of the threat environment. The traditional approach to this has been to focus the most resources on the most crucial system components, thereby addressing the most dangerous threats naturally. This approach, however, requires leaving some less important system components undefended and some less critical threats unaddressed.

Such an approach struggles in the current environment. The problem is that threats change faster than our understanding of the risk. Thus, the profession is promoting a more proactive and adaptive approach to dealing with the current environment. For example, NIST has issued updated guidelines for its risk assessment framework. Special Publication 800-53A, "Guidance for Assessing the Security Controls in Federal Information Systems and

Organizations/Building Effective Security Assessment Plans." This advice marks a shift in emphasis to enterprise-wide, near-time risk management in dynamic environments.

The International Organization for Standardization (ISO) has also issued a revised five-step Risk Management Standard (ISO 31000). ISO 31000 defines risk management as "a set of components that provide the foundations and organizational arrangements for designing, implementing, monitoring, reviewing, and continually improving risk management throughout the organization." It recommends a five-step approach that is particularly relevant to a discussion about enterprise security. These recommendations mirror the best generic practice methods for each cybersecurity function. Therefore, we will use them to illustrate the process:

Step 1: Establish the context – document the organization's core business objectives and define how holistic control supports them.
Step 2: Identify the risks – create a comprehensive list of potential hazards. Risks not identified at this stage will not be analyzed or evaluated later on, so having an overly exhaustive list is preferable to one that is too limited.
Step 3: Analyze the risks – understand criticality and impact. It is possible to leverage the business impact analysis work done by the business continuity team to fill in some of the gaps.
Step 4: Evaluate the risks – characterize the residual level of risk after control treatments have been assessed. Specifically identify any remaining risks that fall outside the organization's risk tolerance, as these will require further treatment decisions. The business's risk appetite and thresholds will provide guidelines for when to avoid, accept, share, transfer, or mitigate risks.
Step 5: Treat the risks – design and implement controls to reduce threats to the organization's achievement of its business objectives and protection strategy. Many risks will require more than one control, such as policies, training, and prevention measures, in order to decrease their expected likelihood and/or impact.

Conversely, some controls may mitigate more than one risk. The notion of "coupling together" the risk controls of various systems as they interoperate must guide this process. The goal is to evaluate risks more holistically. The reality, though, is that we can't move as fast as the threat can push us, so we will always be forced to play catch-up. That's a continuous process. Hence, there has to be a mechanism to make change control more dynamic.

The need for continuous security monitoring and control of an organization's systems is what justifies the electronic elements of the holistic security process. Every control is a consciously designed and deployed condition, strictly aimed at ensuring the trustworthiness of some aspect of the organization across the board. The holistic security process builds the foundation of trust by leveraging the technology's ability to preserve the ongoing confidentiality, integrity, and availability of an organization's virtual assets.

The role of layering

Layering is the practical outcome of segmentation. The concept of layered defenses applies to technological security in much the same way as it applies to the assurance of any physical space, such as a castle. The whole purpose of a defense in depth is to prevent one compromised element from contaminating another part of the system. Functional decomposition is the essence of defense in depth, which is relatively easy to implement when designing a castle, but much more challenging when the medium is electronic and the protection objects are virtual. Therefore, this process should be considered an elegant design exercise.

It would seem to be a simple thing to pre-program the appropriate access decision onto every interface since an interface aims to ensure that every access point, between every defined compartment, is intelligently secured. However, because software systems are both abstract and very complex, the difficulty lies in ensuring that every interface is identified, which is a daunting task in itself, and then adequately safeguarded from every conceivable threat.

In general, the only way to ensure this is through the proper initial design of every electronic control component. Therefore, at the beginning of application development, potential protection requirements must be identified and documented for each module and every interface. Then, adequate security mitigations must be formally specified and coded to address each identified security concern. This is the "baking it in" aspect of the application development process.

Traditional architectural issues, such as complexity and temporal constraints – e.g., real-time demands, interrupt and error handling, and exception handling – must be considered and resolved as part of secure system design. This must then be substantively embodied in code to ensure the system's security.

In practice, developing an effective electronic response requires the designer to identify all relevant issues and then program an appropriate security response. To achieve this, the system's structure must be thoroughly understood, which underscores the importance of formal software engineering methods in the development process. Complex security requirements are established and enforced through formal specification.

This approach is currently the most effective way to ensure that the security response incorporates all the necessary security functionality. It enables the designer to provide a high level of confidence that a component or system will not fail or be breached within a specified period of time in a given environment. The term "robustness" is used to describe that outcome. The "given time" part of the assurance can represent various conditions, such as the number of executions, the number of lines of code traversed, or simply the time elapsed on a wall clock.

The environment is always dependent on external criteria, which are typically dynamic. Currently, most estimates of a system's robustness are based on the various types of tests used to ensure it. Running through a set of testing assumptions can surface the most common problems. However, as the technology matures, causal analysis should also be undertaken.

Causal analysis enables testers to predict points of failure. Causal analysis does not simply test a piece of software to see whether it fails. It looks at the software's structural and development characteristics to identify conditions that are predictive of vulnerability. This technique utilizes historical data, as well as the occurrence of defects, to identify root causes.

The simplest and most effective way to obtain a reliability estimate is to model system behavior. This allows the designer to infer the precise level of assurance from the system's structural characteristics. The ability to do that rests on the use of proper measurement techniques. Good data collected through a standardized measurement process can be turned into a quantitative assurance model.

A quantitative assurance model employs stochastic processes, probability, and statistics to estimate the potential reliability of a given piece of software. These models rely on maximum likelihood estimates, numerical methods, and confidence intervals to underwrite those assumptions. The actual criteria that are used to formulate this are always defined based on stakeholder input as it applies to the environment. One of the more common ways to do this is through fault tree analysis of the sequence and combination of events to identify what might have caused a given failure.

Responding forcefully to attempted security breaches in the same manner as you would to attempted physical security breaches is often very difficult for a variety of reasons. First, identifying attackers is difficult, as they are often in a different jurisdiction from the systems they are attempting to breach. Secondly, they operate through proxies, temporary anonymous accounts, wireless connections, and other anonymizing procedures, which make backtracing difficult. If they successfully breach security, they are often able to delete logs to cover their tracks.

In addition, identifying attackers across a network may require logs from various points in the network. In many countries, the release of these records to law enforcement requires a search warrant. Thus, depending on the circumstances, the legal proceedings can be drawn out to the point where the records are either regularly purged or the information is no longer relevant. Plus, there are always budgetary constraints. The sheer number of attempted attacks is so significant that organizations cannot spend time pursuing every attacker.

Sustaining the attack surface control architecture

Much of the process of assuring the electronic attack surface lies in ensuring the proper configuration and operation of the functions that underlie the organization's embedded computer and network operating systems. Programmed entities enable all of digital computing. These are the system control elements that launch and coordinate the information processing activity. They comprise the installed applications, which are put in place to accomplish the organization's business purpose, the operating system, and the embedded firmware.

These programmed utilities all have a range of purposes. One of these is to provide a set of pre-programmed, automated security functionalities. These functions are generally transparent to the end-user, so they are built into the application, or the operating system/firmware as a set of utilities that launch and run in the background of conventional computer use.

The system administrator then must configure the operation and interaction of those utilities to serve the requirements of the particular situation. The general term to describe this work is system management, or system operations, and the range of potential applications involved is as endless as the commercial market is wide.

Hence, ensuring the secure operation of whatever has been installed on a particular digital device is a constant responsibility, as the application and system software evolve and threats emerge and subside. But there is a straightforward requirement that underlies all of this activity, and which must be ensured as a precondition to any next steps. That involves maintaining trust in the confidentiality and integrity of the data by controlling access privileges for files, directories, devices, and other data or code resident on the system.

Once appropriate access is granted, the session is monitored and controlled by the operating system to ensure continuing compliance. That function is based on established policies and any other relevant conditions that might apply to a given situation. This provides a very high degree of organizational control at the automatic, or system level, because it guarantees that access rights will be directly managed by explicit policies embedded in the central software kernel of the system.

In addition to the focused assurance that this provides, the benefit of embedding security policy directly into the system's functioning is that it makes system resource utilization much more efficient. Building security in means that it is not necessary to invoke a separate program or application when technical protection criteria are evaluated.

The most basic software countermeasure is an application firewall. That utility limits the execution of files or the handling of data by specific programs that are installed on the system. Other countermeasures include

- Conventional firewalls
- Encryption/decryption programs
- Anti-virus programs
- Spyware detection/removal programs
- Biometric authentication systems.

The standard electronic security mechanism for monitoring threats as data passes between layers or segments is the generic firewall. Firewalls embody a defined set of policies that can be implemented in hardware, software, or both. The policies that guide them should state that firewalls will be used to limit access to only required traffic in specified enclaves. For instance, in a database segment, the only traffic that should be allowed is simple communication to and from the endpoint and the database, as per a well-defined communication protocol. Any other type of traffic would be blocked.

The details behind firewall settings at each layer, or segment where they are employed, will be subject to oversight. But this is always a management-based decision, not something made at the information technology operation level. Because firewalls are an essential security device, changes to firewall rules should be approved and implemented in production via a change control board process, just like all other production changes. That level of scrutiny and control will prevent unauthorized changes to firewalls and their protection.

Up to this point, we have been talking about security perimeters between layers, or segments. Boundaries are important because they define the area that must be protected – e.g., protected space, and, as a result, they dictate the degree of actual organizational resource investment that is required to perform the security function.

Extensive boundaries imply a significant resource commitment, while narrower boundaries may require fewer resources. Therefore, the process of boundary setting is an essential part of practical holistic security consideration. The goal of holistic security is to ensure that every security policy is consistently enforced. To do this properly, it is essential to set the protection perimeter in a way that allows for the implementation of defined policies.

To ensure that resources align with the sensitivity requirements of the information, it may be necessary to create a series of interconnected perimeters within the overall system to accommodate the different types of data. If the overall protection scheme contains multiple perimeters, it is referred to as a defense-in-depth. It is called that because several perimeter defenses must be breached for harm to occur. These can be set to enforce a different degree of security depending on what they are intended to protect.

The critical role of assessment

A change in the threat environment is one of the scariest aspects of holistic security. That statement particularly applies to the electronic component, because the continuously moving technological leading edge will always produce new threats over time, thereby making an organization that doesn't accommodate change less secure, since the lack of response to an increasingly dangerous threat environment is a recipe for security lapses.

Even with good architecture, a strong set of controls, and professional operators, the holistic solution will develop holes over time that adversaries can exploit. These holes may be the result of obsolete technologies or an artifact of new, but untested technologies. Either way, the only way to stay on top of the current state of electronic security is through a series of regularly scheduled technical evaluations.

These evaluations verify designs, configurations, and operation of the electronic component of the holistic solution. In addition to routine verification and validation, there are proactive actions that are conventionally referred to as penetration testing, or pen testing for short.

This type of additional assurance is essential. That is because pen tests evaluate the resiliency of the solution against a known set of attack vectors. To facilitate this, a select number of test points and tests are chosen for penetration testing. Specific attacks are launched at these selected points to test for specific vulnerabilities. The results of these tests should verify that the electronic solution is, at a minimum, capable of detecting an adverse event and blocking its ability to compromise the system.

Therefore, running a regular set of penetration test evaluations, at least annually, should be undertaken, with the results communicated to senior management. The real-world nature of the assessment provides substantive verification of the state of the electronic security scheme, at least for the assessment points and tests chosen.

The specific set of tests and points will vary based on previous test results and the critical information associated with a layer or segment. In addition to the periodic pen tests, other reporting opportunities can be utilized to verify network security performance.

Finally, like all other electronic systems, the entire security function should be subjected to a standard internal audit. These audits are used to verify that specified controls are in place, operating correctly, and achieving the business purpose for which they are intended. These periodic audits can verify policies, from simple password policies to complex firewall and IDS rules and provide feedback on the status of the systems as configured. Internal audits can also verify that internal business processes are correctly aligned with the overall security function and that all specified controls are operating as intended and designed.

DOMAIN TWO – BEHAVIORAL SECURITY: ADDRESSING THE HARD PROBLEMS

Know yourself and you will win all battles.

—Sun Tzu

Holistic security is comprehensive security. That is, it is crucial to identify and seal off any unsecured point of potential harm. Electronic security, which is what most people think of when they discuss the cybersecurity function, addresses the newest and, in some respects, the most mysterious aspect of that protection problem. However, it does not, as we have said throughout this text, address obvious points of vulnerability that, by definition, demand a solution. Hence, there is a second domain centered on human behavior that must be mitigated to achieve complete and trustworthy assurance.

Behavioral security revolves around the steps that the organization takes to define a response that is adequately tailored to the specific situation, along with the attendant countermeasures and system management processes necessary to ensure a coordinated organizational control system. That applies to all operational aspects of the business, ranging from strategic policies to routine procedures. As we said, this entire area is based on best practice rather than any form of physical science.

In addition to the necessary technical countermeasures discussed in the prior section, a holistic solution will comprehensively address the organization-wide, strategic, and contextual concerns associated with big-picture legal and regulatory compliance and business continuity, along with instituting effective control over personnel and physical space. The integration of these behavioral control processes with an electronic response is what we refer to as holistic protection.

Cybersecurity systems are a combination of technology, people, and business practices. Each of these entities has a distinct purpose and contributes differently to the ultimate goal of a secure organization. The holistic security process blends the most effective control actions from each of these domains into a single, organized response. Implementing the right mix of security controls requires a delicate balance. Therefore, practical success entails understanding the essential elements and their interrelationships.

As a result, this part of the discussion is based on two fundamental principles. First, written, spoken, and electronic information has intrinsic value. Therefore, any loss of information is a loss to the corporation. Second, the protection of those assets must be continuous. Therefore, holistic security is a systematic and operational process that is integrated into the day-to-day operations of the business. Consequently, it must be designed to address the priority problems in the organizational environment.

Because any attempt to secure intangible assets, in whatever form they may exist – virtual, documentary, or physical – holistic assurance requires a single, coherent approach that builds and maintains a comprehensive and coordinated infrastructure of tangible controls. The reliability of these controls must be objectively demonstrated, and they must continuously evolve to meet the changing environment.

The strategy that implements this must address all security threat requirements – not just the ones that are convenient – but also be systematic and maintainable, as a long-term solution, and directly support and be traceable to the requirements of the business case. The second assumption mandates that security is conducted as a continuous process. As a consequence, "partial" assurance is not an acceptable state.

Hence, the reliability of the security system can be judged by whether all necessary safeguards are in place and operating correctly at all times. That state of continuous assurance requires a deliberately designed architecture of processes and controls, which are all planned, fully integrated, and economically feasible.

The strategy must ensure a trustworthy, fully integrated, long-term assurance capability. In that respect, then, the system must be rationally evolved to meet the changing needs of the environment. Therefore, a proper holistic solution must merge all requisite practices and technical controls into a single, coordinated approach.

However, there are three actual focuses for that control set. First, the controls must ensure the business against large-scale environmental or societal disasters. Then there are the traditional control areas that focus on creating both human and physical security. Finally, because all virtual operations rest on a software base, there is a hybrid technological area aimed at ensuring the organization's code.

The two most significant areas, continuity and compliance, are strategic in nature and focus on big-picture questions, such as disaster planning and ensuring that the organization has met all externally mandated compliance requirements. The traditional areas are focused entirely on ensuring secure conduct within the organization, both among employees and any visitors allowed beyond the security perimeter. Thus, an integrated set of personnel and physical security controls ensures the human behavior and physical assets of the organization.

The last area, secure software assurance, addresses a technological issue by ensuring the absence of exploitable defects in code. That might appear to be a technological activity. Nonetheless, secure software assurance is a collection of best practices that are executed as a systematic and disciplined process. Consequently, it belongs with the controls associated with behavioral security.

All of these areas require designed practices that are carefully aligned with the business purpose, as well as substantive controls that have been established to achieve the planned purposes. Every control must be fully integrated into a synergistic array of mutually supporting security actions that interoperate with the electronic elements of the system to achieve a fully protected organizational environment. The design of this array and its interrelation with the electronic control set is the true art of cybersecurity.

CREATING A SUSTAINABLE ENTERPRISE: CONTINUITY AND COMPLIANCE

It is more important to outthink your enemy than it is to outfight him.

—**Sun Tzu**

THE CONTINUITY PROCESS

Continuity is critical because organizations have built their core functions around the management of information. At the same time, the world is full of threats. Modern continuity processes encompass strategies and steps to ensure the organization's survival in the event of a disaster. This is built around contingency plans that outline the steps to be taken in the event of a disaster. These continuity plans preserve the organization's essential information assets.

The operative word here is the term "essential." Continuity only seeks to preserve assets that are essential to the continued operation of the business purpose. As such, continuity involves three specific activities:

1. Identifying just those information elements needed to return to a predefined operational status.
2. Deciding on the scenarios that might actually cause harm to each of those information elements.
3. Estimating the harm that would result, from which you will get your priorities.

The continuity process is a planned and disciplined organizational response that applies only if other safeguards fail. Hence, continuity is strictly focused on preserving business value. This approach makes the continuity process both proactive and reactive, as the primary goal is to ensure the uninterrupted operation in the event of an interruption.

For example, it makes no difference whether the reason for the disruption was hacker penetration or a force five hurricane; the consequence is the loss of business value for the duration of the stoppage. Thus, continuity seeks to ensure that the effect is minimized, regardless of the cause, to the extent that it maximizes the business purpose.

Because the causes of loss are by definition speculative, all threat assessments are scenario-based. As a result, all continuity planning is built around contingency plans. Logically, the only way to ensure the timeliness and integrity of the response is through good up-front planning. Thus, the preparedness plan outlines a precise set of actions to be taken in the event of a specified disaster. That preparedness plan itemizes the policies and procedures to prevent or minimize damage, as well as the steps to secure or recover organizational information in the event of a harmful incident.

The guiding considerations in contingency planning are timeliness and feasibility. That is because there are an infinite number of threats and a limited amount of resources. Time is the critical decision factor because it represents a real loss of value. That is ... essential systems and the information that they contain must resume operation within a specified period of time, or business value is lost.

Hence, continuity has two goals: to ensure the shortest possible interruption time in the event of a particular occurrence. And also ensure the integrity of the protected information at a specified point in time. The first step in making that assurance is to understand and prioritize the asset base. This is always referenced to the business value and the risks associated with each asset.

In that respect, the continuity process is the necessary lifeboat for any business. It positions the organization to recover lost assets in the event of a disaster. It also entails plans to ensure the continuous availability of the physical components of the system, as well as the ongoing integrity of the information asset itself.

COMPLIANCE

Compliance is any formal process that ensures the requirements of a specification, terms of a contract, law, regulation, or standard are satisfied. Compliance is essential to any organization because it safeguards against the business harm that might result from either intentionally or unintentionally violating a formal mandate. The fact that we find ourselves discussing legal compliance in a book about cybersecurity may be a surprise to traditional practitioners, especially those who concentrate solely on electronic security. However, violations of the terms or conditions of a law, regulation, or contract can bring significant harm to the organization.

That is because litigation is the typical consequence of a failure to comply. As a result, deliberately planned and implemented steps to ensure compliance are an important aspect of protecting the business and its assets from harm.

In practice, the term "compliance" applies to any formally implemented and executed set of actions that ensure fulfillment of the terms of a contract, law, regulation, or standard. Thus, the term "compliance process" describes the organization's formal approach to ensuring conformance with applicable laws, regulations, and contracts.

Compliance processes are an important part of day-to-day cybersecurity operations, because the consequences of non-compliance can be severe.

A failure to comply does not affect the information asset itself. Instead, the harm that ensues from non-compliance affects the organization as a whole. For instance, the incorporation of a few lines of code into a product, which actually belong to somebody else can lead to millions of dollars in fines, plus whatever civil penalties that ensue.

Thus, the unfortunate fact is that whether a violation is intentional or not, companies that fail to comply are legally bound to suffer the consequences. For example, one way that an organization can violate a law is through the illegal use of software. Thus, it is not unusual to hear of settlements in the millions if the violation is company-wide in a major corporation.

The consequences of non-compliance are substantive, and the issue cannot be ignored or left to chance. Thus, every prudent organization must formulate and execute a disciplined process that ensures, with certainty, the identification and elimination of legal violations and non-compliances. Generally, companies that want to ensure compliance must:

- Safeguard Internet users against malicious actions by totally anonymous people.
- Ensure intellectual property rights where there is no real property.
- Investigate crimes where the item that was stolen remains with the owner.
- Maintain confidentiality where the boundaries are unclear.

All of these issues are starting to see regulation, and the outcomes will eventually be factored into all assurance solutions. As such, the factors associated with ensuring adequate legal and regulatory compliance must be understood.

Most of the laws and regulations that have been passed so far concern protecting privacy or ensuring that adequate measures are in place to safeguard virtual systems, for instance, FISMA (2002). They can be classified into four generic categories.

1. Governmental regulations
2. Privacy regulations
3. Laws that regulate computer crime
4. Laws that regulate classified or sensitive information.

Because the legal consequences can be severe, a prudent organization will try to anticipate legal threats. This is typically achieved by instituting routine, best practice-based assurance procedures, which can be proven sufficient to satisfy the due diligence requirement in negligence litigation. However, in addition to the general risk, several specific laws impact privacy, such as HIPAA.

Compliance with any formal law or regulation has to be factored into the equation. Many of them concern defining the rights of individuals to ensure confidentiality. That implies deliberately applied best practice actions to address the stipulations of a given law or regulation. Violations of these can lead to specific penalties, so their dictates must be carefully considered and understood.

Although conformity with legal and regulatory requirements is the most visible aspect of compliance, it is not the most common instance of this activity. That distinction goes to contract compliance. That is because in the real world, most work is done through contracts. That contract might be explicit, or it might be an implicit agreement between an internal customer and an in-house unit. In every case, however, a legally binding agreement of some type is written to specify how the work is to be performed. The role of compliance is to ensure that those terms have been fulfilled.

Because a contract can be made for practically any product or service, there is no single way to define how compliance should be ensured. However, the governing principles are contained in the body of law that defines the rights and obligations of parties who enter into agreements. This is called contract law. The precise responsibilities of all parties are spelled out there. That agreement is then enforced through systematic reviews or audits. Consequently, increasingly rigorous reviews are the traditional method for ensuring legal and regulatory compliance in day-to-day contract management.

ENSURING SECURE SPACE: PERSONNEL AND PHYSICAL SECURITY

> *When the leader is morally weak and his discipline not strict, when his instructions and guidance are not enlightened, when there are no consistent rules, neighboring rulers will take advantage of this.*
>
> —**Sun Tzu**

SECURING THE ORGANIZATION'S PEOPLE

In the case of holistic security, the organized personnel security function embodies a formal set of policies and procedures to assure the actions of the people who work within the organization. This set of organizationally developed and sanctioned statements defines the explicit security responsibilities of all individuals, as well as their resulting accountabilities.

The purpose of a personnel security process is to define the specific actions that must be performed by each individual to achieve satisfactory levels of assurance. These can be classified into three generic categories: routine functions, operational duties, and management responsibilities. It is necessary to document an adequate definition and the required set of actions for each of these areas to ensure an appropriate level of security.

Routine functions protect the computer and its data from threats that may arise from day-to-day activities. These can involve such humble activities as safe housekeeping procedures, which are designed to protect computer equipment or media against petty theft. They can also involve complex technical duties, such as ensuring that the operating system and network are properly configured.

Operational duties, as the name implies, underwrite the day-to-day functioning of the system. This is not a matter of preventative maintenance. It entails monitoring staff activities to ensure that secure work practices are being followed, as well as continuous monitoring of the system to prevent misuse.

Finally, there is the requirement that the personnel security operation must be managed appropriately. So, actions in this category guarantee that the personnel security strategy is implemented correctly. Practices can include taking steps to ensure that each business unit follows the required security procedures. However, they can also include such complex tasks as strategic planning to secure an organization's information function.

Documenting security procedures

Both responsibility and associated accountability must be clearly stipulated to ensure that every individual understands their role and function in the process. Then, if an individual violates those policies, the predetermined accountabilities can be fairly enforced. The only way that a business can establish accountability is through the documentation process. Documentation assures that security activities are both recorded and understood on an ongoing basis. Obviously, as the first condition for doing that successfully, a complete and accurate set of procedures must exist. These are captured in a personnel security manual.

Once the manual has been prepared, it is circulated to everyone in the organization. This creates both a basis for feedback and an awareness of what needs to be done. Every individual in the organization should be able to contribute to the formulation of the official set of procedures, because that buy-in subsequently helps motivate their proper execution. The point is to ensure that every employee in the organization is informed about precisely what is expected of them. If that is the case, then the organization can hold each person accountable for the proper performance of their assigned security tasks.

Accountability is not meant to imply that every individual should be forced to memorize the procedure manual. It means that, at a minimum, everyone in the organization must be aware of the recommended practices that apply to their particular case. The idea is to prevent necessary housekeeping or management procedures from being omitted from an individual worker's daily routine. A procedure manual helps document the specific corrective actions that must be taken in the event of a problem. Obviously, these can only be related to known issues, but since those are the most likely to occur, this ensures that an optimum solution is always available.

For example, if there were frequent network failures, the availability of a proper recovery procedure would ensure that it was brought back into operation in the shortest possible time. At a minimum, every documented procedure should specify the:

- Required steps to be taken
- Expected outcomes and some way to determine that they have been achieved
- Interfaces with other security procedures

ASSIGNMENT OF INDIVIDUAL RESPONSIBILITY

Because consistent performance of security tasks is essential, selected managers must be held responsible for ensuring that all assigned duties are carried out as required. That is an oversight and enforcement function. It involves the explicit assignment of individual accountability and then the regular monitoring of routine security operations.

The rule of thumb is that specific accountability for security should be delegated, in writing, to every individual involved in the creation, handling, or use of an information item. Every designated worker must be trained and knowledgeable in all aspects of the technology used to perform those duties. Additionally, every worker should be kept up to date on all related practices. The aim is to ensure a comprehensive understanding of all security functions within the organization, including management control processes.

RULES OF BEHAVIOR

Personnel security is based on educating employees about what constitutes acceptable behavior. In particular, users must understand the consequences of non-compliance. This is communicated and enforced through rules of behavior. These convey the expected behaviors and accountabilities that apply to each user. Everybody needs to understand those rules before they are allowed to access the organization's information assets. These should be expressed in writing and be available to serve as the basis for security awareness and training operations.

Rules of behavior should clearly delineate the responsibilities and expectations for every individual who uses the system. These must be consistent with general system usage requirements and overall security policies. It is essential to define the thresholds of acceptable risk to adapt the required behavior to each worker properly. This implies that a risk analysis should always be undertaken before these rules are written.

The aim is to ensure that individual behaviors are correctly defined. These rules must take into consideration the requirements of both the people who use the system and the people it serves. They must be sufficiently rigorous to ensure the system's security, while allowing the user optimal flexibility to perform their job correctly. Rules of behavior should define the organizationally sanctioned response to such concerns as

- Individual accountability
- Assignment and limitation of system privileges
- Networking and use of the Internet

The level of rigor of these rules should be directly related to the type and degree of technical security that will be employed. Highly secure operations will utilize a significantly different rulebook than those with less stringent security requirements. Furthermore, both the rule and the reason for doing it must be made clear, particularly where technical constraints are involved. For instance, it is a source of confusion to users when, due to technical considerations, a particular length or form is mandated for a password. That is because most users like to use passwords that have meaning to them.

Therefore, when an employee's dog's name is no longer valid because the system requires eight digits and a number, the potential for unproductive time on the user's part, as well as security breaches, increases. Nevertheless, it can be assumed that if the security justification for restricting the user to a specific format is explained, then the user will be more likely to adapt to the constraint, for instance, by changing their pet's name to Rover101#.

It goes without saying that rules must be enforced. Employing system-based sanctions, such as the temporary or permanent loss of privileges, can ensure this. If such a harsh enforcement approach is used, rules should specifically state how a person whose privileges have been suspended can get them restored. In extreme cases, rules can be enforced through the organization's general disciplinary system. In that case, as with other rules of conduct, sanctions such as fines or dismissal can be imposed.

Individuals who are authorized to use the system but engage in improper activities can cause the most significant degree of harm. Those harmful actions can be intentional. But they can also be accidental. In either case, an appropriate set of technical, operational, and management controls should be developed to detect and prevent harm from its own employees.

PLANNING FOR PERSONNEL SECURITY

For the personnel security function to be most effective, the selected controls and their related procedures must be integrated into day-to-day operations.

That condition is best achieved by making personnel security planning an integral part of overall strategic planning. The goal is to ensure that the level of personnel security control corresponds to the likelihood of harm.

As we have frequently stated, the potential damage that could occur if the information asset is lost, misused, or corrupted by internal workers must be assessed, and a priority must be assigned for its protection. To do this properly, the practical cost of establishing and maintaining the control must be weighed against the likelihood of harm and the frequency of occurrence of each risk.

There are two areas that the personnel security planning function must address. First, the plan should outline the procedures necessary to ensure security in the staffing function. That includes establishing sufficient control over contractor, and/or subcontractor work to ensure that that element of the process is secure. Second, the plan should provide a comprehensive set of procedures to ensure that access to each type of employee is adequately monitored and controlled.

In most organizations, the practical responsibility for personnel security falls within the domain of the human resources function. That is why a single coordinating body with responsibility for holistic assurance is so critical for coordinating between organizational units. The goal of that entity must be to ensure that the human resources staff factors security issues into the process, specifically when hiring and orienting an employee.

Therefore, security considerations must be incorporated into the overall staffing process. The control points for employee hiring can be divided into four primary stages. The rules for each area apply equally to managers, system engineers, users, and even security personnel. The three critical staffing stages are:

1. Job definition
2. Clearance
3. Applicant screening and hiring

Job definition

When a new position is created, the first step is to embed the attendant security requirements in the position definition. That is, the type of sensitivity and the associated level of access required for the work must be unambiguously defined. This must be defined in a generic sense, as it will apply to anyone holding that position and supports the definition of the privileges associated with the position. It underwrites considerations related to the separation of duties.

The principle of separation of duties requires that the work be segmented in such a way that no individual has complete control over a protected process. For example, in most companies, the person initiating the request for a check is precluded from writing it. Instead, the party responsible for authorizations approves the other party's request. This type of control is embodied as a standard security procedure within each position.

Least privilege is a security principle that dictates that individual employees should only be granted the necessary access to perform their duties. For instance, a particular secretarial position might not run database integrity checks. Therefore, access to system-level functions would not be available. On the other hand, a secretary might be required to query the database, and that right would be built into the privileges assigned to that position.

Clearances

It is essential to specify the sensitivity level for every position created, as access to different information assets requires varying levels of security. The clearance level outlines the necessary security restrictions and the authorized access levels for the position. Individuals filling roles with high clearance requirements should always undergo extensive screening to determine whether they meet those criteria.

Controls should be assigned to each position based on the risks and potential injuries that might occur if a security breakdown associated with that role were to happen. It is essential to strike a proper balance of security controls to regulate this effectively. This balancing act is necessary to ensure the efficient day-to-day functioning of the position.

Applicant screening and hiring

Background screening enables the organization to confirm that the prospective employee meets the security criteria for a specific position. For extremely sensitive positions, this background check may involve formal investigations conducted by professional investigators. For most other positions, however, this typically results in nothing more than an electronic records check to confirm the basics of the individual's credentials.

Typical background checks examine aspects such as criminal history, which can be easily obtained from numerous record services. Other factors that might be examined include such things as

- Work history
- Educational history
- Interview or psychographic data
- Legal history
- Financial and/or credit history
- Medical history
- Immigration and/or internal revenue records
- Any observations about their overall behavior.

This degree of inquiry is necessary because employees who have a personal vulnerability are more easily compromised. Therefore, it is essential to ensure that individuals in sensitive positions are not vulnerable to blackmail. Requirements for the rigor of the screening are usually based on the level of sensitivity of the work. For instance, an employer is not likely to conduct an extensive background check for a janitor's position, unless it is located within a highly secure site.

SECURING THE ORGANIZATION'S PHYSICAL ASSETS

Physical security centers on controls to safeguard against physical threats. It is the function that protects facilities and equipment from deliberate or accidental harm from the environment. Some of the technology that underlies physical security, such as microwave intrusion detection, is highly advanced. However, most physical security concepts, such as secure areas and layered defenses, have been in use since the Roman era.

Because physical security seeks to protect tangible objects like equipment, its activities appear to be less "refined" than more exotic technical areas. Thus, in many organizations, physical security is administered separately from the cybersecurity function. That is a dysfunctional approach to assurance, since the access points that pose the greatest risk lie in the physical security domain. The fact is that physical access renders any other security measure ineffective.

No matter how impenetrable the firewall or IDS software, if an attacker can physically access the server, they can compromise it. Proximity enables attackers to accomplish various tasks. They can sit next to a server and run intrusion utilities against a network. Since they are internal, they are behind the firewall and are invisible to most security systems. Without control of the physical space, it is easier to steal the server than to hack into it. In addition, high-capacity memory sticks enable anyone with access to a USB port to download information in seconds. Or even worse, upload unapproved code or data to networks attached to the computer.

In an economic sense, the harm from a major physical disaster, such as a serious fire or flood, is much more catastrophic than the impact of a virus. Finally, because there are so many sources of breach, physical access control is much more involved than electronic access control. For instance, it is easy to monitor the comings and goings of users through a firewall. It is a different matter to ensure the perimeter integrity of every door and window in a large building.

It should be clear from these examples that physical security is both complex and essential to protecting the information asset. In this session, we examine each of the general areas of concern and suggest some fundamental approaches to safeguarding them. The first two factors that have to be understood are the problems of dispersion and diversity.

The problem of dispersion

The role of physical security is to account for and control tangible assets. With the advent of distributed systems, ensuring physical protection has become significantly more challenging. That is the case because network resources are now widely distributed, and that dispersion makes them much more challenging to secure.

Physical network equipment can extend over a wide area. For example, Internet communication originates outside the building. As such, the cable line the birds outside your window are sitting on, and the external interfaces, are just as much a part of your physical network as the modem itself. These external parts may be attacked much more easily than the parts of the system that you keep inside your building. So the question always is ... "Where do you draw the line in the case of physical security protection"?

The problem of diversity

Physical security assures diverse assets. As a case in point, potential targets for control include the obvious: hardware, facilities, equipment, and storage media. But what about the less obvious things, such as written documentation, plans, and agreements? Items in the latter category are likely to represent a more valuable resource than those in the former, and yet they are rarely considered in a physical protection scheme.

This varied collection also has different protection requirements. So, the organization must consciously decide how it will safeguard each of them. It is necessary to consider how each item is to be protected, as each has a distinct role and priority within the overall process. The starting point for that is the construction of an explicit physical asset accounting framework. That structure has to encompass the diverse physical resources of the organization.

This is based on maintaining a perpetual inventory of tangible assets under control, as well as rules for controlling each asset. With that inventory, it is necessary to establish a reliable and secure control perimeter that delineates items within the control structure as well as detailed procedures to guarantee the integrity of workspaces and physical resources within that boundary.

Secure perimeters

The only sure way to safeguard facilities is to create a secure space deliberately. That requires establishing a finite physical boundary and then deploying a set of countermeasures that can be expected to assure the integrity of that perimeter. The goal is to ensure that access to the equipment is controlled and that the organization can effectively respond to intrusions within the defined area.

While it is difficult to protect against every physical threat, there are basic steps that mitigate ordinary risks. That depends on the establishment of the space to be protected. Location is the primary determinant of physical security. It dictates the form of access control. For instance, if the computer is located in a locked office, the business will have to think less about its physical security than if it were sitting in the reception area.

So, the idea is to site equipment appropriately to the risks from unauthorized access. That requirement dictates that computer facilities should not be put in a prominent location in the building. That location should not be conspicuously marked. The principle behind the latter rule is that people authorized to access the system should know where it is located, and those who have not been granted permission should not. This serves as a de facto control technique.

Finally, the perimeter of that location should be formally defined and appropriately safeguarded by effective physical security mechanisms. If there is no clearly established secure area, then the likelihood of a threat increases. To some extent, access and control go hand in hand, as the primary purpose of physical security is to regulate access to secure spaces. In practice, access control is a significant security factor, and it can be a very involved process.

Access has to be granted and monitored. That is, it must be ensured that only the people who have been given access can enter a secure space. This is based on the rule that authorization to access is a privilege that is specifically assigned and enforced, rather than an absolute right. It can be enforced by simple measures, such as locking the door to the computer room and only giving the key to authorized individuals. Also, rules regarding violations of secure space must be enforced.

Implementing control

Control is the mechanism that enforces security. It is established by a formal set of rational controls, which are then monitored for compliance. There are simple mechanisms available to allow organizations to enforce physical controls, such as gates and guards. However, for more advanced requirements, a range of electronic access control mechanisms is available, including microwave monitoring, closed-circuit TV (CCTV), and access control biometrics.

ENSURING THE ORGANIZATION'S CODE

> *Management of many is the same as management of few. It is a matter of organization.*
>
> —Sun Tzu

The deliberate exploitation of programming defects is the most common threat factor for any digital system. Or, in simple terms, any exploitable defect in a software program will allow an attacker to compromise the confidentiality, integrity, or availability of any information that the program handles. There are so many defects in our current code that we need to improve our approach. Therefore, it can be reasonably stated that the security of an organization's information relies on enhancements in how programs are developed and managed.

Minor flaws in programming can lead to a range of adverse consequences, including the exploitation of buffer overflows or the execution of remote procedure calls. These factors can grant an attacker access to any information on a target computer or open the door to a range of malicious code attacks.

Hence, in this final section, we will examine the various methods for addressing software defects. We will demonstrate how the process of developing or acquiring software can cause defects to occur, and we will learn about common ways to identify and fix software defects before they become a source of compromise or exploitation.

The primary objective of software assurance is to identify and eliminate exploitable defects throughout the development, acquisition, and operation of software. Because of its complexity, this task is comparable to "finding a needle in a haystack." In fact, the more accurate analogy might be "finding a particular needle in a stack of needles," since it is almost impossible to tell the difference between secure code and insecure code in a properly running system. In conventional practice, software assurance guarantees that all instances of a software product are

- Trustworthy – there are no exploitable vulnerabilities, either maliciously or unintentionally inserted.
- Predictable – there is justifiable confidence that software, when executed, functions in the manner for which it is intended.
- Conformant – multidisciplinary practices are in place to ensure that software conforms to all requirements and applicable standards.

Ensuring these qualities is almost an impossible task, given the complexity of modern computer systems and the increasing tendency for organizations to develop software through global outsourcing or unvetted supply chains. The only viable solution is to perform software acquisition and development work using a systematic and disciplined process. The means for establishing this process is a set of well-defined, highly structured, and very secure assurance practices that are an integral part of the overall holistic security system.

A PAIR OF NECESSARY DISTINCTIONS

It is necessary to distinguish at this point between the set of activities that characterize the discipline of software assurance and those that logically belong in the domain of the more technical software engineering discipline. This distinction rests on the need to eliminate exploitable defects.

Not every defect is a vulnerability. Therefore, the activities that comprise the process of ensuring the software is functioning properly are not legitimately part of the cybersecurity process. That body of knowledge, which is oriented toward good engineering practice, is generally considered part of the discipline of software engineering.

Nevertheless, all software vulnerabilities result from defects. Therefore, the elements of software assurance relevant to the cybersecurity process aim to identify and remediate defects that constitute security vulnerabilities. Because the focus is identification, not repair, the cybersecurity elements of the software assurance process entail activities that are part of the testing and review process.

SECURING VERSUS ASSURING

The methods and concepts that underlie software assurance have to be understood by cybersecurity professionals to meet their overall security obligations. Given that responsibility, the goals of the software assurance professional and those of the cybersecurity professional differ primarily in what they aim to achieve through the testing and review process.

For software assurance professionals, the goal is to ensure that code runs properly and meets the user's requirements. For cybersecurity professionals, the aim is to identify and remediate only those defects that might lead to the compromise or exploitation of information accessed by that software item. That distinction implies a difference in the type and amount of work that is performed by these two different kinds of professionals.

This distinction may seem minor, given that both processes are oriented toward assurance. Nonetheless, the distinction between ensuring the overall functionality of software and preventing exploitable defects should be kept in mind when establishing a cybersecurity process. That is because the overall process of assuring that a piece of software runs properly and meets user requirements is a vast and entirely separate area of concern, which can drain resources away from any cybersecurity effort.

BUILDING VERSUS MAINTAINING

There is also a need to recognize the distinction between building software and maintaining it. Vulnerabilities enter a software item at three points in the process: construction, distribution, and patching. These can be factored into two areas of business practice – development versus operation.

By definition, development encapsulates any set of activities aimed at writing new code. In practice, development might entail the actual construction of a program. However, it can also include the modification, re-use, or re-engineering of existing code into a new product. Hence, development is typically done using best practices. Thus, the best place to conduct the assurance process is when the software is being built.

Typical sustainment activities include correcting flaws, optimizing existing code, and implementing minor changes. Code may be written here, but the purpose is not to create a new entity. Work in both of these domains is dictated by a set of commonly agreed-on practices, which are designed to build or enhance a software product. That formal set of practices is incorporated into a software process.

THE SOFTWARE PROCESS

Software is a set of programmed instructions that enable a computer to perform practical tasks. Software development encompasses five generic stages: specification, design, coding, testing, and deployment. The first stage, specification, defines the product. There are various ways of providing that definition, including classic specification, prototyping, or even extreme programming. The outcome is always a documented understanding of the functions the software will be required to perform.

The process then proceeds to the design stage. During the design stage, the actual blueprints for the product are developed, and specific decisions are made regarding its construction. There are numerous ways to do a design. However, the only purpose of design is to conceptualize and communicate the structure of the product to the people who will actually build it.

These individuals are typically referred to as "programmers." The function of the programmer is to translate the design into a computer program. A programming language is used to accomplish this, hence the name of the stage, "programming." The only acceptable outcome of the programming stage is a correctly functioning code component.

In most cases, the programming stage is the place where defects are created. These can be accidental, such as buffer overflows, or intentional, like the installation of backdoors and Trojan horses. They typically result from incorrect practice, human error, or malicious intent.

Obviously, the best place to ensure against programming defects is where they are created, at the programming stage. However, the actual programming work is so tricky and involved that it tends to consume all of the time. Therefore, some assurance process is always done during the programming stage. This tests the fundamental correctness of the code rather than searching for sources of threat.

The next stage in the software process is the point where it is most logical to identify and remediate defects directly. That stage is generically termed testing. Due to its purpose, the testing stage is the ideal place for cybersecurity professionals to be involved in software assurance. Accordingly, that is the place where we will begin this discussion.

As we said earlier, defects are not necessarily vulnerabilities. But from a software perspective, all vulnerabilities are defects. Therefore, any vulnerability that could compromise confidentiality, integrity, or availability must be identified and addressed. Testing utilizes documentation generated during previous stages of the software development process to identify and rectify vulnerable code. That documentation guides the subsequent testing work; therefore, its role has to be understood.

The item that is most necessary to the tester is a detailed description of what the software should do. That description should include a definition of the system boundaries as well as the behaviors that the software is meant to exhibit. It is also essential to have a concrete definition of the boundaries and behaviors. This allows the tester to judge whether the software contains the correct set of functions.

It takes a documented point of reference to achieve that level of control. This reference point is commonly referred to as a software requirements specification (SRS), or more often simply as a "specification."

The specification provides a complete, comprehensive, and unambiguous statement of the exact set of behaviors that the system must exhibit. This statement is developed at the beginning of the process. It guides the construction of the product, as much of the testing is oriented toward confirming that the software functions as intended. It also serves as an essential support for the testing phase.

A testing process that focuses only on confirming the existence of behaviors required by the specification does not guarantee that hidden vulnerabilities are not present in the code. Since vulnerabilities are often intentionally placed in code for malicious purposes, it is imperative to identify and eliminate them. Historically, testing has not focused on detecting added functionality. That is one reason why everything, from Easter eggs to malicious items like backdoors and Trojan horses, frequently becomes part of the final product.

CHAPTER SUMMARY: INTEGRATING DIVERSE AREAS INTO A HOLISTIC SOLUTION

As we have seen, the five non-electronic areas are vast in scope and diverse in purpose, and they require a comprehensive and properly interacting set of control functions to mitigate the concerns and threats represented by targeted attacks in each of these areas.

This chapter has been devoted to the practical concerns associated with managing a fully implemented, enterprise-wide, holistic security solution. Here, we discuss the purpose and functionality of all eight generic elements of a holistic solution. Our primary aim is to demonstrate where and how the traditional elements of the holistic process converge to create a single, fully integrated scheme that aligns business purpose with practical protection.

There are four generic classes of considerations that guide the consideration: Attack Surface, Threat Agent, Threat Source, Threat Community, and Threat Consequence. The attack surface refers to the total number of points where an unauthorized user can attempt to enter or extract data from a target object. Threat Agents are groups that can manifest a threat. Threat sources distinguish the beneficiary from the threat agents who actually carry out the attack, and threat communities are subsets of the overall threat agent population that share key characteristics. Threat consequence is a security violation that results from a threat action. That includes disclosure, deception, disruption, and usurpation.

Countermeasures are deliberately designed security controls. When these are applied to protect the system, they are referred to as security services. The goal of holistic security is to ensure that the correct set of countermeasures is deployed to safeguard against every harmful eventuality, and those controls must be mutually interoperating.

In that respect, then, holistic security is built around the twin concepts of convergence and integration, where the only acceptable outcome is a fully harmonized set of control actions that will directly mitigate every priority threat within the overall context of the business purpose. Thus, the primary goal of holistic security is to define and combine every single logically required electronic, human, and physical countermeasure into a unified, comprehensive, and correctly interacting real-time solution.

An organization must reliably secure three distinct attack surfaces for the cybersecurity solution to be effective. Consequently, a proper protection scheme comprises a complete array of intelligently designed and fully integrated best practices that are typically derived from a commonly accepted, industry-sanctioned standard. Those best practices are then suitably tailored to address all identified risks and properly interrelated to serve a specified business purpose.

In cybersecurity, a countermeasure is an action, device, procedure, or technique that mitigates a threat, vulnerability, or attack. It does this by eliminating or preventing it, or by minimizing the harm it can cause. Countermeasures identify and report potentially harmful events, allowing for corrective action to be taken.

The complete set of best practice controls can be factored into eight generic countermeasure areas, which can subsequently be organized into two subdomains. The first sub-domain encompasses all of the traditional technical control areas. These are deliberately focused on securing the electronic attack surface and are generally wholly electronic. As we mentioned, they tend to be viewed as part of the entire cybersecurity operation because they are visible to end users and have a strictly digital focus. These are:

1. Network and communication security countermeasures
2. Application and system software security countermeasures
3. Encryption measures

The second sub-domain is less conventional, but it is nonetheless essential. These are the environmental, contextual, and behavioral countermeasures that the organization establishes to address non-electronic attacks on both human and physical attack surfaces, such as phishing or physical theft. Those fall into five generic categories:

1. Business continuity and disaster recovery planning
2. Legal and regulatory compliance
3. Secure software assurance
4. Personnel security assurance
5. Physical security assurance

Just as electronic controls must be explicitly specified, designed, and substantively implemented, the behavioral controls in these two subdomains also need to be substantiated in order to achieve their specified purpose. All these control areas aim to ensure rational and interoperable assurance of the organization as a whole.

Electronic security is enabled by rigorous control over the enterprise's software assets and the cross-referencing of what each electronic function will do to ensure the business purpose. In general, the only way to ensure this is through the proper initial design of every electronic control component.

Therefore, at the beginning of application development, potential protection requirements must be identified and documented for each module and every interface. Then, adequate security mitigations have to be formally specified and coded to address each identified security concern. This is the "baking it in" aspect of the application development process.

Nonetheless, holistic security is comprehensive security. That is, electronic security, which is what most people think of when they discuss the cybersecurity function, addresses the newest and, in some respects, the most mysterious aspect of that protection problem. But it does not address obvious points of vulnerability. Hence, there is a second domain centered on human behavior that must be mitigated to achieve complete and trustworthy assurance.

Behavioral security revolves around the steps that the organization must take to define a response that is adequately tailored to the specific situation, along with the attendant countermeasures and system management processes necessary to ensure a coordinated organizational control system. That applies to all operational aspects of the business, ranging from strategic policies to routine procedures. As we said, this entire area is based on best practice rather than any form of physical science.

In addition to the necessary technical countermeasures, a holistic solution will comprehensively address the organization-wide, strategic, and contextual concerns associated with big picture legal and regulatory compliance and business continuity, along with instituting effective control over personnel and physical space. The integration of these behavioral control processes with an electronic response is what we refer to as holistic protection.

Cybersecurity systems are a combination of technology, people, and business practices. Each of these entities has a distinct purpose and contributes differently to the ultimate goal of a secure organization. The holistic security process blends the most effective control actions from each of these domains into a single, organized response. Implementing the right mix of security controls requires a delicate balance. Therefore, practical success entails understanding the essential elements and their interrelationships.

Because any attempt to secure intangible assets, in whatever form they may exist – virtual, documentary, or physical – holistic assurance requires a single, coherent approach that builds and maintains a comprehensive and coordinated infrastructure of tangible controls. The reliability of these controls must be objectively demonstrated, and they must continuously evolve to meet the changing environment.

Hence, the reliability of the security system can be judged by whether all necessary safeguards are in place and operating correctly at all times. That state of continuous assurance requires a deliberately designed architecture of processes and controls, which are all planned, fully integrated, and economically feasible. The strategy must ensure a trustworthy long-term assurance capability. In that respect, then, the system must be rationally evolved to meet the changing needs of the environment. Therefore, a proper holistic solution must merge all requisite practices and technical controls into a single, coordinated approach.

Continuity is critical because organizations have built their core functions around the management of information. While at the same time, the world is full of threats. Modern continuity processes encompass strategies and steps to ensure the organization's survival in the event of a disaster. This is built around contingency plans that outline the steps to be taken in the event of a disaster. These continuity plans preserve the organization's essential information assets.

Compliance is any formal process that ensures the requirements of a specification, terms of a contract, law, regulation, or standard are satisfied. Compliance is essential to any organization because it safeguards against the business harm that might result from either intentionally or unintentionally violating a formal mandate.

Personnel security encompasses a formal set of policies and procedures designed to ensure the actions of individuals working within the organization. This set of organizationally developed and sanctioned statements defines the explicit security responsibilities of all individuals, as well as their resulting accountabilities.

The purpose of a personnel security process is to define the specific actions that must be performed by each individual to achieve satisfactory levels of assurance. These can be classified into three generic categories: routine functions, operational duties, and management responsibilities. It is necessary to have an adequate definition and a required set of actions for each of these areas to ensure proper security.

Physical security centers on controls to safeguard against physical threats. It is the function that protects facilities and equipment from deliberate or accidental harm from the environment. Some of the technology that underlies physical security, such as microwave intrusion detection, is highly advanced. However, most physical security concepts, such as secure areas and layered defenses, have been in use since the Roman era.

The only sure way to safeguard facilities is to create a secure space deliberately. That requires establishing a finite physical boundary and then deploying a set of countermeasures that can be expected to assure the integrity of that perimeter. The goal is to ensure that access to the equipment is controlled and that the organization can effectively respond to intrusions within the defined area.

Software assurance is a process, not a technical activity. It identifies and eliminates exploitable defects in the development, acquisition, and operation of software. Because of its complexity, this task is comparable to "finding a needle in a haystack." In fact, the more accurate analogy might be "finding a particular needle in a stack of needles," since it is almost impossible to tell the difference between secure code and insecure code in a properly running system. In conventional practice, software assurance ensures that all instances of a software product are trustworthy, predictable, and conformant.

The only viable way to ensure that is to create a formal design using a systematic and disciplined process that is an integral part of the overall holistic security system. Process controls from all of these behavioral areas, compliance continuity, human and physical security, and software assurance must be integrated into a single synergistic solution that is explicitly aligned with the business purpose to ensure a proper, holistic solution.

Chapter 7

A practical example of holistic architectural process

Figure 7.1 Pencil drawing of a composed commander standing above a battlefield, holding a map in one hand while pointing decisively into the distance. Below him, rows of armored soldiers wait attentively, and rolling hills fade into the background, emphasizing calm leadership, foresight, and strategic direction rather than direct combat.

TURNING SECURITY PRINCIPLES INTO OPERATIONAL REALITY

> *The expert in battle seeks his victory from strategic advantage and does not demand it from his men.*
>
> —Sun Tzu

As we've said throughout this book, the assurance of dependable security relies on the ability to see and make intelligent provisions for the entire elephant.

DOI: 10.1201/9781003603412-7

Or in simple terms, the multiplicity of feasible points of attack demands a comprehensive approach that considers all legitimate sources of threat. In that respect, then, a single exploitable flaw can render a security system ineffective, regardless of how thorough and elegant the deployed response might be. Thus, the security response must be developed through a strategic process of threat identification, risk analysis, and design that proceeds top-down to an actionable set of properly designed and tangible control actions.

And it is not just a defect in the protection scheme that you have to worry about. There is also the matter of the rational arrangement of the control set so that the system itself interacts synergistically, and without any unknown and potentially disastrous interrelationships that might be exploited. Most critical security solutions are composed of several subsystems comprising a large number of integrated components.

Those components must be arranged in a way that satisfies all specified requirements, as well as the business purpose of the organization, and each element must interoperate efficiently and effectively. That solution is only as strong as its weakest link. In essence, then, this is a system solution that has to be ensured to be correct and properly functioning as part of the overall assurance consideration. Finally, there is the ongoing management of that system. Or, in simple terms, are you conducting your day-to-day security protection duties properly, and is the requisite assurance sustainable and sustained throughout the system's lifecycle? This is all part of the holistic security architectural process.

Up to this point, we have been discussing the requirements and principles of a comprehensive, holistic system encompassing security object identification and risk analysis, policy and procedure formulation, and the operation of the eight general areas of cybersecurity protection. We are now going to provide a living example of an open international standard for turning those principles into a working, everyday solution architecture that supports the practical purpose of your business.

THE SABSA MODEL OF LAYERED ARCHITECTURE

SABSA stands for Sherwood Applied Business Security Architecture, and it is arguably the leading methodology for developing business-oriented, risk-based security architectures. SABSA provides a commonly accepted and standardized structure for the creation and implementation of enterprise cybersecurity assurance architectures. It's an open standard, meaning it can be used freely, without a license, by any end-user organization. That makes it perhaps the single most attractive model for architecting a proper, holistic solution.

The SABSA model comprises six layers. Each of these views represents the restricted viewpoint of one of the individuals touching the elephant. Taken together, each layer captures a different view of the problem, much like viewing the same problem from multiple directions, in the hope of capturing the most complete and comprehensive understanding by involving all relevant points of view.

That might oversimplify the purpose somewhat. However, the aim is to integrate all the purposes and perspectives of the organization into a unified understanding, and the steps taken to address each separate view refine the eventual end-product into a single, synergistic solution. That is because the operation of the cybersecurity assurance process has different implications depending on the context in which it is being conducted. That should be intuitively obvious since the privilege and access mechanisms will vary based on the purposes and uses of the requester. The six perspectives of the SABSA Model are:

Layer One: The *Organizational (top) View* is driven by business purpose. Therefore, every strategic contextual issue must be identified and formulated into a coherent strategy that will be addressed through the architectural design process. That includes both current operational planning and long-term strategic business goals.

Layer Two: The *Architectural View* identifies, analyzes, and documents the logical control structure required to achieve a reliable state of holistic protection. In essence, the scope and focus of the protection scheme are clearly demonstrated to guide the detailed design work.

Layer Three: The *Designer's View* designs the defense-in-depth scheme for that particular application. This is the first tangible realization of the holistic protection solution for a given organization. As a consequence, more than the designers are involved in the critical review of the final product. This is where the appropriate organizational stakeholders provided documented input and approval for the final solution, thereby establishing the linkage to the business purpose.

Layer Four: The *Builder's View* is where the conceptual design is substantiated in a complex array of real-world controls that represent the operational security scheme, managed under the security of operations process. This perspective is, in essence, the physical security architecture of a given organization's cybersecurity solution. Therefore, the need to document and relate every element of the system, as well as verify and validate effectiveness, is an ongoing operational commitment. Additionally, this is where provisions for sustainment are specified.

Layer Five, the *Tradesman's View*, is the first variation from the orthodox process that is most commonly associated with virtual system design. The purpose of this level is both practical and necessary, as it focuses strictly on the component level of the solution. It restricts the activities at this level to the creation, implementation, and validation of the discrete elements of the architecture. In essence, this is the modular view. There is no intention to perfect anything outside the module, although all of the specified logical external connections must be verified and information hiding requirements implemented.

Layer Six, the *Security Service Management* view, is also a somewhat nontraditional but logically essential element of holistic security solution formulation. Whatever solution that has been implemented must be operated over time and under all conditions. The state of assurance must be maintained over that period, and all changes must be rationally managed. Therefore, a formal set of considerations must be established and then documented to guide the process.

These considerations must be comprehensive, realistic, and ensure practical organizational control over the security system during its entire functional use. The precise linkage of the holistic solution with the business purpose is established through this six-step process. In effect, the necessary understanding of the functional requirements needed to underwrite business goals for a particular instance can be obtained by following those steps.

THE FIRST STAGE IN THE SABSA PROCESS: GAINING TOP-LEVEL UNDERSTANDING

SABSA requires strict organizational discipline to be implemented effectively. In essence, a properly constructed holistic architecture requires the business to follow all six stages of the SABSA process. The SABSA approach aims to ensure stakeholder trust in the cybersecurity solution, which begins with the detailed definition of the shape of the contextual threat environment. Specifically, that involves providing unambiguous answers to six basic questions: What? Why? How? Who? Where? And When?

"What" is the factor that must be clarified first? The business perspective is referred to as the contextual security architecture in the SABSA Model. That architectural understanding fully aligns with the business context that the particular protection solution will address. The business has many assets, some of which are tangible and some virtual, including business records, electronic business enablers, operational continuity and stability requirements, and compliance with the law.

The primary question in determining what to protect and what not to invest in is "What is the substantive payoff for providing protection?" That is an answer that only leadership can provide. Thus, the responsibility for shaping the system lies with the individuals tasked with aligning business decisions, such as investment in cybersecurity protection, with the organization's stated business goals and objectives.

Strategic alignment entails three large-scale business factors: (1) the specific way that the company chooses to do business, (2) the strategy that effectuates their particular approach, and (3) the explicitly understood and stated purpose and outcomes of that strategy. It can be assumed that the business will function at an optimal level of effectiveness if those three factors are precisely aligned.

A proper alignment strategy will ensure that every control action within the holistic architecture is coordinated and harmonized to achieve the organization's overall business purpose. That requires a comprehensive understanding of all relevant operating factors within the organization and the ability to interrelate those elements into a complete and systematic real-world solution. The operating factors themselves are generally business abstractions, such as the company's market strategy, its business model, and its overall business philosophy. Decisions about how to best protect these factors can only be made by the organization's stakeholders.

As we have stressed, the business perspective can only be legitimately deployed from the top of the organization. The problem arises from the fact that it is common practice for cybersecurity architectures to be designed, developed, and implemented solely from a technical perspective. And because of behavioral factors like social engineering and insider threat, that perspective is four or five levels too low in the hierarchy to enable reliable security. Since the sole, justifiable purpose of the cybersecurity solution is to underwrite and leverage business advantage, all strategic control deployment decisions must be directly aligned with their business purpose. That alignment must be documented and commonly known and accepted within the organization.

The probable outcome of not starting from the top in the architectural development process is a functional disconnect between the system and the organization that it is implemented to serve. That is because the purposes and strategies of the business operation may not be accurately captured in the resultant protection scheme or may not be reflected at all. That makes the entire cybersecurity function look like overhead to the rest of the business.

The Organizational View is critical and must come first because it creates the complete set of business-centered requirements that represent the essential context required to guide the construction and integration of a precisely tailored set of control actions necessary to implement a given level of desired security. It should go without saying that the shape of the security solution should be precisely aligned with the organization's business purpose and the contextual environment in which it operates. Which in turn implies the need for an unambiguous statement of:

- The legitimate type and the threat to the business purpose for all three attack surfaces
- The precise system boundaries, including access control requirements

- The application of the protection scheme within the business operation (e.g., where is it used?)
- System operators, as well as the composition of the user community (e.g., exactly who uses it?)
- The terms and conditions of use, including protection goals (e.g., how it is used?)
- Relevant timing factors that may affect the system's operation (e.g., when will it be used?)

THE SECOND STAGE IN THE SABSA PROCESS: INTELLIGENT ACCESS CONTROL DECISIONS BASED ON RISK

Once the specific business outcomes are determined, the next important factor is scope. This part of the process is essentially a prioritizing activity based on business-driven decisions about value. The holistic cybersecurity lifecycle that we have discussed throughout this text begins at this level. As we have emphasized, the primary purpose of a cybersecurity protection scheme is to ensure the confidentiality, integrity, and availability of the assets that it is set to protect. However, the only rational way to accomplish that is to unambiguously define the objects that explicitly require protection and the specific adverse actions that threaten those objects. This analysis and prioritization of essential business elements fall under the general rubric of defense in depth.

Defense-in-depth structures are defined by the impact of known and sufficiently characterized threats on an itemized set of business assets. Those assets can encompass a broad range of tangible activities, including theft and fraud prevention, legal and regulatory compliance, and business continuity. Assets can also be intangible things, such as brands and branding, as well as intellectual property, which are particularly vulnerable in virtual spaces.

In this respect, this particular stage of the SABSA model is implemented by conducting the same set of activities discussed in the domain of analysis (Chapter 2 of this text): protection object identification, risk analysis, and prioritization. These foundational steps then lead to the definition of the protection perimeter, e.g., defense-in-depth boundary setting, and the development of explicit control mechanisms to enforce proper access privileges.

Although the identification and risk analysis process has a micro-focused and computer-oriented element to it. The actions that characterize this stage are primarily business decisions based on the value of the asset and its particular priority in the business purpose. In fact, the outcome of this stage can only be determined by decisions about the relative importance and alignment of a given protection object with the overall business purpose.

That is because defense in depth is based on evaluating the business worth of any asset, or group of assets, relative to the resources that will need to be expended to protect it. Therefore, the ideal defense-in-depth solution protects only those assets that are critical to the business purpose, and nothing more. The aim is a Goldilocks solution, not too much expenditure … not too little protection … just right.

As we mentioned, this is often a decision made based on organizational politics rather than rationality. Therefore, the definition of the perimeters, or boundaries, of the defense-in-depth scheme must be strongly supported by objective data and observations. To enable this, the standard identification and risk analysis process discussed in Chapter 2 applies at this stage of the SABSA. Therefore, we will not repeat ourselves. However, it is essential to note that there must be strict alignment between the access control decisions and the mechanisms that support them, as well as the business purposes determined in the first stage of the SABSA model. But it is worth noting that the outcome of this process must be ideal alignment between the scope and rigor of the holistic security solution and the organization's business goals and purpose.

THE THIRD STAGE IN THE SABSA PROCESS: EFFECTIVE DESIGN

The third stage in the SABSA process, which is essentially the system design stage, provides a detailed description of the system as it is built. The design view leverages the overall process by which the organization's business requirements are met. Thus, this layer of the SABSA Model is referred to as the conceptual security architecture. It defines the business principles and fundamental concepts that guide the selection and organization of the logical and physical elements at the lower layers of abstraction. As in any design process, this begins with the creation of a tree of components at progressively more detailed levels of composition. The breakdown continues until the designer has satisfactorily represented the business activities and processes that must be assured, including all relevant interactions, transactions, and communications between each business element.

The component tree must isolate and characterize all necessary aspects of the business process for each element, including the existing management processes, governance plug-ins, and supply chain interactions. In the latter case, all suppliers along the component supply chain must be identified and characterized. Finally, all elements of the 'extended enterprise' must be documented, including all business partners and relationships with governmental entities.

Because there is a physical attack surface, it is also necessary to document tangible aspects, such as the location and type of buildings, any relevant geographic factors (e.g., whether the building is located in a floodplain), and access and transportation routes. This information will all be necessary when the physical controls are designed into the total control solution. Additionally, timing and sequencing factors, such as response time and maximum time to restore service, must also be considered. The point being that the development of a holistic design involves much more than determining where the firewall will be placed and how it will be configured.

The architect's view

Holistic security architecture in the SABSA model focuses on developing a Business Attributes Profile, which specifies the essential business requirements of the target organization in a commonly understood and standardized manner. The assurance objectives are derived directly from an analysis of business operational risks as they impact the elements of the Business Attributes Profile. For every significant area of the business identified in the contextual security architecture, there will be a corresponding security strategy, or a group of strategies, that supports it.

The decision support for the architect includes a rigorous cost-benefit analysis, as well as a written justification of the business need to assure a given element, along with a statement of the requisite actions, both technical and managerial, selected from the standard control objectives of the eight common control areas in the holistic model.

The goal of the Business Attributes profile is to provide a high-level technical and management security strategy, as well as a mapping of the control architecture in relation to the overall business purposes. The strategies provide a conceptual framework for integrating the individual control elements that will be implemented at the lower levels in the SABSA process. The mapping of architectural elements ensures that all design components fit together in a way that will effectively support the overall strategic goals of the business. Those strategies must address all of the relevant attack surfaces. That includes the strategy to ensure:

1. Security and sustainment of applications
2. Security and sustainability of the network
3. The maintenance and use of a public key infrastructure (if applicable)
4. Continuity of the business processes and disaster management
5. Legal and regulatory compliance
6. Personnel security, specifically the access control process and utilities
7. Physical protection of all tangible assets, including the locations where they reside

Given item six above, there is an explicit requirement to specify an unambiguous set of security management, roles, and responsibilities for each stakeholder. This is necessary to ensure trust throughout the business operation, as well as between the business and its clients, including the designated person accountable for the asset, and everyone relevant to the protection of the asset. That will range from simple custodians and users, all the way up to service providers and customers.

The assignment of trust is driven by the various policy decisions the organization establishes to govern trust within a given security domain, such as the distinct operational areas within the organization. These policies govern the overall actions of users, managers, and stakeholders within each domain and the overarching trust relationships that comprise the entire system. The essential concept that guides the formulation of security domains, both logical and physical, is that of boundaries, or perimeters, and their interrelationships, which we discussed when laying out the concept of defense in depth.

The designer's view

In essence, the architect is the conceptual artist while the designer is the engineer. The designer converts the architect's conceptual understanding into actuality, in the sense that the designer translates the architect's rendering of the solution into a distinct, rational model that represents the tangible, real-world system. The profession's generic term for this translation process is systems engineering.

Systems engineering involves identifying and specifying the logical architectural elements of an overall system in the form of a specific solution. As we have said, this involves a functional decomposition of the business space into an increasingly more granular array of component subsystems. The resultant component tree models the business as a system of components and subsystems, where primary system security requirements can be identified and specified as a logical set of security controls. This allows for the capture, mapping, and management of requisite interactions between control elements as part of a rational security architecture.

In terms of the logical component tree, the decomposition breaks down the existing real-world business operation into logical layers. The outcome of this decomposition should reflect every major business component, its particular security requirements, and the logical interactions between the component and every other element of the business operation.

In the SABSA model, each decomposed component must satisfy the classic design principles of modularity. Meaning the element must contain one and only one function (coherence), and that no other function overlaps the conceptual boundaries of the module (decoupling). The outcome of this process is a detailed understanding of the control requirements for the decomposed system as well as the control flow between them.

This logical security architecture documents, (1) the specific business information that is to be protected and the protection requirements for each, (2) The related security and risk management controls to be used to secure the business information by attack surface, (3) the specific security actions that will be taken to ensure a consistent and coherent process – e.g., confidentiality protection services, integrity protection services, non-repudiation services, system and software assurance services, (4) the interfaces between modules, including access points and access control methods, that will ensure proper control flow as well as satisfaction of the overall business requirements. This is typically specified by a formal specification of functional requirements as well as a control flow map.

Along with the detailed specification of business and assurance control requirements, the SABSA model also requires that the authorized entities be given documented roles in the process. That includes the specification of authorized users, security administrators, and auditors, along with their inter-relationships, attributes, authorized roles, and privilege assignments. This is typically documented in the form of a trust framework, or authorization 'schema', where the level of confidence that must be established and maintained between system entities is explicitly specified.

From a practical management standpoint, SABSA breaks the organization into security domains, which are essentially subdomains of the secure space. This activity serves as the conceptual basis for formulating a defense-in-depth scheme. Each domain is assigned a different level of protection based on the risk analysis, and the perimeter controls for the domain are designed according to the established level of protection required. The fact that there may be both physical and logical security requirements within a given security domain can lead to the decomposition of the domain into separate sub-domains, based on the electronic, human, and physical controls appropriate to each. Timing is the final aspect of the practical, operational domain formulation, as the requisite timetable and timing have to be established to ensure proper sustainment.

THE FOURTH STAGE IN THE SABSA PROCESS: CREATING THE SYSTEM

The activities in this area are referred to as the system phase if this were a software system development project. It is the stage where concept meets implementation. The person responsible for closing that loop takes the logical specification of requirements and desired interactions and turns that concept into a working version of the real-world controls. Thus, the builder's view is the level at which functional module designs and the conceptual infrastructure are assembled into a physical system, which implements the logical concept as a real-world system. Because those controls are tangible actions that produce documented outcomes, the product of the builder's view is the physical security architecture.

The physical security architecture model describes the control structure of a particular defense-in-depth scheme. It should fully and completely address all priority threats across all three attack surfaces in a logical and resource-effective manner. It should also fully align with and support the business goals and purpose of the organization. All conceptual design actions must be expressed in terms of an explicit physical security control action that reliably mitigates the threat it is intended to address and can be objectively judged based on its documentation and behavior. In total, the physical security architecture is concerned with specifying the:

1. *Business data* model and the security-related data structures.
2. *Decision-making conditions*, policies, practices, procedures, and actions to ensure holistic protection.
3. *Concrete security mechanisms* to enforce the desired protection, including technology and software services, but also including enforceable security procedures and best practices, and an effective physical security plan.
4. *Access control strategy* and organizational roles and responsibilities, as well as human behavior mitigation controls, including awareness and training to ensure understanding and compliance.
5. *Security technology infrastructure*, as it aligns with business strategy and purpose, including the mechanism for explicit configuration management of the technology platform.
6. *Rules for timing and sequencing* security actions and processes within the conventional business operation, including a map aligning those actions with the business purpose.

The business data operation: What to protect

Purpose is the only intelligent starting point for system implementation, and holistic protection systems are implemented to ensure the confidentiality, integrity, and availability of business data. Hence, data and the data structures and mechanisms that process it are the logical starting point for the build. In that respect, then, all meaningful data protection targets, whether electronic or stored in a physical file, must be identified, characterized, and their processing factored into a single, holistic protection concept.

In essence, the builder lays the foundation for the protection scheme by obtaining a precise understanding of the data storage and flow within the business operation, one that is unique to that operation only. This kind of precise understanding is critical because the following two steps in the process involve tailoring a particular set of standard controls to ensure the distinctive purpose of the business operation. That would be impossible if the detailed processing of the information in the operation were unknown.

Setting the course: Policies, procedures, and control actions

All strategic control standards are specified in a way that allows them to be tailored to a given situation. Tailoring is the art of the protection process in that no two business operations are the same. However, the purpose and intent of individual control are to ensure standard best practices. Therefore, the control must be tailored to the situation, which requires a precise understanding of the business intent behind the process it is intended to support.

Thus, a comprehensive set of policies, practices, procedures, and desired outcomes must be formally documented to ensure holistic protection. That documentation typically takes the form of an organizationally sanctioned statement of policy and general procedure that the tailoring process can utilize to specify the explicit actions required to satisfy the intent of those conditions. The builder will then use that policy and procedure document to create the active control set.

Creating the real-world response: Building the control set

The desired outcome of the entire process is a concrete and highly synergistic set of real-world controls. Once the contextual understanding has been ensured. The builder carefully tailors an explicit set of systematic actions that represent the particular solution for the organization at that specific point in time. In essence, this is the cybersecurity system as the organization understands it as a whole.

Users and stakeholders will perform the control actions, whether procedural or embedded in the system, as a tangible part of their day-to-day work. Because the control actions are being performed outside of routine, there is likely very little awareness that these controls are interacting as part of a complex system of interdependent control purposes. Nevertheless, the numerous interactions between stakeholders and users, as well as the control interface, are the one visible thing that all of them can point to when asked to describe the cybersecurity response.

Hence, the fashioning of each control to satisfy the protection purpose it was intended to address, while still directly supporting the business goals and objectives of the organization, is the essential outcome of the entire SABSA process. That is also the reason why the construction and installation of the complete set of controls is such a time-consuming and painstaking process. Given the three attack surfaces and the numerous interdependencies within the control set, this is not something that can be solved by purchasing an off-the-shelf application. It has to be constructed to fit the particular situation it is designed to address.

Ensuring properly mediated access: The access control system

As we mentioned earlier, in many ways, cybersecurity, especially its electronic aspects, can be summed up in two words: "access control." The Saltzer and Schroeder principles are heavily invested in promoting the assignment and enforcement of privilege. In simple terms, the people who ought to have entrée are the only ones who are allowed access. If only trusted individuals are allowed access, then that ensures both confidentiality and integrity.

Thus, access control in many respects involves the assignment and subsequent enforcement of the organization's trust in a specific individual. This is not a matter of simply assigning a password. The level of confidence has to be verified by the organization and then monitored to ensure that satisfactory trust has been maintained. It also involves vetting actions on the physical interface to ensure that the individual is only accessing spaces to which they have been authorized. The creation and maintenance of a formal trust process is part of the organization's duty to establish protection in the first place.

Electronic architecture: Ensuring electronic protection

Most of cybersecurity is viewed as electronic since the asset is stored, processed, and accessed as electronic information. Given the extensive set of physical gadgetry necessary to process and transmit data, the SABSA model explicitly emphasizes the need to create and sustain the components of the electronic platform.

This applies explicitly to the assurance that the technology used to carry out all essential processes aligns with the organization's overall business strategy. In essence, this means that every technological element must be justifiable in terms of the value it adds to the business purpose. Additionally, all installed systems must be mapped to their operational use in support of the ongoing business process.

The operational plan: Getting the timing right

Finally, assuming all the conditions above have been satisfied, it is essential to specify what constitutes the rules for system use. No matter how well-designed the system may be, it can still be rendered practically useless if the business does not utilize it properly. Therefore, the required actions to conduct business using the elements of the holistic protection scheme have to be specified for all stakeholders within the conventional business operation.

This typically begins with a map that records and aligns all necessary security actions with the stated goals and objectives of a specific business operation. In essence, there is a clear understanding of the relation between the overall business purpose and the actions that have been designed and implemented to ensure it. The chief advantage of this map is that the organization's decision-makers can use it to determine if they are deviating from the intent and purpose of the system and recommend corrective action. It also allows decision makers to specify corrective action where needed.

THE FIFTH STAGE IN THE SABSA PROCESS: MODULE IMPLEMENTATION

This stage would be called programming and testing if this were a software project, as it focuses entirely on the module creation and validation level of the build, producing a tangible, verifiable end product. That product is one of the "N" number of system modules identified and characterized at the system definition phase (SABSA level four). In essence, this is the stage where the rubber meets the road, and the outcome is the organization's operational protection system.

From an execution standpoint, this is a disaggregated process in that each build team concentrates on implementing a single component of what can be a large and complex system. It is a down-focused, highly involving, and detailed creation process. The team's efforts are focused entirely on ensuring the logical and functional correctness of the module they have been assigned to construct, and there is very little consideration given to how that fits with the business purpose or any of the larger conceptual requirements of assuring holistic protection.

The work is guided by the detailed design documentation that was developed, which was the point of the prior four stages. The guiding principles are the rational programming practices associated with the software engineering profession. Additionally, along with programmed logic controls, there are also real-world actions, such as employee vetting and privilege assignment, as well as gate guard protocols, that must be specified.

Therefore, each person tasked with defining their specific component piece should be a specialist in the subject matter area. They should be familiar with and able to apply the specific practices necessary to achieve the purpose of their particular component module. Thus, programmers, human behavioral specialists, and even physical security specialists may be called on to participate in this part of the process. The outcome of their combined set of individual components is the organization's holistic security architecture, comprising all the elements, which are then integrated up an integration ladder into the operational security solution for that organization. That architecture contains a complete set of:

1. *Operational controls* for all aspects of the protection scheme, including all asset repositories and virtual and physical processes that interact with them.

2. *Risk management process* and associated practices, including the mechanism for incident response, controlled change, and evolution of the holistic protection scheme.
3. *Standards, industry best practices, and technical tools* that have been utilized to formulate the control architecture and underwrite its operation.
4. *Behavioral management controls* to secure the human and physical attack surface, including everything from codes of conduct down to human resource protocols.
5. *Roles, responsibilities, and specific accountabilities* for every member of the organization concerning their role in standard cybersecurity practice.
6. *A code of conduct* including the timing and applicability requirements for standard operational situations.

The operational control system

At the top, the organization's functioning control response is nothing more than an integrated set of control actions in modular form. These modules, when correctly integrated, constitute the holistic control response, and they are, in effect, the organization's cybersecurity system. The complete set of control modules works together to achieve the desired level of security, and they are fully aligned with the business purpose in their operation.

Each module must obey the principles of modularity in that its (internal) actions will accomplish one, and only one, purpose, and its operation does not depend on something that happens external to the module (decoupling). The sequence and timing of module operation are determined by the events to which it is set to respond, and the interrelationship with other modules in accomplishing a given task is engineered into the element's functioning based on a design decision.

The threat and risk management process

The primary purpose of the holistic control system is to safeguard the organization's assets against known threats. Therefore, the actual day-to-day functioning of that process must be explicitly tied to the components of the solution. In essence, the "where, how, and why" of that organization's specific risk management solution must be mapped in detail to the control scheme and the associated business purpose.

Primarily, the conceptual aspects of this are handled by the design documentation. But the real-world elements of risk management are justifiably part of the implementation process. Therefore, practical activities such as incident response, change management, and back-end testing must be specified in detail and associated with the practical control aspects and business purpose they are intended to implement. This is typically represented in a detailed risk management plan, an organizational artifact that is maintained as the overall holistic system evolves.

The basis for the control architecture

The selection of the common standard for control architecture is an artifact of the design process. However, the actual association with the generic control requirements of a standard model is a necessary aspect of tailoring those controls to the specific protection and business purpose. Thus, strict attention must be paid to documenting the interrelationship between a control requirement and its realization in that particular instance.

This association is typically achieved through a detailed map that connects the best practice requirements outlined in the standard model with the tangible realization of those requirements in a specific practical situation. The usual way of presenting this is through a detailed table that directly associates each generic control requirement with the components and organizational actions that have been specifically tailored to achieve it.

Control actions

The contingent action of each control must be unambiguously described down to the who, what, when, and where. This micro-focused aspect of the holistic security process is an essential requirement, as some aspect of the business as a whole, or perhaps the entire organization, will be required to perform each control step. Therefore, explicit instructions for doing that have to be provided.

These instructions are typically encapsulated as protocols in a best practice procedure manual, which is maintained as an organizational resource and which individual workers are expected to reference in the performance of their business duties.

The role of training, awareness, and even formal education practices in ensuring understanding and compliance cannot be overemphasized, as organizations constantly undergo staffing changes. Thus, in addition to documenting the control actions, it is essential to have a robust training function to ensure ongoing understanding and compliance.

Assignment of accountability

The explicit assignment of roles, responsibilities, and accountabilities is the other side of the coin for the security protocols documented in the procedure manual. This assignment must link each role in the organization to its corresponding duties in executing the holistic security process, and it must align specifically with the general business purpose of each role. This is where the Saltzer and Schroeder principles are implemented as real-world functions.

The assignment process itself is a function of management decision-making. However, the communication and oversight of requirements are management duties that must be explicitly delegated and documented as having been successfully performed. This must be recorded and publicly available, and targeted training and awareness programs must be formulated to support it.

Making things explicit

The assignment of oversight and management protocols is part of the holistic system master plan. The connection between individual duties and security objectives is typically established by a general statement of codes of conduct, followed by the explicit assignment of tasks in the job description for each position within the organization as a whole. This is usually captured in the procedure manual for each security objective within the general business operation.

The procedure manual is an organizational artifact that demands strict organizational control from the top. That is because it is the single mechanism for assigning accountability. Thus, any violations of procedure as outlined in the manual are something that the organization can handle as part of the disciplinary process. In many respects, there is no rational discipline without a detailed and fully enforceable set of stated procedures to underwrite it.

THE SIXTH STAGE IN THE SABSA PROCESS: SUSTAINMENT

The first five stages of the SABSA process produce a tangible solution that is as complete, accurate, and tied to the business purpose as possible. However, that entire stage process has an endpoint in the final solution. So, the question is ... What happens after the holistic system is fully integrated into conventional business operations? That is the purpose of sustainability planning and operation. In many respects, this is an entirely different process from the development of the solution, since it is aimed at continuously ensuring the state of the system is correct and relevant to the business purpose.

The job of the sustainment operation is to ensure the system operates as designed and built, and to address the inevitable tweaks and evolution of the control processes it implements. This is a critical aspect of the operation since, without rational control over the change process, even a perfectly designed system can fall apart over time as the business evolves. The assurance of the system's correctness as built is essentially a classic configuration management challenge. However, SABSA refers to it as the Service

Management Security Architecture, which is an excellent reflection of its business orientation.

Nonetheless, whether the orientation is toward organizationally facing service aspects of ensuring correctness or the internal process for control over change as it inevitably occurs, there is a standard process for ensuring long-term sustainment that is consistently implemented in whatever context sustainment is necessary.

In concept, the sustainment process refers to the organization and maintenance of assets in a system. Its objective is to control changes made to components in a way that preserves the system's integrity. Sustainment depends on the first five stages of the SABSA process to define the object to be sustained. It also requires a separate decision-making process to authorize actions taken to change a previously created system object.

This first aspect – e.g., working with the system as built – is the cornerstone of the sustainment process. That is because the system is the structure that will be sustained as logically correct. The second element is also essential, as it requires the organization to always know the status and configuration of the product at a given time and, accordingly, to make rational decisions about changes. These two conditions are practically implemented through three interdependent management activities. These activities are:

1. *Change Process Management*, which is made up of change authorization, verification control, and release processing.
2. *Baseline Control*, which is composed of change accounting and control library management.
3. *Configuration Verification*, which includes status accounting to verify compliance with changes as authorized.

The control scheme, or control map, formulated as part of the holistic system development process, is a prerequisite for sustainment management because it establishes the "day one" configuration of the control system. Once established, that scheme, or map, is maintained throughout the lifecycle. Sustainment itself is specifically defined and formally implemented through a sustainment plan that is part of the original system planning process. At a minimum, this plan should specify the process for identifying and authorizing change requirements, as well as the method for reintegrating changed objects into the new protection scheme.

The hierarchy and composition of the authorization process must also be defined. The process of change is controlled by management authorization given at various levels of the organization based on the priority of the affected item. Thus, the authority, scope, and responsibility associated with the decision maker need to be linked to the change request, based on at least three levels of sensitivity: high, medium, and low. Additionally, there must be a mechanism for monitoring the operation of the holistic security scheme, as well as a means for providing timely analysis and information to support the authorization function.

The purpose of the sustainment process is to establish and maintain the integrity of virtual assets, making them available to relevant parties. The specific aim of change control within this purpose is to ensure the completeness, consistency, and correctness of each item in the larger holistic protection scheme. Thus, once the sustainment process has been established, change management controls every modification to any control in the functional security system. That change control mandate applies system-wide and to every item within the protection scheme for the entire lifecycle operation.

In essence, the sustainment process receives change requests from any element of the organization. This is typically something that is noticed during the day-to-day business process, and which the requester feels needs to be changed. That request is then analyzed to evaluate the impact(s) of the change, which are documented, and the analysis is sent to the designated decision maker for that type of change to be approved or rejected.

In conjunction with this, the sustainment process maintains a detailed record of the status of all components of the protection system, including the operational history of each element. The status accounting records the current status of the item to be changed. That status report typically includes things like versions (if any) of the item, its location, and its role in the larger map of controls.

Once a change is made, it is verified as correct before being integrated back into the operating security scheme. Of course, this must wait until the change has been made by the individual or unit designated to make it. In practice, the verification and delivery of a changed product, along with its documentation, is a formally controlled process that produces a revised version of the protection scheme. If that is the case, then sustainment will also update the map to incorporate the revised version, while maintaining a record of the old version as backup and for historical analysis. If executed properly, the sustainment process assures the ongoing effectiveness of the holistic security scheme throughout its lifecycle.

Finally, the SABSA model also includes a view that ensures the architecture as built is complete, consistent, robust, and 'fit-for-purpose' in every way. This is usually an auditing activity that is established by plan in the beginning and carried out as scheduled. The SABSA approach assumes that the architecture model as a whole supports these needs. Along with sustainment, this sub-view establishes that security is being applied systematically and appropriately.

CHAPTER SUMMARY

Up to this point, we have been discussing the requirements and principles of a comprehensive, holistic system, encompassing security object identification and risk analysis, policy and procedure formulation, and the operation of the eight general areas of cybersecurity protection. Here we provide a living example of an open international standard for turning those principles into a working, everyday solution that supports the practical purpose of your business.

THE SABSA MODEL OF LAYERED ARCHITECTURE

SABSA is arguably the leading methodology for developing business-oriented, risk-based security architectures. SABSA provides a commonly accepted and standardized structure for the creation and implementation of enterprise cybersecurity assurance architectures. It comprises six layers. Each of these views represents the restricted viewpoint of one of the individuals touching the elephant. Taken together, each layer captures a different view of the problem, much like viewing the same problem from multiple directions, in the hope of capturing the most complete and comprehensive understanding by involving all relevant points of view. Thus, the six perspectives of the SABSA Model are:

Layer One: The *Organizational (top) View* is driven by business purpose. Therefore, every strategic contextual issue must be identified and formulated into a coherent strategy that will be addressed through the architectural design process. That includes both current operational planning and long-term strategic business goals.

Layer Two: The *Architectural View* identifies, analyzes, and documents the logical control structure required to achieve a reliable state of holistic protection. In essence, the scope and focus of the protection scheme are clearly demonstrated to guide the detailed design work.

Layer Three: The *Designer's View* designs the defense-in-depth scheme for that particular application. This is the first tangible realization of the holistic protection solution for a given organization. As a consequence, more than the designers are involved in the critical review of the final product. This is where the appropriate organizational stakeholders provided documented input and approval for the final solution, thereby establishing the linkage to the business purpose.

Layer Four: The *Builder's View* is where the conceptual design is substantiated in a complex array of real-world controls that represent the operational security scheme, managed under the security of operations process. This perspective is, in essence, the physical security architecture of a given organization's cybersecurity solution. Therefore, the need to document and relate every element of the system, as well as verify and validate effectiveness, is an ongoing operational commitment. Additionally, this is where provisions for sustainment are specified.

Layer Five: The *Tradesman's View* is the first variation from the orthodox process that is most commonly associated with virtual system design. The purpose of this level is both practical and necessary, as it focuses strictly on the component level of the solution. It restricts the activities at this level to the creation, implementation, and validation of the discrete elements of the architecture. In essence, this is the modular view. There is no intention to perfect anything outside the module, although all of the specified logical external connections must be verified and information hiding requirements implemented.

Layer Six: The *Security Service Management* view is also a somewhat nontraditional but logically essential element of holistic security solution formulation. Whatever solution that has been implemented must be operated over time and under all conditions. The state of assurance must be maintained over that period, and all changes must be rationally managed. Therefore, a formal set of considerations must be established and then documented to guide the process.

These considerations must be comprehensive, realistic, and ensure practical organizational control over the security system during its entire functional use. The precise linkage of the holistic solution with the business purpose is established through this six-step process. In effect, the necessary understanding of the functional requirements needed to underwrite business goals for a particular instance can be obtained by following those steps.

THE FIRST STAGE IN THE SABSA PROCESS: GAINING TOP-LEVEL UNDERSTANDING

SABSA requires strict organizational discipline to be implemented effectively. In essence, a properly constructed holistic architecture requires the business to follow all six stages in the SABSA process. The SABSA approach aims to ensure stakeholder trust in the cybersecurity solution, which begins with the detailed definition of the shape of the contextual threat environment. Specifically, that involves providing unambiguous answers to six basic questions: What? Why? How? Who? Where? And When?

"What" is the factor that must be clarified first? The business perspective is referred to as the contextual security architecture in the SABSA Model. That architectural understanding fully aligns with the business context that the particular protection solution will address. The business has many assets, some of which are tangible and some virtual, including business records, electronic business enablers, operational continuity and stability requirements, and compliance with the law.

The primary question in determining what to protect and what not to invest in is "What is the substantive payoff for providing protection?" That is an answer that only leadership can provide. Thus, the responsibility for shaping the system lies with the individuals tasked with aligning business decisions, such as investment in cybersecurity protection, with the organization's stated business goals and objectives.

Strategic alignment entails three large-scale business factors: (1) the specific way that the company chooses to do business, (2) the strategy that effectuates their particular approach, and (3) the explicitly understood and stated purpose and outcomes of that strategy. It can be assumed that the business will function at an optimal level of effectiveness if those three factors are precisely aligned.

THE SECOND STAGE IN THE SABSA PROCESS: INTELLIGENT ACCESS CONTROL DECISIONS BASED ON RISK

Once the specific business outcomes are determined, the next important factor is scope. This part of the process is essentially a prioritizing activity based on business-driven decisions about value. The holistic cybersecurity lifecycle that we have discussed throughout this text begins at this level. As we have emphasized, the primary purpose of a cybersecurity protection scheme is to ensure the confidentiality, integrity, and availability of the assets that it is set to protect. However, the only rational way to accomplish that is to unambiguously define the objects that explicitly require protection and the specific adverse actions that threaten those objects. This analysis and prioritization of essential business elements fall under the general rubric of defense in depth.

Defense-in-depth structures are defined by the impact of known and sufficiently characterized threats on an itemized set of business assets. Those assets can encompass a broad range of tangible activities, including theft and fraud prevention, legal and regulatory compliance, and business continuity. Assets can also be intangible things such as brands and branding, and intellectual property, which are particularly at risk in virtual space.

In this respect, this particular stage of the SABSA model is implemented by conducting the same set of activities discussed in the Domain of Analysis (Chapter 2 of this text): protection object identification, risk analysis, and prioritization. These foundational steps then lead to the definition of the protection perimeter, e.g., defense-in-depth boundary setting, and the development of explicit control mechanisms to enforce proper access privileges.

Although the identification and risk analysis process has a micro-focused and computer-oriented element to it, the actions that characterize this stage are primarily business decisions based on the value of the asset and its particular priority in the business purpose. In fact, the outcome of this stage can only be determined by decisions about the relative importance and alignment of a given protection object with the overall business purpose.

That is because defense in depth is based on evaluating the business worth of any asset, or group of assets, relative to the resources that will need to be expended to protect it. Therefore, the ideal defense-in-depth solution protects only those assets that are critical to the business purpose, and nothing more. The aim is a Goldilocks solution, not too much expenditure … not too little protection … just right.

THE THIRD STAGE IN THE SABSA PROCESS: EFFECTIVE DESIGN

The third stage in the SABSA process, which is essentially the system design stage, provides a detailed description of the system as it is built. The design view leverages the overall process by which the organization's business requirements are met. Thus, this layer of the SABSA model is referred to as the conceptual security architecture. It defines the business principles and fundamental concepts that guide the selection and organization of the logical and physical elements at the lower layers of abstraction. As in any design process, this begins with the creation of a tree of components at progressively more detailed levels of composition. The breakdown continues until the designer has satisfactorily represented the business activities and processes that must be assured, including all relevant interactions, transactions, and communications between each business element.

The component tree must isolate and characterize all necessary aspects of the business process for each element, including the existing management processes, governance plug-ins, and supply chain interactions. In the latter case, all suppliers up and down the component supply chain must be identified and characterized. Finally, all elements of the 'extended enterprise' must be documented, including all business partners and relationships with governmental entities.

THE FOURTH STAGE IN THE SABSA PROCESS: CREATING THE SYSTEM

The activities in this area would be referred to as the system phase if this were a software system development project. It is the stage where concept meets implementation. The person responsible for closing that loop takes the logical specification of requirements and desired interactions and turns that concept into a working version of the real-world controls. Thus, the builder's view is the level at which functional module designs and the conceptual infrastructure they reside in are assembled into a physical system, which implements the logical concept as a real-world system. Because those controls are tangible actions that produce documented outcomes, the product of the builder's view is the physical security architecture.

The physical security architecture model describes the control structure of a particular defense-in-depth scheme. It should fully and completely address all priority threats across all three attack surfaces in a logical and resource-effective manner. It should also fully align with and support the business goals and purpose of the organization. All conceptual design actions must be expressed in terms of an explicit physical security control action that reliably mitigates the threat it is intended to address and can be objectively judged based on its documentation and behavior. In total, the physical security architecture is concerned with specifying the:

7. *Business data* model and the security-related data structures.
8. *Decision-making conditions*, policies, practices, procedures, and actions to ensure holistic protection.
9. *Concrete security mechanisms* to enforce the desired protection, including technology and software services, but also including enforceable security procedures and best practices, and an effective physical security plan.
10. *Access control strategy* and organizational roles and responsibilities, as well as human behavior mitigation controls, including awareness and training to ensure understanding and compliance.
11. *Security technology infrastructure*, as it aligns with business strategy and purpose, including the mechanism for explicit configuration management of the technology platform.
12. *Rules for timing and sequencing* security actions and processes within the conventional business operation, including a map aligning those actions with the business purpose.

THE FIFTH STAGE IN THE SABSA PROCESS: MODULE IMPLEMENTATION

This stage would be called programming and testing if this were a software project, as it focuses entirely on the module creation and validation level of the build, producing a tangible, verifiable end product. That product is one of the "N" number of system modules identified and characterized at the system definition phase (SABSA level four). In essence, this is the stage where the rubber meets the road, and the result is the entire organization's operational protection system.

From an execution standpoint, this is a disaggregated process in that each build team concentrates on implementing a single component of what can be a large and complex system. It is a down-focused, highly involving, and detailed creation process. The team's efforts are focused entirely on ensuring the logical and functional correctness of the module they have been assigned to construct, and there is very little consideration given to how that fits with the business purpose or any of the larger conceptual requirements of assuring holistic protection.

The work is guided by the detailed design documentation that was developed, which was the point of the prior four stages. The guiding principles are the rational programming practices associated with the software engineering profession. Additionally, along with programmed logic controls, there are also real-world actions, such as employee vetting and privilege assignment, as well as gate guard protocols, that must be specified.

Therefore, each person tasked with defining their specific component piece should be a specialist in the subject matter area. They should be familiar with and able to apply the specific practices necessary to achieve the purpose of their particular component module. Thus, programmers, human behavioral specialists, and even physical security specialists may be called on to participate in this part of the process. The outcome of their combined set of individual components is the organization's holistic security architecture, comprising all the elements, which are then integrated up an integration ladder into the operational security solution for that organization. That architecture contains a complete set of:

7. *Operational controls* for all aspects of the protection scheme, including all asset repositories and virtual and physical processes that interact with them.
8. *Risk management process* and associated practices, including the mechanism for incident response, controlled change, and evolution of the holistic protection scheme.
9. *Standards, industry best practices, and technical tools* that have been utilized to formulate the control architecture and underwrite its operation.
10. *Behavioral management controls* to secure the human and physical attack surface, including everything from codes of conduct down to human resource protocols.
11. *Roles, responsibilities, and specific accountabilities* for every member of the organization concerning their role in standard cybersecurity practice.
12. *A code of conduct* including the timing and applicability requirements for standard operational situations.

THE SIXTH STAGE IN THE SABSA PROCESS: SUSTAINMENT

The first five stages of the SABSA process produce a tangible solution that is as complete, accurate, and tied to the business purpose as possible.

However, that entire stage process has an endpoint in the final solution. So, the question is ... What happens after the holistic system is fully integrated into conventional business operations? That is the purpose of sustainability planning and operation. In many respects, this is an entirely different process from the development of the solution, since it is aimed at continuously ensuring the state of the system is correct and relevant to the business purpose.

The job of the sustainment operation is to ensure the system operates as designed and built, and to address the inevitable tweaks and evolution of the control processes it implements. This is a critical aspect of the operation since, without rational control over the change process, even a perfectly designed system can fall apart over time as the business evolves. The assurance of the system's correctness as built is essentially a classic configuration management challenge. However, SABSA refers to it as the Service Management Security Architecture, which is an excellent reflection of its business orientation.

Nonetheless, whether the orientation is toward organizationally facing service aspects of ensuring correctness or the internal process for control over change as it inevitably occurs, there is a standard process for ensuring long-term sustainment that is consistently implemented in whatever context sustainment is necessary.

For Product Safety Concerns and Information please contact our EU representative GPSR@taylorandfrancis.com
Taylor & Francis Verlag GmbH, Kaufingerstraße 24, 80331 München, Germany

www.ingramcontent.com/pod-product-compliance
Ingram Content Group UK Ltd.
Pitfield, Milton Keynes, MK11 3LW, UK
UKHW022130190926
475702UK00013B/1734
* 9 7 8 1 0 3 2 9 9 3 0 8 9 *